C000178898

# ROYAL EDUCATION

*Frontispiece: Queen Charlotte with her two eldest sons, Prince George (George IV) and Frederick, Duke of York*, Allan Ramsay, *c.* 1764. On the spinet, a copy of John Locke's *Some Thoughts Concerning Education* (1693).

# ROYAL EDUCATION
## Past, Present and Future

PETER GORDON

AND

DENIS LAWTON

FRANK CASS
LONDON • PORTLAND, OR

*First published in 1999 in Great Britain by*
FRANK CASS
Newbury House
900 Eastern Avenue
London IG2 7HH

*and in the United States of America by*
FRANK CASS
5804 N.E. Hassalo Street
Portland, Oregon 97213-3644

*Website*: www.frankcass.com

Copyright © 1999 P. Gordon and D. Lawton

British Library Cataloguing in Publication Data
Gordon, Peter, 1927–
Royal education: past, present and future
1. Great Britain – Kings and rulers – Education – History
I. Title II. Lawton, Denis, 1931–
370.8′621

ISBN 0–7146–5014–5 (cloth)

Library of Congress Cataloging-in-Publication Data
Gordon, Peter, 1927–
  Royal education: past, present, and future / Peter Gordon
and Denis Lawton.
    p . c m .
  Includes bibliographical references (p.  ) and index.
  ISBN 0-7146-5014-5 (cloth)
  1. Upper class – Education – Great Britain – History.
2. Great Britain – Kings and rulers – Education – History.
I. Lawton, Denis. II. Title. III. Series.
LC4945.G72G67  1999
371.826′21–dc21
                                                          99-18362
                                                          CIP

*All rights reserved. No part of this publication may be reproduced, stored in or introduced into a retrieval system or transmitted in any form or by any means, electronic, mechanical, photocopying, recording or otherwise, without the prior written permission of the publisher of this book.*

Printed in Great Britain by
The Cromwell Press, Trowbridge, Wilts.

# Contents

# List of Illustrations

# Acknowledgements

We would like to thank the many individuals and institutions who have assisted us during the writing of this book. We are grateful to the staffs of a number of libraries for their courtesy and efficiency in answering our queries, particularly the British Library, the London Library, the Institute of Historical Research and the University of London Institute of Education Library. Francis Dimond, Curator of the Photographic Collection, The Royal Archives, Windsor Castle, and Nicole Mitchell, Picture Library Manager, Royal Collection Enterprises, Windsor Castle, made the choosing of photographs a pleasurable task. Philippa Youngman, Joyce Broomhall and Andrew Humphrys helped in many ways towards the production of the final manuscript, and Pauline Gordon was of great assistance in compiling the index. Our greatest debt, however, is to our wives, Tessa Gordon and Joan Lawton, who have provided valuable support as well as practical help at all stages of the project.

## Picture Credits

We would like to thank the following organisations for kindly granting us permission to reproduce original photographs and illustrations in this book:

Frontispiece; plates 1, 4, 5, 8, 9, 10, 11, 13, 14, 15, 16. Source: The Royal Collection © Her Majesty Queen Elizabeth II.
Plates 3, 6, 7. Source: Courtesy of the National Portrait Gallery, London.
Plate 17. Source: © Hulton Getty Picture Collection.
Plate 18. Source: Popperfoto.

While efforts have been made to obtain permissions for all copyrighted material reproduced in this book, we apologise for any omissions, which can be rectified in later editions.

# Preface

THERE WERE MANY different reasons for writing this book, some more important than others. First, the subject is strangely neglected: many standard historical texts pay little, if any, attention to education, including the education of the monarchy. This is surprising because the topic is interesting on a number of levels. For example, the education received by a future king or queen tells us a good deal about what decision-makers thought about education, and how they interpreted education in terms of the needs of those destined to be the sovereign. We are presented with both a contemporary view of the nature of education and a view of the nature of monarchy. Historians and others should also be interested in how both those kinds of view change over time. At another level, it is possible to make some tentative judgements about the relation between what was intended by an educational programme, and what was actually achieved. If the programme failed, was it the fault of the planning or the implementation or the quality of the teaching?

A second aim of the book is to explore the notion of choice. Most parents, when considering the education of their children, are constrained by what is available or by what they can afford. The education of many (but not all) future monarchs has been decided without such constraints. So why were certain decisions made? What was the thinking about education behind them? What were the results of what we might in retrospect sometimes regard as bizarre choices? At a time in our social and educational history when choice is seen to be increasingly important, there is some invaluable data here waiting to be analysed. A related aspect is concerned with how such choices have changed over time, and why.

More speculatively, we shall explore the influence that education seems to have had on royal personalities, perhaps even on the course of history. We often make assumptions about the significance of making certain educational choices, but how important was it in reality that Queen Elizabeth I was taught to speak French and Italian fluently and was well versed in Latin? Is it possible that Roger Ascham, Elizabeth's tutor, chose a Greek curriculum, including new insights into the interpretation of the Bible, which might have pushed Elizabeth a little further in the direction of Protestantism? We know, for example, that her brother Edward's tutors were carefully vetted for their religious views.

So far we have been considering what education might have done for royalty; an equally important topic may be what the royals have done for education. If we go back far enough in our history there was a strong tradition of kings being involved in education. Alfred the Great, for example, saw it as part of his role to be a patron of learning and to encourage monastic schools. Because so few people, even in the clergy, could read Latin, he set about translating some of the key texts into English. Patronage then meant spending time and money, not merely acting as a figurehead. That tradition continued into later centuries: perhaps Henry VI's most lasting achievement as king was establishing Eton College in 1440, and King's College, Cambridge, a year later.

The Tudors were all actively concerned with education: in Chapter 2 we shall see that they were themselves well educated, but they were also great patrons of schools and colleges. Lady Margaret Beaufort, Henry VII's mother, founded St John's and Christ's colleges at Cambridge, and established the Lady Margaret professorships of divinity at both Oxford and Cambridge universities. Henry VII himself, although notoriously mean, left money for the completion of King's College, as well as personally supporting the scholarship of Polydore Vergil. Henry VIII, Edward VI and Elizabeth I carried on the Tudor tradition of active support for schools and colleges, including some new foundations.

By the twentieth century, that tradition had been lost: members of the royal family are still willing to be chancellors of universities and to open new school buildings, but the idea of using royal money to establish a new Gordonstoun or to support an Atlantic College seems unlikely. Even Prince Charles, who has used some of his own income for the Prince's Trust and has ideas about education, has not re-established the practice of financing new foundations. This may be because the welfare state has made both schooling and higher education available to all, so that it has become simply a state concern, but that is not necessarily the whole answer. We shall see in Chapter 8 that the growth of the welfare state has not prevented the royal family from extending their role in charities such as the Save the Children Fund; so why should they not have a more positive financial role in education, especially when Prince Charles, for example, has frequently criticised standards in public education? Education is arguably more important now than it ever was, and perhaps no harm would come from a royal initiative – of the right kind. Some critics of the monarchy have contrasted the enthusiastic art collecting of the Stuarts and Hanoverians with the sad fact that Queen Elizabeth II has added so little to public collections; royal interest in schools and public education is also much more circumscribed than it was. Are education and art collecting in the same category of valuable lost traditions?

Some aspects of royal patronage have survived; others have simply faded away. It is perhaps misleading, however, to attempt to make direct comparisons between Tudor attitudes to education and those of the Windsors, unless we hedge the comparisons around with qualifications about changing contexts. For that reason we shall begin the book not with education but with a chapter on how the monarchy itself has evolved; then in Chapters 2 to 7 we shall proceed to discuss the education of the monarchs, starting in Chapter 2 with the education of the Tudors. Finally, we have Chapter 8, which not only attempts to generalise on the basis of 500 years' evidence but also looks forward to possible future developments.

After we had started this book, the whole question of the future of the monarchy became a public debate. The behaviour of some members of the royal family caused concern, and it was even suggested that Prince Charles might not become king. Then the circumstances leading up to the tragic death of Princess Diana caused some commentators to put forward the view that the monarchy was in need of modernisation. Some of these issues have a link with education, and the events must be referred to, but they are not the major concern of this book.

# 1  *Continuity and Change:*
## *The English Notion of Monarchy*

IN WRITING THIS book our main intention was to explore some aspects of royal education and how it has changed. In order to do that we must analyse the historical context of education: in other words, we must first explain why sovereignty in Britain has changed over the centuries. For that reason, this chapter will contain little reference to education; it will be concerned with the institution of monarchy, and how our perception of it has changed over the last five centuries.

Anyone visiting one of our royal palaces such as Windsor Castle, can buy a very informative booklet by P. W. Montague-Smith[1] who shows the unbroken line of the British monarchy from Cerdic, the King of the West Saxons, in AD 534 . He also shows, in a section headed 'The Continuity of Kingship', the order of succession today – from Prince Charles (the heir apparent, or first in line of succession), to Prince William (second in line), to Prince Henry (third in line) and so on. The author stopped at number 30 but he could have gone on for several pages. It all gives the impression of clear-cut rules of succession, almost of inevitability.

Of course, the rules were not always as clear as this. Continuity has been generally less in evidence than change. The laws of succession have altered considerably over time and have moved steadily from uncertainty to certainty. Montague-Smith gives us one relatively recent example of change: the Act of Settlement (1701) eliminated from the succession Roman Catholics and those married to Catholics, so Prince Michael of Kent sacrificed his position as number 17 in line when he married a Catholic. The Royal Marriages Act (1772) introduced other

1

restrictions and there have been much more fundamental changes over the centuries.

For example, when William the Conqueror died he left three sons – Robert, William Rufus and Henry (in birth order). Students, attempting to interpret eleventh-century events through their knowledge of current practices, sometimes ask why Robert, the eldest son, did not become King of England when William I died. The answer is quite simply, or perhaps not so simply, that the rules of succession were very different then. We know that William I's own claim to the throne was partly based on his assertion that King Edward the Confessor had named him as the heir to the throne of England. Naming a successor is no longer part of the process of succession (although a great deal of ceremony was still thought to be necessary in 1969 when Queen Elizabeth II gave the title of Prince of Wales to Charles). In the Middle Ages, however, the practice of a king naming his successor was often crucial. So it was with William I, who named his first-born as Duke of Normandy but nominated William Rufus as his heir to the English throne. Henry, the third son, received a large cash settlement in silver coin as a consolation prize. But younger sons did not always accept their inferior position gracefully: they frequently led revolts against their elder brothers, especially if a king showed signs of incompetence. When William II died in very mysterious circumstances from a 'hunting accident' in the New Forest, his younger brother Henry, who was not far away, immediately rode with his followers to Winchester to claim the royal treasure. Having taken possession of the treasure, Henry then moved swiftly to London to make arrangements for his coronation, which took place only three days later. From the point of view of the evolution of the monarchy there are three aspects of this story which are of interest. First, some nobles objected that Henry's elder brother, Robert, Duke of Normandy, might have had a better claim. Henry's ingenious reply was that he had been 'born in the purple' – that is, he was born after his father became king in 1066, whereas Robert had been born when William I was only Duke of Normandy. This argument showed how flexible the rules then were. The second point of interest is that it was clearly important for Henry to be crowned as soon as possible, for at least two reasons. The Coronation signalled that Henry was acceptable to the great Anglo-Norman barons, illustrating the fact that the idea of a king being 'elected' was not completely obsolete. Third, the ceremony of the coronation, involving being anointed with sacred oils by a bishop, symbolised acceptance by the Church, and also was thought to endow the King with superhuman qualities. Thus Henry I became king in accordance with several different criteria: inheritance, possession of the royal treasure, 'election' by the aristocracy, and, last but not least, being crowned. For those who might still have thought that Robert had a better claim, Henry defeated his elder brother in 1106 at the battle of Tinchebray, imprisoned him for the rest of his life, and took over the Duchy of Normandy for himself. In the end, might was still right.

The major difference between twelfth-century kingship and the present position is that heredity has become much more important, probably all-important, hence the significance of the 'line of succession'. Gradually, and especially with the development of democracy and constitutional monarchy (that is, reigning without real power of ruling the country), the 'blood' factor has become the decisive one. Monarchs can still be 'disqualified' if, for example, they become mad like George III, or break important rules or conventions of kingship like Edward VIII. But it would now be quite inconceivable for anyone not in the line of succession to take over as king or queen. Constitutional monarchs nowadays, even more than their predecessors who had real power, need to be able to demonstrate an unchallengeable pedigree. The coronation is still an important ceremony but its function is now purely symbolic, although, as we shall see, enthusiastic monarchists sometimes make claims for supernatural effects.[2] The importance of royal symbolism should not be underestimated, as we shall see, but it need not involve the supernatural.

It will be necessary for us to pay close attention to the changing notion of the English monarchy and to changing theories of kingship. Although Tudor kings and queens did not possess absolute power, they were much nearer than their twentieth-century counterparts to absolute monarchy; by the end of the sixteenth century, however, successive Parliaments had already constrained royal powers to some extent. The trend was not all in one direction: for Henry VIII it is certainly true that,

3

in order to get the Reformation legislation he wanted, it was necessary to call Parliament frequently and to put himself in its power. On the other hand, Henry's royal status was significantly enhanced: because the King was no longer subordinate to any other authority on earth, he was now directly accountable to God alone, and this closeness to God reinforced the notion of divine right of kings.[3] We must be careful to make a distinction between the real power of monarchs and their royal status. It may be true that 'power is where the money is and all the rest is theatre', but theatre is very important in royal matters, and ideas about closeness to God were by no means irrelevant; even in the twentieth century, as late as 1956, 35 per cent of subjects believed that Queen Elizabeth II was chosen by God. It may indeed be the case that as monarchs have lost real power, they have increased the trappings of royalty: the symbols and emblems of an exalted status.

James Stuart, when still James VI of Scotland, made his own contribution to the theory of kingship in his book *The True Law of Free Monarchies* (1598) which was a justification of one of his favourite doctrines, the divine right of kings. James quoted the Bible as his authority: the Book of Samuel showed that God told the Israelites that the King had the right to make use of their property and their children as he saw fit. The King was not answerable to them but to God himself. In 1610 James, in his speech to Parliament, made the bold claim that

> Kings are justly called gods, for that they exercise a manner or resemblance of divine power upon earth. For if you will consider the attributes to God, you shall see how they agree in the person of a king. God hath power to create or destroy, make or unmake at his pleasure, to give life or send death, to judge all and to be judged nor accountable to none, to raise low things and to make high things low at his pleasure, and to God are both soul and body due. And the like power have kings: they make and unmake their subjects; they have power of raising and casting down; of life and of death; judges over all their subjects, and in all causes, and yet accountable to none but God only. They have power to exalt low things, and abase high things, and make of their subjects like men at the chess.[4]

But James had implicitly accepted a contractual element between king and subjects when he became King of England, and after his experience of the English Parliament, as we shall see in Chapter 3, he was forced to modify his practice, if not his theory, even further. Charters, such as Magna Carta (1215) and other concessions to the nobility, were privileges granted by the sovereign, but in practice such privileges tended to become permanent as part of the common law. The coronation ceremony included a public promise by the monarch not to take away privileges granted by predecessors. Although there was no written constitution, the King was effectively bound by precedent, and when James's son, Charles I, tested divine right against the power of custom, he paid for this belief with his life. Monarchs have to be sure that their notion of kingship is shared by their subjects, then and now. This has clear educational implications.

Various versions of the absolutist view of monarchy continued to be held throughout the seventeenth century. For example, Thomas Hobbes in *Leviathan* (1651) justified absolutist government, not in terms of divine right, but as a kind of contract. Some time before he died in 1653, Sir Robert Filmer, a well-connected graduate of Trinity College, Cambridge, asserted his own royalist position in *Patriarcha* (published posthumously in 1680). He claimed that absolute monarchy was the only God-given form of government; there was no alternative. G. D. H. Cole once referred to *Patriarcha* as a 'silly book',[5] but it was influential at the end of the seventeenth century. Filmer's position was attacked by the philosopher John Locke, who rested his argument in *Two Treatises on Government* (1690) on the existence of the natural rights of all men: life, liberty and property. Locke offended royals and royalists by saying that rebellion could sometimes be justified, if a king violated his subjects' natural rights.

Apart from these philosophical discussions, the execution of Charles I in 1649 and the Commonwealth experiment clearly had an effect on what the people believed about what kings could and should do. In the seventeenth century the dispute about royal powers had four specific aspects: the ability of the King to raise taxes without the consent of Parliament, the right to a private royal army, the right to set up royal courts of justice in addition to those in existence, and the right to suspend laws passed by Parliament or to exempt some subjects from obeying the laws of the land. The dispute was resolved in 1688 by the so-called 'Glorious Revolution' and in the Bill of Rights (1689), which Parliament drew up as a set of rules for William and Mary; future kings and queens were firmly reminded that they were subject to the law. After that there was a steady limitation of royal power corresponding to the development of democracy in the nineteenth and twentieth centuries. Part of that story is the move away from absolutism and divine right to constitutional monarchy and responsible government. To be a constitutional monarch is less dangerous – few have suggested executing Edward VIII or Prince Charles – but there is a difficult set of rules for monarchs to learn. In that respect education and training have become more important; in later chapters we shall want to examine how well future kings and queens were prepared for the task of playing a role in a 'game' whose rules were continually changing.

It is now difficult to find a coherent theory of monarchy, and public opinion often seems to be confused. A generation ago some were arguing for a Scandinavian-type monarchy whereby members of the royal family would move around the country more like ordinary citizens – even on bicycles. The theory behind this version of monarchy was that since a constitutional monarch has no real power, then there is no reason why the family should be treated with great reverence. That Scandinavian model has not yet been accepted in Britain. Instead, we have members of the royal family treated as superstars: veneration without power. In the 1950s, Dermot Morrah, a palace courtier,[6] tried to explain and justify this reverence by arguing that the monarchy possessed a quasi-religious quality symbolising the timelessness of the British way of life. Kingsley Martin, then editor of the *New Statesman*,[7] mocked this view, which was similar to a statement made earlier by Archbishop Temple at the Coronation of George V. Temple had claimed that the King was the 'incarnation of his people'. This idea was repeated at the accession of Elizabeth II, when the 1953 Coronation was again represented as a sacrament. *The Times* of the day contained the following passage:

> Today's sublime ceremonial is in form and in common view, a
> dedication of the State to God's service through the prayers and

benedictions of the Church. That is a noble conception, and of itself makes every man and woman in the land a partaker in the mystery of the Queen's anointing ... In her is incarnate on her coronation the whole of society, of which the State is no more than a political manifestation.[8]

Prisoners were said to have gained spiritual benefit as a result of seeing the Coronation on television; and a clergyman said that the Coronation was a miracle that might save civilisation. Kingsley Martin unkindly likened this mystical view to the belief of the South Sea Islanders who saw the coronation of their king as a magical rite which enabled him to control the winds and the rain.[9] A similar point was made, more positively, by Enoch Powell: 'Our monarch is not a crowned president. She is anointed. She represents a supernatural element in the nation.'[10]

It is probably true that there are fewer people today who would justify the continuation of the monarchy in such religious terms. In their sociological analysis of the Coronation in 1953, Shils and Young attempted to produce evidence to support the view that society needs more than rational procedures to sustain its existence.[11] Their sociological explanation was based on Durkheim's theory that society is more than the sum of all its members: there is a collective consciousness which periodically needs some kind of communal event to reaffirm the moral values of society. Even in modern society certain royal occasions may have this effect of reaffirming some of the collective sentiments and collective ideas which form part of the culture. This is not quite the same as Enoch Powell's argument or Morrah's magic, but it goes beyond the legal and the rational. Other sociologists have disputed their interpretation.[12] More recently, the funeral of Princess Diana confirmed the view that we should beware of completely rational explanations of or justifications for the monarchy. Before discussing the question of the appropriateness of future monarchs' education, we need to analyse the changing role of sovereigns.

It is also necessary to note that the Crown as an institution has rarely been completely secure, and to avoid extinction the monarchy has changed. Elizabeth I's long reign gave an appearance of stability in the sixteenth century, but the seventeenth century witnessed not only the execution of a king but the development of an alternative to the monarchical principle; and for much of the seventeenth and eighteenth centuries the monarchy was extremely unpopular: 'A Scot, a Dutchman and finally a German sat on the throne of xenophobic England'.[13] After 1689 there was always a Stuart rival, a Pretender, waiting in the wings. In 1701, as it was considered important to exclude those Roman Catholic descendants of James II, Parliament decided that after the death of William III and Queen Anne, the succession would pass to Sophia, Dowager Electress of Hanover, or to her Protestant heirs. Parliament accordingly passed the Act of Settlement in 1701 which also declared that ministers should be 'responsible' for decisions made by the sovereign. In effect this was stating that the sovereign acted legitimately only on the advice of ministers. This trend towards parliamentary control was reinforced when George I became king and after 1717 did not attend meetings of the Cabinet. Instead, the chair was taken by the most senior minister, later to be called the Prime Minister. A sovereign might still try to run the country but had to do so through 'agents' or 'king's friends' in the House of Commons.

The gradual loss of royal power in England was encouraged by several other factors in the eighteenth century. The first was the growth of the party political system, which meant that ministers were selected not by the King but by a party, the Whigs or the Tories. The pretence that ministers, including the Prime Minister, were appointed by royal authority continued, and until very recently new ministers were required to kiss the royal hand as a symbol of personal loyalty and obedience. The reality was that ministers were chosen by the party in power, and a royal dismissal of a Prime Minister was never attempted after William IV. This shift of power from sovereign to party was facilitated by the individual unpopularity of most monarchs in the eighteenth century, and by specific events such as the South Sea Bubble in 1720, which discredited the King. David Cannadine[14] has argued that the behaviour of George III's children made them the most unloved royal generation in English history. George IV's marriage to Queen Caroline and his treatment of her became a public scandal; cartoons abounded, and on the death of George

IV *The Times* editorial said that no-one wept for him. The reason for the unpopularity of the Hanoverians was only to some extent due to their unattractive behaviour: they were not yet seen to be above politics, so George III was partly blamed for the loss of the American colonies, and William IV attracted criticism because he was known to be opposed to the 1832 Reform Act, which extended the parliamentary electorate. The solution for the royals was to appear to be above politics and to lead personal lives which were less open to public criticism. Both took time to achieve.

With the accession of Queen Victoria in 1837 there was a revival of popular support for an attractive young queen, but Victoria did interfere in politics on many occasions,[15] and, worse still, after the death of Prince Albert in 1861 she 'became invisible'. She went into a prolonged period of mourning for 20 years, refused even to open Parliament and was the object of much critical comment in the press and elsewhere. She was referred to in some newspapers as 'Mrs Brown' (a reference to her relationship with her Scottish ghillie John Brown) or 'Queen of the Whigs' and was regarded as a joke rather than as head of state. Additionally, the lifestyle of the future Edward VII did not endear him to his mother's subjects, some of whom feared a return to the low moral standards of the Hanoverian kings. Moreover, republicanism grew in strength after Queen Victoria withdrew from public life. Although it probably never became a majority view, 84 republican clubs were founded in the three years following 1871.[16] Republican politicians such as Sir Charles Dilke[17] may have been more inclined to tolerate the Queen's unconstitutional interferences, thinking that she would not be succeeded by her disreputable son, Edward, to whom even the royalist Bagehot referred as 'the unemployed youth'.

One view of the monarchy that emerged was a kind of crypto-republicanism: the King or queen as head of a state which was in all but name a republic. This compromise has recently been vigorously condemned by such contemporary critics of the monarchical principle as Tom Nairn, who associates the continued existence of the Crown with a host of reactionary social customs and practices.[18] For many twentieth-century republicans, the royal family is not just a symbol of an antique, feudal past, but a means of propping up hereditary and class privileges which work against democratic modernisation: 'Monarchy is a weapon in the hands of capital and privilege.' According to this view we should not see the public perception of monarchy as something which has simply developed naturally: there is evidence that, since 1789, the popular view has been carefully manipulated by politicians who feared the consequences of a republic. Disraeli has often been credited with popularising Victoria as the 'Queen Empress', but Gladstone before him had exploited public opinion, for example, at the time when the future Edward VII appeared to be dying of typhoid; and politicians with republican views, such as Dilke, were ruthlessly brought back into line by Gladstone.[19]

Meanwhile, the monarchy had survived, and from the beginning of his reign, Edward VII became almost a model of constitutional behaviour. Unlike his mother he rarely interfered in political matters, and the crown was passed on, probably stronger than ever to his son, George V. George, coached by his Private Secretary, Lord Stamfordham,[20] was usually just as careful as his father to obey the rules of constitutional monarchy, although he sometimes sailed close to the wind.[21] Some have blamed courtiers for giving the kind of advice which has delayed progress in modernising the monarchy and even for putting the institution at risk.[22] We shall return to that question in Chapter 8. For many writers the reign of George V was, despite his imperfect education, one of almost almost perfect constitutionalism. His public behaviour was usually exemplary, even if he was a bully within the family; he never shirked his duties and he enjoyed ceremony and pageant. But he feared for the future, thinking that the future Edward VIII, despite his upbringing, would rock the royal boat.

Many others thought that Edward VIII might destroy the Windsor dynasty. Had he remained as king, the chances of a republic might have been increased; but the politicians, Prime Minister Stanley Baldwin in particular, had no intention of running the risk of that threat to the established order. George VI was a safe, if somewhat unprepared, alternative. Following the abdication, there was a period of about a half a century of enthusiastic royalism before scepticism once more returned.

The development of such a secure throne from the Hanoverians to the Windsors and the change of public opinion during that time needs further analysis. The change in popular status of the royal family did not just happen: it was constructed. A partial explanation has been provided by Cannadine, who argues persuasively that many discussions of the royal family, including the Shils and Young paper already referred to, are weakened by inadequate historical contextualisation.[23] It makes no sense to compare, say, the Coronation of George I with that of Elizabeth II without taking into account a number of contextual factors at both times, including the power of the monarchy, the personal standing of the King or queen, the economic and social structure, the media, technology and fashion. (The same principle, as we shall see, applies to making educational comparisons, although Cannadine's paper does not attempt to cover that field.) Cannadine proceeds to show how the changes in ritual can be divided into four phases: first, the 1820s–70s, when royal ceremonies ranged from farce to fiasco; second, 1877–1914, the period during which Victoria was not only made visible once more but also enjoyed the status of Queen Empress, and played a full part in royal Jubilees and other pageantry – 'invented traditions'; third, 1918–53, a settled period of English constitutional monarchy flourishing when other royal regimes had disappeared, with lack of power compensated for by splendid rituals and pageants made available to a mass audience by the media; finally, from 1953 a further period of the Windsors, not yet finished. Pimlott has also commented that 'the reduction of the royal family to picturebook iconography did not diminish public enthusiasm: indeed, by removing all remaining partisan elements, it enhanced it'.[24]

The importance of Cannadine's analysis is that it shows clearly that in England diminishing royal power can be correlated with increasing royal splendour and popular appeal; it also shows that the association did not happen by chance but was constructed, not necessarily consciously, by politicians (and writers such as Bagehot) who wanted to preserve the social order and feared that a republic might destroy it.

In passing, we might also observe, from an educational point of view, that this kind of analysis does not feature in school textbooks, where the history of the monarchy tends to be treated blandly, often presented in an almost Whiggish way as a graceful move from absolutism to a happy, democratic, constitutional monarchy. The Commonwealth interregnum (1649–60) is often glossed over as an unfortunate, temporary mistake, and the problems of James II in 1688 are shown as the result of the behaviour of a king who was both foolish and a Catholic. It is likely that the curricula of many princes has taken that line and that republican arguments have been given little weight. We shall see, for example, in later chapters, that the views of Bagehot have been given more attention than they deserve in the preparation of future monarchs.

Returning to the question of how the public perception of royalty has changed, especially since the end of the eighteenth century, we need to ask who were the shapers of public opinion concerning the monarchy in the late nineteenth century and twentieth century. At this stage we might even indulge in some hypothetical questions. During the reign of Victoria, for example, if Gladstone and then Disraeli had not intervened, the Queen might have continued to be 'invisible' and the republicans grown in strength so that Edward VII never became king; or later on, if George V had not been so carefully advised, he might have interfered in political processes and been forced into an impossible constitutional position. Or his son might have been allowed to marry Mrs Simpson, intervene in the complex international situation, and cause the end of the House of Windsor. The fact that none of these things happened was not just chance; it was the result of the intervention of various individuals and groups of individuals.

There were probably at least four groups. We have already mentioned the politicians who wished to avoid a republic: they include Tories such as Disraeli and Baldwin, Liberals such as Gladstone and Lloyd George, and Labour politicians such as MacDonald, Attlee, Wilson and Blair. The second group consists of courtiers and advisers: Lord Esher[25] was responsible for much of the change in ceremony and wanted to make these occasions appealing to the public, using ceremonies such as coronations, weddings and funerals as spectacular events which reinforced a certain public image of the royal family. Lord Stamfordham saved

George V from inappropriate behaviour; Sir Alexander Hardinge[26] made sure that Edward VIII did not destroy the House of Windsor; and there have been many others to whom we shall refer in Chapter 8. The third group was the newspaper proprietors, who had exercised remarkable self-censorship from the end of the nineteenth century (the beginning of the popular press) to the short reign of Edward VIII. The fourth group is the BBC (and, later, commercial television), starting with Lord Reith, the BBC's first director-general, who had very firm views about the established order and who supervised very carefully any references to the royal family, taking a personal interest in the early Christmas broadcasts which started in 1932. This tradition has continued with such orthodox figures as the broadcaster Richard Dimbleby, who used radio and later television very skilfully to present a reverential view of the monarchy. That attitude was maintained by the media even into the troubled 1980s and 1990s.

This analysis provokes such questions as, for example, 'why does the Queen ride to the opening of Parliament in a coach rather than a Rolls Royce?' or 'why, when most of the nobility were trading in their coaches for cars, did Edward VII commission an even more splendid royal coach?'.[27] Such questions are also related to the future public image of the monarchy, to which we shall return in Chapter 8. Meanwhile, what has this to do with royal education? First, it seems to be true that as royal power has declined, visibility and veneration have increased. If that is indeed the case and such a paradox is not found to be incompatible with democracy, then careful educational planning will be needed in the very near future. Second, in our investigation of royal education, we need to look particularly at how adequately this aspect of royal upbringing has been planned and executed in the past. Third, we will need to examine, in later chapters, whether education of the royals is being modernised in the same way as other aspects of the royal lifestyle.

We need now to return to the account of the changing notions of the royal family. In the 1980s and 1990s there was a decline in popularity: questions were asked about royal finances, and there were criticisms of the behaviour of the 'young royals' which were extensively reported in the popular press. It may be that some of the royal family had underestimated the importance of mystique and magic for the British monarchy. For a sovereign who reigns but does not rule, the symbolism and theatre associated with the role are crucial. Words like 'mystique' and 'magic' have frequently been used, ever since Bagehot wrote about the Victorian constitution. Perhaps the current level of expense on the monarchy can only be justified in terms of magic and mystique. But should modern monarchy cling to magic and mystique? By 1997 support for the monarchy had for a time sunk to below 50 per cent.[28] At this point 'the firm' decided that it was necessary to make positive plans for better public relations. In late 1997 and early 1998, the Way Ahead Group, set up in 1994, comprising the Queen, Prince Philip, the Prince of Wales and Princess Anne, discussed various possible ways forward. It was decided to employ a public relations/market research organisation to diagnose the problem more fully. It was also decided to appoint a highly paid full-time director of communications to manage future events more effectively. Peter Lewis, director of public affairs at Centrica, the supply arm of British Gas, was appointed in June 1998. The research commissioned by Buckingham Palace showed that many members of the public represented in the 'focus groups' thought that the royal family was wasteful, out of touch (because of their traditions and upbringing) and badly advised. One part of the remedy discussed was slimming down the 'working' royal family, thus reducing costs. It was observed that the Windsors cost roughly twice as much as contemporary continental royal families. Action was called for. It had already been decided to sacrifice the royal yacht; now even the royal train was targeted for royal economies. And were five palaces really necessary (as well as Balmoral and Sandringham)? the Queen also wrote to her lord-lieutenants asking them to tell those involved in royal events that bowing and curtsying should be regarded as optional. A certain kind of informality became the order of the day.

This discussion by the Way Ahead Group was a timely precaution: at the time of writing, the abolition of the hereditary principle for the House of Lords is part of the Labour Government's legislative programme. If that were to happen, it is

14

likely that the hereditary monarchy would also be open to closer scrutiny. It may be that only improved education and training for future royals could save the institution. In 1977 Philip Howard could assert that 'the Prince of Wales has been sensibly educated for his demanding constitutional and symbolic role, and promises extremely well.'[29] Twenty years later there were more who, like John Grigg some three decades ago,[30] question the adequacy of the education provided for Charles and other royals.

The changing nature of the British monarchy raises interesting questions about the upbringing and preparation of future constitutional kings and queens, including their formal education. It might be useful to attempt to envisage an ideal programme for the ideal monarch. It would, of course, change considerably over time, but even so it might be possible to map out a programme in terms of general principles. In addition to a good general education, which is now regarded as the right of every citizen, what else is desirable? Dermot Morrah said that the education of a future king 'must be directed with an imaginative eye to the future; yet it must be firmly anchored in the experience of the past. It must look to the inevitability of change as reign follows reign; yet it must conceive of change always as organic growth and not as revolution.'[31] Chapters 2 to 7 will give readers opportunities to review the education received by the royals from the late fifteenth to the end of the twentieth century. It is hoped that consideration of past examples may throw some light on contemporary issues. At this stage we need only note that although many reforms, financial and constitutional, have been started, they have not, as yet, included much new thinking on education. We shall return to these issues in Chapter 8, after we have reviewed five centuries of royal education.

## NOTES

1. P. W. Montague-Smith, *The Royal Line of Succession* (Pitkin, 1986). Montague-Smith had previously been editor of *Debrett's Peerage*.
2. D. Morrah, *The Work of the Queen* (William Kimber, 1958). Morrah's view was that in the late 1950s the Queen was seen as a representative of the Commonwealth, drawing strength from the magical roots of kingship. But the Queen also symbolised ordinary life.
3. The divine right of kings had a long history, not only connected with the papacy, but also with the Holy Roman Empire. The doctrine asserted that hereditary monarchy is approved by God, monarchs are accountable to God alone and rebellion against a

lawful king is blasphemous.
4. The references to James I are included in A. Hughes (ed.), *Seventeenth Century England: A Changing Culture*, vol. I (Ward Lock, 1980), pp. 27–9.
5. G. D. H. Cole, *Politics and Literature* (Hogarth Press, 1929), p. 47.
6. Morrah, *The Work of the Queen*. B. Pimlott, *the Queen: A Biography of Elizabeth II* (HarperCollins, 1996), p. 293, said that Morrah had a reverential, semi-religious theory of monarchy (which John Grigg called 'British Shintoism'). Nevertheless, Pimlott thought that Morrah's views influenced court thinking on the promotion of the monarchy.
7. Kingsley Martin, *The Crown and the Establishment* (Hutchinson, 1962).
8. Ibid.
9. Ibid.
10. Quoted by Philip Howard, *The British Monarchy in the Twentieth Century* (Hamish Hamilton, 1977). Howard went on to say that a third of the Queen's subjects in the UK said that they believed that she was chosen by God.
11. E. Shils and M. Young, 'The Meaning of the Coronation', *Sociological Review*, 1, 2 (1953).
12. N. Birnbaum, 'Monarchies and Sociologists: A Reply to Shils and Young', *Sociological Review*, n.s., 3,1 (1955), pp. 5–23.
13. M. Kishlansky, *A Monarchy Transformed: A Monarchy Transformed, 1603–1714* (Allen Lane, 1996), p.1.
14. D. Cannadine, 'The Context, Performance and Meaning of Ritual: The British Monarchy and the "Invention of Tradition", c.1820–1977', in E. Hobsbawm and T. Ranger (eds), *The Invention of Tradition* (Cambridge University Press, 1983), pp. 101–64.
15. Victoria did not fully understand the constitutional position. As we shall see in Chapter 5, her education had not prepared her for the delicacy of reigning but not ruling: she expected to rule. Only gradually did she learn to accept Prime Ministers of whom she personally disapproved. And she still wanted to influence policy; in this she was encouraged by Prince Albert. Later she was particularly hostile to Gladstone and objected strongly to his Irish Home Rule policy. Gladstone was, however, a monarchist and made the best of a difficult situation, about which the public was completely unaware. To have made known his difficulties would have been to have run the risk of a republican solution which Gladstone would have detested. In 1880 when the Queen did not want to appoint Gladstone as Prime Minister, it was made very clear that the Liberal Party would not serve without him. This was a good illustration of the fact that power had moved from crown to Parliament, party and the electorate. Victoria may have found it difficult to understand why she could not have her own way in 1880, whereas in 1894, when Gladstone retired, she could choose his successor, Lord Rosebery, without consulting his party. In theory, but not always in practice, appointing a Prime Minister remained part of the royal prerogative. This ambiguity was not resolved until all parties adopted the practice of electing their leaders. After Victoria no sovereign ever refused to appoint a Prime Minister. This was important because it reinforced the public perception of the sovereign being above politics.
16. Richard Williams, *The Contentious Crown: Public Discussion of the Monarchy in the Reign of Queen Victoria* (Ashgate, 1997).
17. Sir Charles Dilke (1843–1911), Liberal politician, MP, 1868–86 and 1892–1911. He was regarded as a radical on many issues, including the abolition of the monarchy, but public hostility encouraged him to moderate his public utterances about the royal family.
18. Tom Nairn, *The Enchanted Glass: Britain and its Monarchy*, 2nd edn (Vintage, 1994 [1988]). The 1994 edition includes an Introduction aimed at bringing the topic up to date.
19. Nairn, *Enchanted Glass*, p. 342.
20. Stamfordham, Arthur Bigge, 1st Baron (1849–1931). Son of a Northumberland parson, educated at Rossall School and the Royal Military Academy. Private secretary to King George V.
21. In 1910 the Liberal Prime Minister, H. H. Asquith, faced with the problem of the House

of Lords behaving 'unconstitutionally' by refusing to pass a Money Bill, proposed to restrict the powers of the House of Lords by the Parliament Bill. The danger then would have been that the Lords might simply have refused to pass that bill too. To avoid that possibility, Asquith told the King that if the Lords refused to pass his bill, he would ask for a general election to be called, and that if he won he would like the King's promise to create a sufficient number of Liberal Peers to ensure that the bill could not be blocked by the Lords. Stamfordham advised the King against making such a promise. This was regarded as controversial, even dangerous, advice.

22. Courtiers act as a kind of safety-net, advising monarchs how to avoid constitutional problems, but they have also often encouraged the Crown to hang on to as much power as possible. See Chapter 8, especially Laski's discussion of Private Secretaries.
23. Cannadine, 'Monarchy and Tradition', in Hobsbawn and Ranger, *The Invention of Tradition*, pp. 106–7.
24. Pimlott, *the Queen*, p. 13.
25. Reginald Brett, 2nd Viscount Esher (1852–1930). Son of a lawyer, Master of the Rolls, educated at Eton and Trinity College, Cambridge. Private secretary to Lord Hartington (later Duke of Devonshire). Liberal MP 1880–85, Secretary of the Office of Works, 1895–1902, which included responsibility for royal palaces. He was greatly esteemed by Queen Victoria and Edward VII, who appointed him Governor of Windsor Castle, where he reorganised the royal archives and published an edition of Queen Victoria's letters.
26. Sir Alexander Hardinge, later 2nd Baron Hardinge of Penshurst (1894–1960), the son of Charles 1st Baron Hardinge of Penshurst, Viceroy of India. Educated at Harrow and Trinity College, Cambridge; served in the Grenadier Guards. Assistant Private Secretary to George V, 1920–36; Private Secretary to Edward VIII, 1936.
27. Cannadine's analysis, 'Monarchy and Tradition', of this period is excellent.
28. Opinion poll published by the *Guardian*, 12 August 1997.
29. Howard, *British Monarchy*, pp. 202–3.
30. J. Grigg, 'A Summer Storm', in Jeremy Murray-Brown (ed.), *The Monarchy and its Future* (George Allen & Unwin, 1969). In this paper Grigg was reflecting on an article he had written in 1957 (when he was still Lord Altrincham), which had caused a good deal of discussion at the time.
31. D. Morrah, *To Be a King* (Hutchinson, 1968), p. xiv. Morrah was Arundel Herald Extraordinary and sub-titled his book 'A Privileged Account of the Early Life and Education of HRH the Prince of Wales, Written with the Approval of HM the Queen'.

# 2 *Renaissance, Reformation and the Education of the Tudors*

THE BEGINNING OF the reign of Henry VII, 1485, is often taken to be a convenient point to start discussing the modern history of England. Henry's victory over Richard III at the battle of Bosworth effectively brought to an end the Wars of the Roses, and Henry's reign can be seen as a time when the modern state and many of its institutions, at least in England and Wales, were developed. In Italy, the rediscovery of many Greek and Latin texts had, throughout the fourteenth and fifteenth centuries, been of some influence in changing attitudes and tastes in a variety of fields, not simply the literary. In England and in other parts of western Europe there had also been indications of dissatisfaction with the religious establishment, including the papacy, from at least as far back as John Wycliffe and the Lollards in the last quarter of the fourteenth century. Both these influences, the Renaissance and the Reformation, were to bring about considerable changes in educational thought in general and, as we shall see, in the education of future kings and queens of England in particular.

J. D. Mackie began his well-known text *The Earlier Tudors* by asserting that the Renaissance was not an event but a process.[1] He went on to show that it was a long process, in some respects stretching back into the Middle Ages. The Renaissance as the transition from the Age of Faith to the Age of Reason was only part of the story. Similarly, humanism involved more than the emergence of individualism, or the spirit of criticism challenging simple acceptance of doctrines and beliefs.

The term 'Renaissance' is ambiguous, and we should remember that it was not used until the eighteenth century. The origins of the Renaissance were associated with the rediscovery of and revival of interest in classical Greek and Latin texts. Many writers have stressed Renaissance achievements in art, architecture and sculpture, but the Renaissance was also significant for new ideas, especially of the kind that cast doubt on traditionally accepted truths or 'common sense', for example, those of Machiavelli in statecraft (political philosophy), or later, Galileo in science. Erasmus, the Dutch humanist, can be seen as a later example of Renaissance thought spreading to the north-west of Europe. His edition of the Greek New Testament published in 1516 provided an interesting link with the Reformation. The Greek version showed up errors of translation in the Latin Vulgate text, which provided support for those potential reformers who wished to say that it was the Bible, not the Church or the Pope, which should be regarded as the authority in religion. The study of Latin and Greek texts with a concentration on the discussion of meaning, was the basis of Erasmus's educational programme, but he also advocated a critical study of good modern literature. Like other humanist teachers, he believed that pupils should enjoy learning and that it was part of the teacher's task to know how to make the work interesting to individuals with different backgrounds.

The Reformation is another complex term. It is accepted that there was a series of events in the sixteenth century which caused the Protestants to break away from the Roman Catholic Church. That much is not controversial; but the causes of the Reformation and the relative importance of those causes are much more open to debate. There were aspects of the Catholic Church which had been under criticism for many years: corruption, nepotism, the sale of ecclesiastical offices, the exploitation of superstitions by such practices as indulgences and pardon. Some put the doctrine of transubstantiation into the same category as superstitions and ignored papal instructions about such beliefs. All of these problems might have been put right by internal reform, but there were political pressures in Germany (and later in Henry VIII's England) which eventually ended the ideal of a single united Roman Catholic Church led by the Pope. Henry VIII's children, the future King Edward VI, Queen Mary and Queen Elizabeth, were educated in ways that caused them to have quite differing attitudes to the Reformation, ranging from the extreme

Protestantism of Edward to Mary's inclination to burn Protestant heretics, even though they had all experienced some key aspects of Renaissance education.

Many of the ideas about educational reform originated in Italy. Fifteenth-century Italy experienced a rise in prosperity which increased demand for the educated and qualified. Universities failed to keep up with this demand and most were old-fashioned in what they offered. New schools were founded, often in the homes of scholars, where there was direct communication between teachers and students, and new material was taught. One famous example was the Academy of Vittorino Rambaldone da Feltre at Mantua, which set a pattern for the education of Italian aristocrats of both sexes that influenced many later writers.[2] These included Baldassare Castiglione, author of *Il Cortegiano* ('The Courtier') (1528), which set out the requirements for an educated nobleman, as well as Sir Thomas Elyot and Roger Ascham, all of whom contributed to new thinking about the content and methods of education.

For both da Feltre and Castiglione, education was more than learning: it was 'breeding', which was not the same as birth or blood. Gentility was not a matter of correct conversation or clothes, what we might now call etiquette, it was 'the whole being of man'.[3] These qualities could be taught: suitable sports could give the body suppleness and grace, and the gentleman must excel without seeming to do so. Castiglione talked of *sperzatura* or 'nonchalance', which survived into twentieth-century England as the hallmark of the independent ('public') school and Balliol man's 'effortless superiority'. Similarly, in England Sir Thomas Elyot's *The Boke Named the Governour* (1531), which will be discussed later, was a programme designed for the upbringing and education of the sons of gentlemen. Being written by someone who was an enthusiast for the English language, it made Renaissance ideas on education available to a wide readership. Equally important was the fact that such an education was not to be administered solely by the clergy.[4]

In all the examples mentioned above, the recommended curriculum changed from the medieval *trivium* (grammar, rhetoric and logic) and the *quadrivium* (arithmetic, geometry, astronomy and music) to a balanced programme of physical, intellectual, spiritual and aesthetic development, although it may be anachronistic to think of such clearly defined areas of experience at this stage: literature and music were thought to have moral purposes, as were physical activities of the right kind. The physical included fencing, riding, hunting, hawking and dancing; the intellectual focused on Greek and Latin texts but also on contemporary poetry and prose. The other arts were also important, and it was regarded as desirable not only to appreciate music and painting but also to be a performer if possible. However, the most important difference between Renaissance education and the medieval *trivium* and *quadrivium* was that in all aspects of the curriculum pupils were encouraged to understand and to exercise their critical faculties rather than simply to memorise.

It was against this background of social and intellectual ferment that the Tudors were educated. Their views on education, how they were educated, and how they wanted their children educated were all part of the Renaissance and Reformation picture.

## HENRY VII (1457–1509)

Less is known of the details of Henry VII's upbringing than that of his children and grandchildren. He was born Henry Tudor, Earl of Richmond, on 28 January 1457 at Pembroke Castle in Wales. His father, Edmund Tudor, who died three months before, was married to Lady Margaret Beaufort, Countess of Richmond, a great-great-granddaughter of Edward III. His mother was not quite 14 when Henry was born and she married twice more. Lady Margaret was a remarkable woman in many ways. Politically, she plotted the overthrow of Richard III in order to place her son on the throne and engineered Henry's marriage to Elizabeth of York, which cemented the two rival Houses. She was also a highly cultured person, who spoke French fluently, was well versed in literature, translating into English Thomas à Kempis's *The Imitation of Christ*, and was a patron of the arts. Lady Margaret was responsible for the founding of two Cambridge colleges, Christ's in 1505 and St John's in 1511 and endowed Lady Margaret professorships of divinity at both Oxford and Cambridge universities.[5] Although Henry was to be separated from her for many years, there was a close bond between them, strengthened by a mutual love of literature and the visual arts. In one of his letters to his mother, Henry wrote, 'I shall be glad to please you as your heart desire it, and I know well that I am as much bounden to you so to do, as any creature living for great and singular motherly love and affection that it hath pleased you at all times to bear me.' In return, she called Henry 'my good prince, king, and only beloved son'.[6]

Henry became a ward of William, Lord Herbert Raglan, for a decade and his upbringing was largely undertaken by his uncle Jasper, Earl of Pembroke. Because of his Lancastrian royal connections, Henry was regarded as a political threat after the outbreak of the Wars of the Roses in 1455. When the Yorkists recovered the throne for Edward IV in 1471, Jasper and his nephew fled to France. Edward unsuccessfully attempted to get hold of Henry, 'the only imp now left of Henry VI's brood'.[7] The education of Henry, an intelligent and thorough person, as an Anglo-Welsh nobleman was already beginning to be influenced by the new Renaissance theories of education. Latin and French authors were very important, and one of his tutors, an Oxford scholar, Andreas Scotus, said that he had never seen a boy who exhibited so much quickness in learning. In France he continued his education; it was said that, as a fluent French speaker, he developed a taste for reading French classics, which he retained in later life. Henry also acquired the conventional skills in hawking and hunting. He was described a century later by the philosopher-statesman Francis Bacon as follows:

> He was a comely personage, a little above just [average] stature, well and straight limbed, but slender. His countenance was reverend, and a little like a Churchman: and as it was not strange [cold/arrogant] or dark [hiding thoughts or feelings], so neither was it winning or pleasing, but as the face of one well disposed. But it was to the disadvantage of the painter, for it was best when he spoke.[8]

Henry's love of art led to his commissioning leading Flemish painters to provide him with pictures[9] and we have the superb chapel in Westminster Abbey and the work at St George's Chapel, Windsor as evidence of his taste. He established many links with Renaissance Europe, especially Italy, where he attempted to legitimise his rule by allying himself with Rome.[10] There was much diplomatic activity and frequent contact with papal representatives, but it was Henry's admiration of humanist scholars which bore its greatest rewards. One particular favourite was an Italian, Polydore Vergil, who came to England in 1501 as deputy-collector of Peter's Pence (a contribution to the Pope). A historian of the universities of Bologna and Padua where he had studied, Vergil was presented with a Leicestershire living, and later became naturalised. Henry commissioned him to write a history of England, *Anglica Historia*, which devoted a chapter to each monarch from the reign of William the Conqueror to Henry's own reign, a practice copied subsequently by many historians. It was a good choice of authorship and although the book did not appear in print until 1534, it became an influential source for many writers, including Shakespeare; in 1589 it became required reading in all schools.

One outstanding humanist, Desiderius Erasmus, who was born in Amsterdam, made two visits to England during Henry's reign, in 1499 and 1506, and visited the King at court in the company of Sir Thomas More. Erasmus himself wrote a number of education textbooks, such as *De Ratione Studii* ('On the Correct Method of Study') (1511), *De Civilitate Morum Puerilium* ('On the Politeness of Children's Manners') (1526), and *De Pueris Statim ac Liberalitur Insitutendis* ('On the Liberal Education of Boys') (1529). He was impressed with what he saw in the capital, declaring London, not Oxford or Cambridge, to be the country's most important educational centre. 'There are in London', Erasmus wrote to a friend, 'five or six Latin and Greek scholars of deepest learning such as not even Italy could now show'.[11] There he established friendships with some of the leading English humanists, including John Colet, the founder of St Paul's School, and Thomas Linacre, who was both a physician and a classical scholar and briefly tutor to Prince Arthur before his early death, and William Grocyn, one of the earliest men to introduce Greek literature into England.[12] Henry was on friendly terms with Italian princes, such as the Dukes of Milan, Ferrara and Urbino. He greatly admired the Duke of Urbino as a patron of the arts and education and in 1506 appointed him to the Order of the Garter. It was received on his behalf by Baldassare Castiglione, the future author of *Il Cortegiano*. In return, Castiglione brought Henry as a gift from the Duke a painting of St George and the Dragon by one of Urbino's most brilliant artists, Raphael.[13]

Henry's love of France was apparent at his court. Indeed, the Spanish ambassador in London wrote to Ferdinand IV in 1498, 'He would like to govern in the French fashion, but he cannot. He is subject to his Council.'[14] Henry also looked to France for significant people for his court. Bernard André, a blind friar, had been introduced to Henry before he was king. Shortly after the Battle of Bosworth, André was given a religious post in England. He soon began lecturing at Oxford and was later appointed as England's first royal historiographer.[15] André wrote extensively; his most famous poem, *Les Douze Triomphes de Henry VII*, in 79 stanzas, was illustrative of the classical nature of the New Learning. André also acted as tutor to Henry's sons, Arthur and Henry. It is not surprising that their education was planned to reflect the new humanism.

Henry's experience of exile as a youth played an important part in the formation of his character. His ability to speak French enabled him to follow diplomatic events in Europe and he was able to act accordingly. He was adept at making rapid decisions and was something of an opportunist. While of necessity he established close links with Europe in order to ensure the survival of the Tudor dynasty, he was active in introducing humanist educators into England and was one of the most important patrons of his era.[16] The fruits of this new development will be seen in the education of the royal children.

## HENRY VIII (1491–1547)

Henry's education had begun early. Only a few weeks after his birth at Greenwich on 28 June 1491, he was sent to Eltham Palace, one of his father's country houses, where he was joined by his 5-year-old brother Arthur, the heir to the throne, and 1-year-old sister Margaret. The detailed regulation of the nursery was dictated not by their mother, but by their grandmother, Lady Margaret Beaufort.[17] The royal children's mealtimes were supervised by a physician and his food was tasted for poison. The royal arms were everywhere displayed.

Lady Margaret was also responsible for the appointment in 1498 of Henry's future tutor, John Skelton, one of the greatest English poets of his time. Born about 1460, Skelton studied at Cambridge and was then employed in Lady Margaret's household school before entering her son's service. She probably calculated that Skelton, an extrovert noted for his wit and irreverence, would be a good match for her equally outgoing grandson.[18] Skelton, who had already translated Cicero's letters and Diodorus Siculus's *History of the World* into English, was an excellent teacher, giving his charge a sound classical education. He instructed Henry in the works of Livy, Caesar, Ovid, Terence and Tacitus, though he ignored the study of Greek literature. He remained tutor to the two princes until the death of Arthur in 1502. Some notion of the progress of the royal education can be gleaned from the well-known visit of Erasmus, together with Sir Thomas More, to the 8-year-old Henry at Eltham. More presented the Prince with some of his writings, but Erasmus had not prepared an offering. Afterwards Erasmus, who had noted 'already something of royalty in his [Henry's] demeanour', received a letter later that day 'challenging something from his pen'. Thereafter, they exchanged Latin correspondence with each other. William Blount, Lord Mountjoy, who introduced the Prince to humanists visiting England, assured Erasmus that a letter written by Henry to him in perfect Latin on the death of Philip the Fair of Castile was Henry's own unaided work. His mastery of Latin continued into adulthood. Cardinal Bainbridge wrote in 1513, 'There cometh no letters from any other prince unto his Holiness [Leo X] to be exhibited in the Consistory than be judged more elegantly written than they be.'[19] His book attacking Luther, written eight years later, was almost entirely in his own hand. Skelton, who decided to take holy orders because of his post as royal tutor, wrote a manual in 1501 for his pupils, *Speculum Principis* ('A Prince's Mirror'), which stressed the importance of religious and moral instruction. It advised that Henry should keep all power in his own hands and 'choose a wife for yourself; prize her always uniquely'. Pleased with what he had achieved in educating the Prince, Skelton boasted in verse:

> The honour of England I learned to spell
> I gave him drink of the sugared well
> Of Helicon's waters crystalline,
> Acquainting him with the muses nine.[20]

Henry was also proficient in French, being taught by either Giles Duwes, author of a French grammar and an alchemist, or Bernard André. He learnt Spanish and understood Italian. Besides his mastery of languages, Henry is also remembered for his musical skills. By Tudor times music formed an increasingly important part of court and state ceremonials, as the inventory of Henry's enormous collection of musical instruments testifies. He was an accomplished performer on the lute, recorder, virginals and the organ, enjoyed singing and was a composer and arranger of vocal and instrumental pieces; no fewer than 34 of his compositions have survived. In 1517 it is reported that he listened for four hours on end to the organ playing of Dionysius Memo, the celebrated organist of St Mark's, Venice.[21]

The daily routine of his education must have been a taxing one. After rising early to hear matins sung, he would have attended mass at 6 o'clock, followed by a light meal accompanied by wine or ale. Lessons included mathematics, logic, law, languages and tales of chivalry. About 10 a.m. dinner was served, to be followed by activities in the martial arts, either jousting or fighting on horseback or on foot with blunt weapons or learning to use two-handed swords or battle-axes. Another meal followed at four in the afternoon, then music lessons with chess or gambling in the evenings. One interesting aspect of Henry's education was that it was shared with a group of other children who were in some ways related. Throughout this process, Henry was closely watched in order to ensure that he acquired the qualities necessary for kingship – courtesy, urbanity and dignity.

Henry, like his father, encouraged the presence of humanists at court and in the universities. There is a telling letter on the subject, even allowing for hyperbole, written by Lord Mountjoy to Erasmus shortly after Henry became king in 1509:

> Oh, my Erasmus, if you could see how all the world here is rejoicing in the possession of so great a prince … The other day he wished he was more learned. I said, that is not what we expect of your Grace, but that you will foster and encourage learned men. Yea, surely, said he, for indeed without them we should scarcely exist at all.[22]

In such a climate, education flourished. John Colet, Dean of St Paul's, founded a public school, St Paul's, in London in 1512 and it proved to be a model for the future. It differed from existing schools in that it was not intended for the education of the clergy but rather for the enlightened education of children. The curriculum reflected this aim and Colet produced textbooks to encourage the new methods of teaching.[23] The universities also flourished with the New Learning. Cardinal Wolsey planned to gather the best intellects in Europe to teach at his new Cardinal College, later renamed Christ Church, at Oxford, which was established in 1528. After Henry assumed royal supremacy, diocesan funds were appropriated for educational purposes in order to reconstitute or extend existing schools as the need for educated public servants grew. Henry's Scheme of Bishoprics provided for 'Colleges newly erected by the King's Highness'. At Canterbury, for instance, the existing school was reconstituted as the King's School in 1542 and at other cathedral cities such as Winchester, Worcester, Gloucester, Peterborough and Durham, colleges were either contemplated or revived.[24] Henry also had plans to expand an existing college at Cambridge, King's Hall. Its Great Gateway, which he built, now the entrance to Trinity College, contains a statue of him.

Henry inherited the crown of a country which was much more stable and prosperous than it had been in 1485. His elder brother Arthur had died suddenly at the age of 15 in 1502, leaving Henry as a popular, almost undisputed, heir to the throne. If we attempt to assess the effects of his education on his subsequent reign we are faced with two kinds of difficulty. First, historians have differed considerably in their assessment of Henry's qualities as a king; second, even if that assessment were less controversial, it would still be foolish to speculate too boldly on how much education had contributed to his alleged successes and failures. Henry's character was a complex one. He was widely read in literature and theology and was a gifted musician and a linguist. On the other hand, he suffered from over-powering egoism. Quite clearly what Henry mainly lacked was a strong enough sense of justice. This may have been due to a failing in his education or to an innate tendency or to the problem of acquiring royal power. What seems clear is that his moral training was not sufficiently strong to enable Henry to overcome the temptations with which he was later faced. Early in his reign he sacrificed the lives of Dudley and Empson while retaining the

1. *Henry VIII and Family,* unknown, *c.* 1545. From left to right: Mary I, Edward VI, Henry VIII, Jane Seymour and Elizabeth I. Jane Seymour, mother of Edward VI had died in childbirth eight years previously.

money which had resulted from their malpractice: his treatment of Wolsey and Thomas Cromwell later in the reign was equally unscrupulous. His egoism also tempted him into expensive wars and into debasing the coinage, the effects of which he may or may not have understood. In addition, Henry borrowed vast sums so that he left the country almost bankrupt on his death in 1547 at the age of 56.

Many of Henry's failings, however, could arguably be ascribed to his earlier years. He was never given any responsibility for affairs of state during his father's lifetime, a remarkable parallel some four centuries later with the future Edward VII. The early death of Henry's elder brother Arthur led Henry VII to deny his second son the opportunity of training for kingship. (It should also be remembered that the King had lost four other children as well as his wife during his lifetime.) He had as a youth been kept under strict supervision with limited freedom of movement and restricted access to others of his own age. Always a stern father, Henry VII ordered that his son should never speak in public except to answer one of the King's questions. Possibly the King considered that Prince Henry was in need of firm discipline. As one historian has commented, 'Whatever the truth of the matter, a modern may well shake his head over this story of evident repression of an ebullient youth and conclude that it explains a good deal of the flamboyance and waywardness of the grown man.'[25]

### EDWARD VI (1537–53)

Edward, the son of Henry's third wife, Jane Seymour, was born on 12 October 1537 at Hampton Court Palace. She died a few days after his birth and Edward was only 9 when his father died. The education of Edward VI is reasonably well documented, with more detail available than for most monarchs, probably for two reasons. The first is that because Edward only lived until the age of 15, biographers have been obliged to look closely at all aspects of his boyhood, including his education. The second reason is that not only were some of Edward's tutors interested in the theory of education as well as its practice, but, fortunately, they wrote about these matters as well. Thus we have letters and the writings of Ascham, and the extensive correspondence of his tutors, Cox and Cheke, as well as some comments made by Edward himself in his *Chronicle* and elsewhere. Edward has generally been regarded as well educated. What was missing from his upbringing was an emotional sensitivity. His curriculum was thorough and disciplined but lacked the Renaissance concern for poetry and the arts. Edward was certainly not *l'uomo universale*; he was too close to fanaticism to fit the Renaissance ideal, but many historians have admired his youthful dignity and his attempts to be a just king.

We know that Henry VIII took a close interest in all aspects of his only son's upbringing. Henry was almost obsessed with the need for everything connected with the Prince to be done correctly and diligently, from the maintenance of the royal nursery to the preparation of food. Henry was similarly concerned with the detailed arrangements for Edward's upbringing and early education. In May 1538, Henry appointed Lady Mary Bryan, who had been governess to Edward's sisters, Princess Mary and Princess Elizabeth, to supervise his upbringing for the next six years. She was a warm-hearted and efficient person but easy-going, providing a comfortable environment for the education of the future king.

When he was 4, Edward began his first lessons, consisting of Greek and Latin entirely by the oral method. The Prince's curriculum was much influenced by the publication a few years earlier in 1531 of Sir Thomas Elyot's *The Boke Named the Governour*. It was dedicated to Henry VIII and, claiming that the upper classes did not hold learning in such high esteem as they had 50 years earlier, it urged that men with power and money should ensure a thorough Christian education for their children. The great novelty of the book was that it was written entirely in English. Henry thought highly of Elyot – he was twice ambassador to Charles V of Spain – and his theories of education were applied to Edward's schooling. Elyot forcefully expressed his views on the standard of teaching which prevailed at the time. 'Good Lord', he wrote, 'how many good and clear wits of children be now a days perished by ignorant schoolmasters?'[26]

Elyot recommended that all men except physicians should be excluded from the nursery but at the age of 7, a man tutor should be appointed whose first task was to 'know the nature of his pupil'. As a humanist, he advocated the importance of high-born children learning classical languages. The pupils should be 'sweetly allured' into learning, using play-way and conversation methods, and Latin was to be taught 'in the most gentle manner'. His Latin–English dictionary of 1538 was the first such work to be compiled by an Englishman. Elyot believed that even small boys would readily learn Latin, Greek and French provided they were not burdened with the tedious study of grammar. A somewhat more rigorous regime was to follow after the child's early years. The content and style of classical writings were to be digested. Elyot particularly recommended the study of poets, with oratory and rhetoric added from the age of 14. Cosmography also featured in the curriculum to illustrate classical history, and from the age of 17, the pupil, he suggested, should become acquainted with moral philosophy. To balance this heavy intellectual programme, Elyot stressed the need for physical activities such as dancing, hunting, riding, fencing, swimming, wrestling, shooting, hawking and archery, in order to develop various skills which would build both character and courage. Deportment was another essential feature.

Up to the age of 6 Edward was, in his own words, brought up 'among women'. His first tutor, Dr Richard Cox, a moderate Protestant, had been recommended by Archbishop Cranmer. Cox was a former Provost of Eton and Dean of Lincoln, and while still Edward's tutor he became the first Dean of Christ Church, Oxford.

When Edward began reading it was from a horn book in which the letters were illustrated in colour. Penmanship came later and continued under the supervision of Roger Ascham. Edward was trained in two kinds of handwriting; first the simple 'Roman' hand which was used for ordinary correspondence and then the very elaborate 'engrossing' style that took many years to perfect.[27] Occasionally Edward and Elizabeth worked together with Ascham on this task.

Edward recovered from his first serious illness in 1543 when he was six. He was suitably encouraged by Cox and other masters who taught him many other subjects. By the following year, his Latin and Greek were good enough for him to translate and compose easily; his reading in English was mostly from the Bible. Like his father he was very fond of music and he studied singing and musical composition under Dr Christopher Tye, the notable composer, and the lute and probably other instruments under the Flemish musician, Philip van Wilder. He enjoyed a range of outside sports, including tennis, and some indoor games such as cards, chess and backgammon which were later discouraged by Ascham because they involved gambling.

Cox tried to use progressive methods of teaching, making a military game out of learning syntax and grammar. After a time Edward got bored with it and Cox was faced with a great enemy, 'Captain Will', who must be defeated. 'I think', Cox wrote, 'that only [one] wound shall be enough to daunt both Will and all his fellows.' Eventually, Cox resorted to corporal punishment and thereafter obtained obedience from his royal pupil.

In 1544 when Edward was 7, an additional tutor was employed, Sir John Cheke, a brilliant Greek scholar and the first Regius Professor of that subject at Cambridge. Greek was then little known in England and Cheke was eager to promote a wider knowledge of the language.[28] At 30, he was a much younger man than Cox and a more stimulating teacher who believed in modern methods. Among his many distinguished students were William Cecil the statesman, and Ascham. Cheke enlarged his horizons by introducing the Prince to some of his Cambridge friends. When it was thought that Edward needed companionship, a small private school of about 14 children was set up at court under Cheke's supervision. Among Edward's fellow pupils were Henry Brandon, Duke of Suffolk, who was some years his senior, Sidney, Earl of Warwick and James Butler, Earl of Ormonde. Barnaby Fitzpatrick, a high-spirited and intelligent youth, became a friend of the Prince and was reputedly Edward's proxy for correction. One benefit of this system, according to legend, was that the Prince would not be personally chastised but would be intimidated by witnessing the punishment of his colleagues.[29] This period, from 1544 to 1547, was probably the happiest of his life. In the latter year he became king on the death of Henry VIII, but his educational programme continued. Cox retired in 1549 and Cheke, now Provost of King's College, Cambridge, became chief tutor.

In addition to attending Council and other formal meetings, Edward was now studying passages from Cato, Aesop and Cicero as well the Old and the New Testaments. Cheke had established a good working relationship with the new king. According to his earliest biographer, Cheke was 'always at his elbow, both in his closet and in his chapel, and wherever else he went, to inform him and teach him'.[30] Cheke told that Edward was beginning Plutarch's *Apophthegms, Morals and Lives* and had started geometry and Italian, as well as having regular geography, history and Latin lessons. He also showed promise in philosophy and logic, music and astronomy. There were serious gaps in his curriculum, though, as it contained very little imaginative literature such as the works of Sir Thomas Malory or Geoffrey Chaucer which were being read by other young people at this time. A good pen picture of the Prince is afforded in the posthumous *Life and Raigne of King Edward the Sixth* by an early seventeenth-century historian, Sir John Hayward:

> These his acquirements by industrie were exceedingly both enriched and enlarged by many excellent endowments of nature. For in disposition he was milde, gracious and pleasant, of an heavenly wit, in body beautifull, but especially in his eies, which seemed to hue a starrie livelynes and lustre in them, generall he seemed to be as Cardane [an Italian philosopher] reported of him A MIRACLE OF NATURE.[31]

Some formal letters written by Edward have been preserved. In one to the Queen he asked her to beg his half-sister Mary to 'attend no longer the foreign dances and merriments, which do not become a Christian Princess'. This has been taken as evidence of his growing Puritanism. Edward's views on religion became harsh, bordering on the fanatical. His English lessons were mainly from the Bible. In the first year of his reign he made a special study of the books of Proverbs, Ecclesiastes and the four Gospels. Before he was 11, Edward was convinced, partly by Cheke, that heretics should be reasoned with and punished but not burned. He thus avoided the wholesale religious executions that characterised Mary's reign.

In 1550, when Edward was almost 12½ years old, Cheke suggested to him that he should keep a *Chronicle* which started with his own birth. Edward continued to make entries until November 1552, seven months before his death. It is not a personal diary, but a formal political account of foreign and military affairs, with some discussion of religious controversies and other civil and economic matters. Nevertheless the *Chronicle* displays the King's love of words, which he used with considerable skill and linguistic daring, coining many words which are still in use today.[32] Edward was now translating Cicero's *Philosophy* into Greek and the works of Demosthenes and Isocrates into Italian and French. His fluency in French was due to his tutor, Jean Belmaine, a Calvinist who probably influenced the development of his pupil's strongly held Protestant sentiments.[33] When Edward showed signs of ill-temper, Cheke would remind him that 'Every fault is greater in a king than in a mean man.'

He was expected to read ten chapters of the Bible every day, and was conversant with the current theological debates and issues of his time. After religion his main concern was with an important aspect of economics at the time, that of the currency. His adviser on the matter was Sir Thomas Gresham, the founder of the Royal Exchange, and Edward showed much greater financial prudence than had his father during his reign. Although his formal education was intended to end when he was 14, he continued to enjoy his studies with Cheke and others. From the beginning of 1553 his death was seen to be approaching. Edward continued to the end of his life to study, especially religious texts. Amongst his last readings were Tye's *Acts of the Apostles in Rhyme* and Thomas Sternhold's *Psalms in Metre*, both recently published and dedicated to him. It is an appropriate memorial to Edward's scholarship that, with the reallocation of charity funds for educational purposes following the Chantries Act of 1547, 27 of the new endowed schools should bear his name.

## MARY I (1516–58)

The education of Mary Tudor posed problems which previous sovereigns had not faced. Although her father Henry VIII and her mother Catherine of Aragon produced many children, only Mary survived infancy. It seemed at the time that she could possibly become the first Queen of England in her own right since Boadicea.

Mary was born on 20 February 1516 at Greenwich Palace. From the earliest age, she was almost exclusively attended by women. Lady Margaret Bryan was an early governess, to be replaced in 1520 by Mary's godmother, Margaret Pole, Countess of Salisbury, and her household moved with her on the frequent visits to other royal residences. Catherine, who was described by Erasmus as 'a miracle of female learning',[34] oversaw the early education of her daughter. She was well qualified for this task, having benefited from a good humanist education in Spain, and she was anxious that Mary should equally benefit from the New Learning. However, there is little evidence that in the first four years of her life Mary was subject to any formal instruction, except being taught the alphabet by her mother. When Mary was seven, Catherine invited a fellow Spaniard, Juan Luis Vives, to suggest a plan of action for Mary's future education.

Vives was born in Valencia in 1492 of a noble family. His own upbringing was marred by the stern discipline of his mother. Recalling an early long separation from her he wrote, 'When I was come home, I could not perceive that she ever longed for me. Therefore there was nobody that I did more flee, or was loth to come nigh than my mother when I was a child.'[35] Vives attracted the attention of Erasmus as a scholar, and, with the support of Wolsey and More, arrived in England in 1523. To what extent his own experiences coloured his views in writing his book commissioned by Catherine for her daughter entitled *De Institutione Faeminae Christianae*, translated into English as *The Instruction of a Christian Woman*, is now hard to say. In the preface, Vives declared, 'Your dearest daughter Mary shall read these instructions of mine, and following in living. Which she must needs do, if she order herself after the example that she hath at home with her, of your virtue and wisdom.' The book was designed as a blueprint for a future monarch who would have all the virtues expected of her. Vives envisaged education as a form of protection against immorality, noting that woman is by nature 'the devil's instrument, and not Christ's'. He followed his friend Erasmus in stating that 'nothing so completely preserves the modesty of young girls as learning', for without it 'many from simplicity and inexperience have lost their chastity before they knew that such an inestimable treasure was in danger'.[36] Vives warned against allowing her to read love poems, especially Ovid, who inclined women to silly fancies and to lust, or medieval romances. Instead, he recommended religious texts, especially the Bible. For obvious reasons, teaching was to take place in the home and not in the company of others.

Catherine requested Vives to outline a curriculum which would meet most of these requirements. As a result he wrote *De Ratione Studii Puerilis* which supplemented the previous work. The New Testament was to be read morning and night together with the works of the early Christian poets and other suitable authors. For an understanding of government, Plato's dialogues were recommended as well as More's *Utopia*. The classics should figure prominently, with Justinius, Plutarch and Valerius Maximus being recommended for history. Both Latin and Greek should be learned by reading appropriate texts. Certain 'heathen' poets, such as Seneca and Horace, were permitted. On the matter of teaching, Vives was one of the first writers to base education on psychology. 'Observe the child and adopt your aims and methods to his needs' was his main principle.[37]

Vives's advice on female education was an unsentimental one. As he wrote, 'The daughter should be handled without any cherishing. For cherishing marreth sons, but it utterly destroys daughters.' Nevertheless, given that equality of educational opportunities between the sexes at the time was not an issue, Vives's views were in many respects enlightened. He differed from other humanists in recommending that mothers, rather than tutors, should instruct their offspring in infancy. Vives also believed in lifelong education for both boys and girls, and recommended a wide range of choice in reading materials.[38] It is unlikely that Vives himself ever taught Mary, but his precepts were closely followed during her subsequent education. He fell into disfavour with the King in siding with Catherine after the divorce proceedings and never returned to England after 1528.

Thomas Linacre was appointed as Mary's Latin tutor at the same time as Vives's arrival in England. The post may have been a sinecure because of his other multifarious activities as a medical man and a classicist. Linacre's biographer relates that he was also Mary's physician but was unable to fulfil this role because of his own failing health. Anxious to render a suitable service to her, Linacre composed for the 7-year-old princess a book entitled *Rudimenta Grammatices* ('The Rudiments of Grammar'), published in 1524.[39] It was dedicated to Mary and was a guide to Latin grammar, written in English. The book was subsequently widely used in grammar schools. Linacre died the following year aged 64.

One of her main tutors was Richard Fetherston, who was chaplain to Catherine. It seems that he took over much of the teaching from Catherine when Mary was 7. Recommended by Vives, Fetherston accompanied the Princess when Henry sent her, together with her household and the council, to Wales in 1525. The Queen wrote to her on her departure:

> As for your writing Latin, I am glad that ye shall change from me to Master Federston, for that shall do you much good to learn by him to write aright. But yet sometimes I would be glad when ye do write to Master Federston of your own enditing, when he hath read it that I might see it. For it shall be a great comfort to me to see you keep your Latin and fair writing and all.

Mary was still Henry's only legitimate heir and her journey in the West Country and the Welsh Marches as Princess of Wales were intended to prepare her for her future role. At the same time, she continued with her studies. The Countess of Salisbury, after a spell of time in the King's disfavour, was once more Mary's governess, and accompanied her on this visit. Detailed directions were issued to her council on how the Princess should pass her time:

> At seasons convenient, to use moderate exercise for taking open air in gardens, sweet and wholesome places and walks … and likewise to pass her time most seasons at her virginals or other instruments musical, so that the same be not too much, and without fatigation or weariness to intend to her learning the Latin tongue and French. At other seasons to dance, and among the residue to have good respect unto her diet, which is meet to be well prepared, dressed, and served with comfortable, joyous and merry communication in all honourable and virtuous manner; and likewise unto the cleanliness and well wearing of her garments and apparel, so that everything about her be pure, sweet, clean, and wholesome.

Another member of the household concerned with her lessons was Giles Duwes, who had probably introduced Mary's father to the French language. Duwes, a former Royal librarian, was a witty and lively teacher. He prepared a French grammar for Mary, An *Introductorie for to lerne to rede, to pronounce, and to speke French trewly*, which contains several imaginary dialogues between the Princess and Duwes, messengers from Henry VIII and foreign rulers on a range of topics, including piety and courtly love, as well as a mock epitaph on the death of French through indifference.

Many outside observers commented on Mary's accomplishments, not only flattering courtiers. For example, Mary was visited by a Venetian delegation who reported, 'This Princess is not tall, has a pretty face and is well proportioned with a very beautiful complexion and is 15 years old. She speaks Spanish, French, and Latin ... is well grounded in Greek, and understands Italian but does not venture to speak it. She sings excellently and plays several instruments.'[40]

There is other evidence of her educational progress and accomplishments. At the age of 13, Mary translated *The Prayer of St Thomas of Aquinas* from Latin into English, which can be seen in the British Library. Less is known about her grasp of Italian and Spanish, though at one stage she secretly corresponded with her mother in the latter language. The picture painted by a French bishop of Mary at the age of 20 being knowledgeable in theology, philosophy, music, several foreign languages and mathematics is probably an exaggerated one, but nevertheless indicates the wide field of her intellectual interests.

In attempting to trace the influence of Mary's education on her subsequent role as monarch, a number of factors must be borne in mind. From early childhood she was isolated from her mother and the company of other children and was supervised with unusual intensity by her household. Her childhood was a solemn one, with few emotional outlets and little record of laughter or being indulged with toys or other games.[41] Her mother's strong Catholic convictions were doubtless transmitted during Mary's childhood and reinforced by readings from religious texts. She remained convinced in her religious beliefs throughout her life, leading to the highly unpopular and personally disastrous marriage with Philip of Spain in 1554.

To add to her emotional deprivation, Mary was sent away from her parents for various reasons, both political and domestic. She was separated from Catherine after Henry abandoned her for Anne Boleyn in 1531 and Mary was only allowed to see her once in the remaining five years of Catherine's life. Mary's relationship with her father deteriorated because of her refusal to obey him after the divorce and she was declared illegitimate; she received little sympathy from her stepmother, Anne Boleyn. Mary also gradually lost those who had been largely responsible for her upbringing through the departure of Vives from England after he fell into disfavour, the death of Linacre and the execution of her governess, the Countess of Salisbury, on Henry's orders as well as that of her tutor, Richard Fetherston. Some of these events may well account for the intolerance she displayed in the persecution of her Protestant subjects during the five years she was queen and which earned her the soubriquet 'Bloody Mary'. It does seem however, in the end, that one of the consolations of Mary's sound education was her ability to find solace in her studies. One of her last recorded acts, when she was tired and ill, was to begin a translation of Erasmus's paraphrase of the Gospel of St John, though it lay unfinished on her death on 17 November 1558 at the age of 42.

## ELIZABETH I (1533–1603)

There is little doubt that Elizabeth succeeded in becoming one of the best educated of the Tudors, in spite of many early handicaps. She was born on 7 September 1533 at Greenwich Palace, the daughter of Henry VIII and his second wife, Anne Boleyn. Henry wanted a son, and it was not thought likely at the time that one day she would reach the throne. It is believed that Anne had planned to give her daughter a humanistic education, and it is known that she entrusted Elizabeth's care to her chaplain, Matthew Parker, a former promising Cambridge scholar and future Archbishop of Canterbury. However, any such plans came to an end with the execution of Anne in 1536 after being accused of adultery with five men, including her own brother. Elizabeth, not yet 3 years old, had lost both her mother and her legitimacy, being declared a bastard on Henry's marriage to Jane Seymour, 11 days after Anne's execution.

Elizabeth was now put under the care of Lady Bryan at Hunsdon House in Hertfordshire, along with her sister Mary. Lady Bryan complained to Thomas Cromwell, the King's principal adviser, that because of reductions in the household budget, the little princess was lacking in suitable clothes. She also complained that Elizabeth was being obliged to take her meals in

(more than euer i did) i do confesse,
that i haue broken myne othe, and
promesse. Alas thou haddest cho
sen me for thy wife. and didest sett
me vp in great dignitie, and hon
noure. (ffor what greatter hōnour
may one haue than to be in the
place of thy wife. wich swittely ta
keth reste nere to the) of all thy
goodes, quene, maistres, and lady.
and also in suretie, both of body
and soule. i so vile a creature, be
ynge ennoblished by the. Nowe
(to tell the truth) i had more, and
better than any man, can desyre

2.    Elizabeth I's handwriting, aged 11, 1544.

the hall instead of being given an appropriate nursery diet:

> My lord, Mr Shelton [Sir John Shelton, the steward of the house]
> would have my Lady Elizabeth to dine and sup every day at the
> board of estate. Alas! my lord, it is not meet for a child of her age
> to keep such rule yet. I promise you, my lord, I dare not take it
> upon me to keep her Grace in health an' she keep that rule. For
> there she shall see divers meats, and fruits, and wine, which it
> would be hard for me to restrain her Grace from. Ye know, my
> lord, there is no place of correction there; and she is yet too young
> to correct greatly.[42]

Few details of her childhood are known. After the birth of her
half-brother, Edward, in 1537 to Jane Seymour, who died in
childbirth, Elizabeth and Mary took part in the christening
ceremony; because of her age, Elizabeth had to be carried by a
nobleman. Both sisters were pawns in the diplomatic game of
attempted marriages to French and Habsburg princes and in
spite of her illegitimacy, the Act of 1544 put Elizabeth in line of
succession after Edward and Mary. Elizabeth, despite her
treatment at his hands, always held her father in high esteem and
was fascinated by his power and wealth. She also admired him
greatly for his stance against the Pope and his becoming head of
the Church as well as of the State.[43]

These years must have been full of anxiety for the young
Elizabeth. Henry had briefly been married briefly to Anne of
Cleves in 1540 and this was followed by marriage to Catherine
Howard, who was executed two years later. The sixth and final
marriage of Henry in 1543, to Catherine Parr, brought about
many changes in the lives of the three royal children.

Catherine Parr's own educational attainments were modest,
but because of her interest in the education of women, she
ensured that the tuition to be received by her stepdaughter was
as well supervised as that for Edward (Mary was by this time 27
years old). Catherine's household was described at the time as 'a
school of virtue for learned virgins [where] it was now a common
thing to see young virgins so trained in the study of good letters
that they willingly set all other vain pastimes at naught for
learning's sake'.[44]

Elizabeth was already proficient at Latin and Italian by the
time she was 10. Her first letter to Catherine Parr dated July 1544,

was in Italian, mainly as a school exercise,[45] and with her stepmother's encouragement Elizabeth flourished. She expressed her gratitude to Catherine by sending her as a New Year's gift for 1545 a translation of a mystical poem by Marguerite d'Angoulême, Queen of Navarre, entitled 'The Mirror or Glass of the Sinful Soul'.[46] As Elizabeth wrote in an accompanying letter, 'I translated this little book out of French rhyme into English prose, joining the sentences together as well as the capacity of my simple wit and small learning could extend themselves.' Elizabeth shared her lessons with her brother Edward, receiving sound tuition in the classics from John Cheke, French from Jean Belmaine and Italian from Battisti Castiglione, using her skills to produce a version in all three languages of Catherine Parr's own *Prayers and Meditations*.

Elizabeth's education was disrupted by a series of astonishing events following the death of Henry VIII in 1547. Within a few weeks, Catherine surprised the court by marrying Sir Thomas Seymour, the younger brother of Edward, the latter of whom had appointed himself to the position of Lord Protector to the young king. Thomas, who was jealous of his brother's position, insisted on being raised to the peerage and given the title of Lord High Admiral. He had hoped to marry the 14-year-old Elizabeth, but on realising the impossibility of this plan, instead successfully courted Catherine Parr.

During the following year, Elizabeth lived with Seymour and Catherine at their Chelsea house. He soon began to visit Elizabeth's bedchamber in the morning, slapping her back and buttocks and sometimes appearing barelegged in his night gown. On one occasion in the garden, Seymour tore Elizabeth's dress to pieces while Catherine pinioned Elizabeth's arms. There is little doubt that the Princess was flattered by the older man's attentions. The farce came to a sudden end about Whitsun 1548, when by chance the now pregnant Catherine came across the couple 'all alone, he having her in his arms'. The following day, Elizabeth was sent off to Sir Anthony Denny's household at Cheshunt, together with her new tutor, Roger Ascham. After Catherine's death that same autumn, Seymour pursued his plans to seek Elizabeth's hand in marriage, but he was arrested in January 1549 for high treason and executed in March.

It has been suggested that the architect of Elizabeth's later education was Sir Anthony Denny,[47] a favourite of Henry VIII who had been educated at St Paul's School and St John's College, Cambridge. Denny had acquired the leases of many rich demesnes at Waltham Abbey, Essex, after the dissolution of the monasteries and lived at nearby Cheshunt.[48] He was probably instrumental earlier in the appointment of his relative, Catherine (Kat) Ashley as Elizabeth's governess; she quickly won the Princess's confidence and remained a close friend for many years. Kat's main task was to guide her in modesty and virtue and to teach her female accomplishments. Needlework, for instance, was mastered to such an extent that Elizabeth was able to present her brother with a cambric shirt 'of her own working'. Kat's husband, John Ashley, was a friend of Roger Ascham; the latter had in 1546 recommended his favourite pupil, William Grindal, a fellow of St John's College, Cambridge to be a Greek tutor to Elizabeth. Ascham had praised Grindal for his intelligence and judgement and Grindal inspired Elizabeth in her study of the language for the next two years. He was still in his early twenties when he died of the plague in 1548.

Elizabeth was able to persuade Catherine and Seymour that Ascham should become her tutor despite the fact that they had other plans for her. Ascham remained in Elizabeth's employ, with interruptions, for the next two decades. Ascham, who taught Greek at St John's College, Cambridge, had made his name through his book *Toxophilus, the schole of Shootinge*, published in 1545 and dedicated to King Henry. It was one of the first scholarly books published in English, in Ascham's own words, 'this English matter, in the English tongue, for Englishmen'. Ascham praises archery as a suitable pastime for noblemen, stating that 'The best wits to learning must needs have much recreation, and ceasing from their books, or else they mar themselves.' The book is an interesting example of a blend of humanism with the best of the old training of chivalry.[49]

Ascham's better known book *The Scholemaster*, addressed to both gentlemen and gentlewomen, was published in 1570 after his death. It deals with his philosophy of teaching and the best methods to adopt for encouraging children. In the preface to the book, Ascham states that the subject arose out of a discussion with Sir Richard Sackville, who recalled his own unhappy schooldays when he was taught by the threat of the rod. Ascham calls for

41

'gentleness in teaching' as 'gentleness allures to learning'. He himself had used this approach with the young princess, as can be gathered from the advice which he gave to Kat Ashley:

> Good Mrs, I would have you in any case to labour, and not to give yourself to ease. I wish all increase of virtue and honour to that my good lady whose wit, good Mrs Astley, I beseech you, somewhat favour. The younger, the more tender; the quicker, the easier to break. Blunt edges be dull, and dure much pain to little profit; the free edge is soon turned if it be not handled thereafter. If you pour much drink at once into a goblet, the most part will dash out and run over; if you pour it softly you may fill it even to the top, and so her grace, I doubt not, by little and little, may be increased in learning, that at length greater cannot be required.[50]

The second part of *The Scholemaster* dealt with the 'plaine and perfite way of teachyng children to understand, write and speake the Latin tongue'. Ascham spent each morning with Elizabeth studying passages from the Greek New Testament followed by reading the tragedies of Sophocles or speeches by Isocrastes and Demosthenes. The afternoons were devoted to Latin authors, mainly Livy and Cicero, together with the works of the Early Fathers, such as the *De disciplina virginum* of St Cyprian. Ascham's method was not confined to the dry teaching of grammar and syntax. He was eager that Elizabeth studied the style of classical authors in order to improve her own, at the same time acquainting her with the character of the writers themselves. He also introduced her to 'double translation', whereby, for example, a passage from Livy would be turned into English and then back again into Latin. Ascham's teaching, according to his biographer, was an attempt to realise in a perfect subject the educational ideal which he had formed while tutoring at Cambridge.

> He sought to mould the mind and character of his apt pupil by combining the best learning contained in the classics with the saving doctrines of Christianity. This meant for him ... guiding her according to Aristotelian precepts of natural virtue, in order that she might achieve true *areté*, and at the same time inculcating Christian piety by having her read the Bible and selected patrisitic writings.[51]

The curriculum was not a narrow one with undue concentration on book work. As Ascham had declared in his

There is little doubt that, while undertaking her educational studies, Elizabeth was affected by the Seymour episode. Her governess, Kat Ashley, had been interrogated by Sir Robert Tyrwhitt, the head of Elizabeth's household, and she had confessed to witnessing Seymour's amorous approaches to the Princess. Subsequently, Elizabeth herself was closely questioned but denied any improper behaviour on her part. She was then moved in the next few years from place to place, such as to Hatfield and Ashridge, and scrupulously avoided being caught up in the events of Lady Jane Grey's brief queenship. Her isolation following the failed rebellion of Sir Thomas Wyatt in Mary's reign further reinforced her determination to remain seemingly neutral. She henceforth covered her personal vulnerability with a display of virtue accompanied by a modesty of dress, distancing herself from any whiff of scandal in her private life.

However, it is clear that Elizabeth benefited from the Renaissance view that the nobility, including rulers, both male and female, should be educated to a high standard and in her time was considered something of a bluestocking. She encouraged local initiatives in education – there were some 360 grammar schools by 1600 – and she took a close interest in the development of Sir Thomas Gresham's College in the City.[54] Elizabeth's knowledge of languages, as we have seen, was impressive. This helped to establish her as a figure of importance in the diplomatic world when unmarried queens were not generally acceptable. She had learned a good deal of statecraft from her formal studies which stood her in good stead in her struggle for survival in a turbulent age and she was politically astute. She herself symbolised the unity of Church and State. Such a policy was only possible because she avoided the extreme religious positions of Edward and Mary. She understood the doctrinal controversies very well and while there would seem to be no reason to doubt her sincere belief in some of the Protestant views which she acquired from her tutors (she once wrote that 'she had never been taught the doctrine of the ancient religion'),[55] it was very convenient for her to be able to merge them into a consensus of religious settlement.

On the negative side, one criticism that has been made of Elizabeth is that she shared the Tudor family problem of being

44

unable to make up her mind. Sometimes, of course, this was a cunning ploy to avoid taking a decision which would cause trouble. But there were other occasions when her indecision was extremely frustrating to her advisers. The ever-faithful William Cecil, Lord Burghley, her principal minister, was frequently driven to the point where his patience was almost exhausted. In the case of the execution of Mary Queen of Scots, Elizabeth not only found it difficult to decide, but having yielded to pressure to have Mary executed, then blamed an assistant secretary for exceeding his authority. One recent biographer of Elizabeth, after examining the possible effect of her education on her subsequent actions, concluded:

> It might be well argued that Elizabeth's coldly calculating view of politics and her secular view of the function of religion in society owed something to her reading of the classical moralists. There is little evidence that the substance of their argument affected her practice of politics. She was familiar with at least one work of Erasmus, but there is little evidence that his humanist moralism touched her feelings. Machiavelli – had she read him – would have been more congenial to her way of proceeding. Her cool pragmatism owed more to her own harsh experience than to any bookish instruction.[56]

The Tudor monarchs were all well educated. All of them owed much to Renaissance educational ideas. In addition, Elizabeth and Mary benefited from the sixteenth-century view that girls should be as well educated as boys. The continuity of Tudor royal education was provided by Renaissance ideals and theories as well as the practical work of such inspired teachers as Ascham and Vives. On the other hand, royal education during the Tudor period changed dramatically, largely on account of the religious ideas of the Reformation and Counter-Reformation, swinging from the Catholic orthodoxy of Henry VII and Henry VIII to narrow Protestantism under Edward VI; back to the old faith under Mary, and finally a splendid English compromise with Elizabeth I.

By the beginning of the seventeenth century, education in England had changed considerably, and so had the notion of sovereignty and the public perception of kings and queens. The price paid by Henry VIII for his divorce was much greater parliamentary influence and power. In the seventeenth century this would have serious implications for monarchs and for the education of monarchs. We shall explore these issues in the next chapter.

NOTES

1  J. D. Mackie, *The Earlier Tudors, 1485–1558* (Oxford University Press, 1952), p. 1.
2. See M. E. Cosenza, *Biographical and Bibliographical Dictionary of the Italian Humanism in Italy, 1300–1800* (Boston, MA: G.K. Hall, 1962), vol. 4.
3. J. H. Plumb, *The Penguin Book of the Renaissance* (Penguin, 1964), p. 272.
4. M. J. Tucker, 'The Child as Beginning and End: Fifteenth and Sixteenth Century English Childhood', in L. de Mause (ed.), *The History of Childhood* (Souvenir Press, 1976), p. 246.
5. For details of her university benefactions, see M. K. Jones and M. G. Underwood,*the King's Mother: Lady Margaret Beaumont, Countess of Richmond and Derby* (Cambridge University Press, 1992), pp. 202–31.
6. A.F. Pollard, *The Reign of Henry VII from Contemporary Sources* (Longman, Green, 1913), p. 220.
7. Quoted in S. B. Chrimes, *Henry VII* (Eyre, Methuen, 1972), p. 18.
8. J. Weinberger (ed.), *Francis Bacon: The History of the Reign of King Henry the Seventh* (Ithaca, NY: Cornell University Press, 1996), p. 6.
9. G. Temperley, *Henry VII* (Constable, 1917) p. 314.
10. N. Beckett, 'Henry VII and Sheen Charterhouse', in B. Thompson (ed.), *The Reign of Henry VII* (Stamford, Lincs.: Paul Watkins, 1995), p. 128.
11. E. E. Reynolds, *Thomas More and Erasmus* (Burns & Oates, 1965), p. 53.
12. K. Charlton, *Education in Renaissance England* (Routledge & Kegan Paul, 1965), p. 51.
13. D. Starkey, 'The Legacy of Henry VIII', in D. Starkey (ed.),*Henry VIII: A European Court in England* (Collins and Brown, 1991), p. 11.
14. C. H. Williams, *England under the Early Tudors* (Longman, Green, 1925), p. 149.
15. R. L. Storey, *The Reign of Henry VII* (Blandford Press, 1968), p. 6.
16. M. V. C. Alexander, *The First of the Tudors: A Study of Henry VII and his Reign* (Croom Helm, 1981), p. 165.
17. M. L. Bruce, *The Making of Henry VIII* (Collins, 1977), p. 35.
18. C. Erickson, *Great Harry* (Dent, 1980), p. 28. It has been noted that both Henry VII and Henry VIII made a deliberate change of policy by not appointing noble masters for their sons, so that the political fortunes of the masters should not compromise the future of the children. In addition, 'The rise of the schoolmaster as against the knightly master chimes with the growing emphasis in the Renaissance on the study of Latin grammar', N. Orme, *From Childhood to Chivalry: The Education of English Kings and Aristocracy 1066–1530* (Methuen, 1984), pp. 23–4.
19. J. Bowle, *Henry VIII: A Biography* (Allen & Unwin, 1964), p. 29.
20. J. Ridley, *Henry VIII* (Constable, 1984), p. 7.
21. D. Greer, 'Henry VIII', in *The New Grove Dictionary of Music*, vol. VIII (Macmillan, 1980), p. 485.
22. Quoted in J. D. Mackie, *The Earlier Tudors, 1485–1558* (Oxford University Press, 1952), p. 235.
23  J. Simon, *Education and Society in Tudor England* (Cambridge University Press, 1967), p. 76.
24. Foster Watson, *The Old Grammar Schools* (Cambridge University Press, 1916), p. 23.
25. J. J. Scarisbrick, *Henry VIII* (Eyre & Spottiswoode, 1997 [1968]), p. 7.
26. Sir John Elyot, *The Governor*, ed. A. T. Eliot (Ridgway & Sons, 1834 [1531]), p. 40.
27. H. W. Chapman, *The Last Tudor King* (Cape, 1958), p. 51.
28. C. R. Markham, *King Edward VI* (Smith, Elder, 1907), p. 6.
29. J. G. Nichols (ed.), *The Literary Remains of King Edward the Sixth*, vol. 1 (New York: Burt

Franklin, 1857), p. lxx.
30. J. Strype, *Sir John Cheke* (Oxford: Clarendon Press, 1821 [1703]), p. 22.
31. B. L. Beer, *The Life and Raigne of King Edward the Sixth by John Hayward,* vol. 1 (Kent State University Press, OH, 1993), p. 34.
32. W. K. Jordan (ed.), *The Chronicle and Political Papers of King Edward VI* (Allen & Unwin, 1966), p. xvi.
33. W. K. Jordan, *Edward VI: The Young King* (Allen & Unwin, 1968), p. 42.
34. R. K. Marshall, *Mary I* (HMSO, 1993), p. 7.
35. H. F. M. Prescott, *Mary Tudor* (Eyre & Spottiswoode, 1953), p. 26.
36. C. Erickson, *Bloody Mary* (Dent, 1978), p. 43.
37. Foster Watson, 'Juan Louis Vives', in *Encyclopaedia and Dictionary of Education,* vol. IV (Pitman, 1922), p. 1743.
38. M. Dowling, *Humanism in the Age of Henry VIII* (Croom Helm, 1986), p. 224.
39. J. N. Johnson, *The Life of Thomas Linacre,* ed. R. Graves (Edward Lumley, 1835), p. 232.
40. W. Roll, *Mary I* (Englewood Cliffs, NJ: Prentice-Hall, 1980), p. 174.
41. D. Loades, *Mary Tudor: A Life* (Oxford: Blackwell, 1989), p. 38.
42. Quoted in F. A. Mumby, *The Girlhood of Queen Elizabeth* (Constable, 1909), p. 17.
43. N. Williams, *The Life and Times of Elizabeth I* (Weidenfeld & Nicolson, 1972), p. 19.
44. Quoted in C. Erickson, *The First Elizabeth* (Macmillan, 1983), p. 58.
45. G. B. Harrison (ed.), *The Letters of Queen Elizabeth* (Cassell, 1935), pp. 4–5.
46. P. Collinson, '"Windows in a Woman's Soul": Questions about the Religion of Queen Elizabeth I', in *Elizabethan Essays* (Hambleden, 1994), pp. 93–4.
47. M. Dowling, *Humanism in the Age of Henry VIII* (Croom Helm, 1986), p. 234.
48. K. Bascombe, 'Sir Anthony Denny', in D. Dean (ed.), *The Worthies of Waltham,* Part 2 (Waltham Abbey Historical Society, 1978), pp. 1–2.
49. S. J. Curtis and M. E. A. Boultwood, *A Short History of Educational Ideas* (University Tutorial Press, 1965), p. 14.
50. Quoted in D. Ryan, *Roger Ascham* (Oxford University Press, 1963), p. 104.
51. Ibid., p. 106.
52. J. A. R. Giles (ed.), *The Whole Works of Roger Ascham,* vol. III (John Russell Smith, 1864), p. 143.
53. Quoted in D. Cressy, *Education in Tudor and Stuart England* (Edward Arnold, 1975), p. 110.
54. A. L. Rowse, *The England of Elizabeth* (Macmillan, 1950), pp. 496, 528.
55. A. Somerset, *Elizabeth I* (Fontana, 1992), p. 10.
56. W. MacCaffrey, *Elizabeth I* (Edward Arnold, 1993), p. 7.

# 3 *Puritanism, Revolution and the Education of the Stuarts*

WHEN ELIZABETH DIED in 1603, James Stuart, who was already James VI of Scotland, became James I of England. He inherited from Elizabeth a nation that was prosperous, stable internally and no longer having powerful enemies abroad to threaten the security of the kingdom. But not far below the surface tranquillity there were potential difficulties. One of them was religious. Another problem for a monarch who believed in the divine right of kings was the growing tendency of Parliament to assert its authority and insist that it too had rights. This trend continued throughout the seventeenth century and into the eighteenth. Mark Kishlansky has recently suggested that not only the monarchy, but all aspects of political and social life were transformed during this period:

> The modern disciplines of biology, chemistry and physics ... William Harvey, who discovered the circulation of the blood; Robert Boyle who posited the existence of the chemical elements; and Isaac Newton, who propounded the theory of gravity. And these were but the shooting stars in a firmament so vast that the Royal Society was created to survey it.[1]

By steering a middle way between reform and tradition, Elizabeth had secured a lasting religious settlement; the Thirty Nine Articles were generally, but not universally, acceptable to her subjects. Among those who were not content with the settlement were those now referred to as Puritans. This was a term rarely used in the early seventeenth century and then usually in a pejorative sense. Puritanism was a way of life as well as an ideology; its characteristics were thrift, sobriety, asceticism

48

and sometimes hypocrisy. The Puritans in Elizabethan and Stuart England wanted to purify the Church of England of any remaining popish practices such as statues of saints, kneeling for communion and anything under the heading of the biblical condemnation of idolatry. Another aspect of Puritanism was its simplicity of worship. This was, of course, potentially antagonistic to the idea of royalty that there should be splendour and display in all public events, including religious ceremonies. Rather than the mass, particularly high mass with candles, crucifixes, incense and the veneration of the host, Puritans preferred long sermons, the explication of key biblical texts, simple prayers and psalm-singing.

There was a link between some aspects of Puritan belief and the growth of democratic theory and practice, although it should not be exaggerated. Puritans believed in direct communication between individuals and God; they were opposed to church hierarchies, as embodied in bishops and popes, and to aristocracies; the predestined elect were not socially differentiated in this life. Inevitably such beliefs called into question the privileges of kings and the nobility. By the end of Elizabeth's reign, Puritanism had spread considerably and there were many in influential positions, at Oxford and Cambridge, for example. There was a clear connection between Puritanism and education. Reading the Bible was an essential activity for any Protestant; it was important that all should be given the opportunity not only to learn to read but also to be educated more widely.

## JAMES I (1566–1625)

The circumstances surrounding the childhood of the future James VI of Scotland and James I of England could not have been more dramatic. His mother, Mary Queen of Scots, had returned to her native country following the death of her husband, Francis II of France, and she subsequently married Henry Stuart, Lord Darnley. In March 1566, when she was six months pregnant with James at Holyrood, Mary witnessed the murder of her secretary and supposed lover, David Riccio, by Darnley and his followers.

James was born on 19 June 1566 at Edinburgh Castle. Even at his baptism six months later there were tensions. The two sponsors were Charles IX, the King of France, representing the

Catholic faith and thus Mary's own religion, and Queen Elizabeth, representing the Protestant faith. News of his birth had been ill-received by Elizabeth. Sir James Melville was sent from Scotland to convey the information to the Queen, who was at Greenwich, where he found her 'in great mirth, dancing after supper'. Melville continued:

> But so soon as the Secretary Cecil whispered in her ear the news of the Prince's birth, all her mirth was laid aside for that night; all present marvelling whence proceeded such a change; for the Queen did sit down, putting her hand under her cheek, bursting out to some of her ladies, that the Queen of Scots was mother of a fair son, while she was but a barren stock.[2]

Within a few weeks, his father, Darnley, was dead, killed by a gunpowder explosion when he was lying ill his house. Mary was suspected as one of the plotters and when she married the Earl of Bothwell shortly afterwards, she placed her own life in danger. The Protestant lords formed an army in Stirling and vanquished Mary's supporters without a fight at Carberry Hill. Bothwell fled abroad and Mary was captured and sent to Loch Leven Castle. She escaped and fled to England where she suffered imprisonment until her execution in 1587; James never saw his mother again. She was forced to abdicate the Scottish throne, appointing her half-brother, the Earl of Moray, as Regent and her son, Prince James, as king. The Coronation took place on 29 July 1567 in the parish kirk of Stirling when James was 13 months old. This event did nothing to bring to an end the turmoil in the country. Moray was assassinated in 1570 and the regency was given to James's godfather, the Earl of Lennox; in the following year, Lennox was mortally wounded in an armed fight, and his death was witnessed by the little boy. Lennox's successor, the Earl of Mar, died of natural causes the following year and the fourth and last Regent, the Earl of Morton, was later executed on the charge of having caused Darnley's death many years earlier.

Such a sequence of events in James's childhood left its mark, not least on his lack of experience in understanding family life. Any close links with his mother were impossible and in any case, James had already been placed in the care of the Earl of Mar and his wife. The regime at Stirling Castle was a strict one; the countess (who continued to be responsible for the young king

3. *James I and VI aged 8*, attributed to Rowland Lockey, *c.* 1574.

after her husband's death) displayed little affection towards her charge. Mary, through her correspondence, took an interest in her son's early education. In January 1570, when James was 4, Mary wrote to the countess, 'Thinking now tyme that he begyn to learne to knaw sum thing of reiding and wryting, we have send hym ane A.B.C. and example how to forme his lettres.'[3] For his part, James retained a love for the mother he never knew. He assured her 12 years later, when she suggested an act of 'Association', under which she would become joint sovereign of Scotland with James:

> On your part I beg you very humbly to believe that I have never had nor will have other will than to recognize you as my mother and as the one from whom all honour that I can receive in this world will come, and with the aid of God and time you will recognize that my affection does not tend to anything but to honour and respect you and execute your commandments, and to follow the overtures that it has pleased you to make touching our union and association.[4]

A large household had been assembled at Stirling to administer to the needs of the young King. The Earl and Countess were instructed to ensure

> that every one within the said bill ordinary of the household resorts to the ordinary preaching and prayers, and that godly and honourable conversation may be a pattern of learning to so notable a personage as His Majesty James, that no example of ungodly and light behaviour be given by any person, whereof the imitation might do hurt to His Highness tenderness.[5]

Baby talk was thus firmly excluded. The infant King's daily food allocation was a generous one: two-and-a-half loaves of bread, one quart and one pint of ale and two capons.

James's formal education began when he was 4 years of age. It was entrusted by the Privy Council mainly to two scholars of very contrasting dispositions, George Buchanan and Peter Young. Buchanan, a historian, humanist and poet, was not a good choice for a tutor. Then 64 years of age and in indifferent health, he was more concerned with his own studies than in teaching a young child. He was apt to be irritable and would easily lose his temper. James was a timid boy and was somewhat overawed by

51

Buchanan. The latter was described by a contemporary as 'rehearsing at all occasions moralities, short and instructive, whereof he had abundance, inventing where he wanted'.[6] Later in life, talking of a person in high office, James confessed 'that he ever trembled at his approach, it minded him so much of his pedagogue'.[7] Once when the young James was noisily working with one of his classmates, John, the Earl of Mar, son of the Regent, Buchanan, disturbed from his books, entered the room and punished James so abruptly that the countess began to protest at his laying hands on the King and received a typically coarse answer in reply: 'Madam', said Buchanan, 'I have whipped his arse; you may kiss it if you please.' Nevertheless, James had great respect for Buchanan's learning. He informed the Venetian ambassador in 1603 that Buchanan had instructed him in the merits of the constitution of Venice. James's fluency in Latin was due to his tutor, a fact he acknowledged:

> All the world knows that my master, Mr George Buchanan, was a great master in that faculty. I follow his pronunciation both of the Latin and the Greek, and am sorry that my people of England do not the like; for certainly their pronunciation utterly spoils the grace of these two learned languages.[8]

By contrast, Peter Young, then only 26 years of age, educated at St Andrews and in Calvinist Geneva, provided sympathetic and encouraging support for the King. Whereas Buchanan was a bachelor and a misogynist, Young married three times. Young remained James's favourite counsellor throughout the King's life, being given posts as almoner and ambassador, and was later knighted.

Between them, Buchanan and Young set out to provide an education which would make James the most learned monarch in Europe. The regime, which was shared with three companions, was an arduous one. Before breakfast, there were readings from Isocrates, Plutarch and the New Testament and afterwards Livy, Cicero or modern history. In the afternoon lessons in logic and rhetoric were given as well as arithmetic, cosmography and Greek. Under Peter Young's guidance, James became steeped in formal theology. The Bible was read at all meals and James formed a taste for discussing and debating doctrinal matters which he carried over into adulthood.

Buchanan, an early advocate of the theory of constitutional monarchy, dedicated his book *De Jure Regni apud Scotos* (1579) to his pupil. In it, Buchanan developed a very modern concept of the duties and responsibilities of a monarch whose powers were held as a trust from the people he governed.[9] Buchanan offered the book as 'an importunate and authoritative monitor ... to whom if you shall yield obedience, you will obtain tranquillity for the present, and for the future everlasting glory'.[10] Later, James was to reject this notion in favour of the divine right of kings. David and Adam Erskine, Commendators of Drybrugh and Cambuskenneth, were responsible for James's physical and social training.

A magnificent library was established by Buchanan and Young for the young king, representing many branches of knowledge. Apart from the many Latin and Greek texts in their original languages, there were translations in English, French and Italian. History, science, military strategy and theology were well represented, as well as well-known books on the education of princes, such as those by Elyot, Ascham and Castiglione, and treatises on government. The library was augmented by his mother's collection from Holyrood, consisting mainly of French and Italian poetry. James was a natural scholar and rapidly absorbed all that was placed before him. Buchanan praised the King when he was 16, remarking, 'At this early age you have pursued the history of almost every nation and have committed many of them to memory.'[11]

Physically, James was not attractive, probably largely due to the conditions surrounding his birth. He was of medium build with broad shoulders, spindly legs and one foot turned outwards; as a result of childhood rickets he had a shuffling gait. He had staring eyes, a face pitted from a childhood attack of smallpox and narrow jaws which made for difficulties in eating. James's slovenly dress, uncouth way of talking and poor table manners did not add to his attractiveness. He loved physical exercise; his favourite sport above all others was hunting, where his physical handicaps were of lesser importance. Although he possessed two golf clubs and recommended golf to his son, there is no evidence that he played the game himself.

James poured his vast knowledge into writing, publishing no fewer than seven books before 1600. His first venture was in the realm of poetry. Inspired by Alexander Montgomerie, a court poet, James produced his first verses when he was 15. Three years later, in 1584, he wrote his first treatise, printed as *The Essayes of a Prentise in the Divine Art of Poesie*.[12] Other works included *Daemonologie* (1597), *The Trew Law of Free Monarchies* (1598) in which he developed his ideas on the divine right of kings, a number of religious works and perhaps his best-remembered piece of writing, *A Counterblaste to Tobacco* (1604).

Of outstanding interest, however, is the extensive work, with its Greek title *Basilikon Doron* (in English *A King's Gift*) (1599), and subsequently translated into a number of other languages. It was expressly written for his eldest son, Henry, Prince of Wales, a gifted and artistic youth who was to live for only 18 years. The book is divided into three parts: the first was 'a King's duetie towards God in Religion'; 'the second part of my booke teaches my sonne howe to use his office in the administration of justice and politicke government'; the third 'contanying a King's outwarde behaviour in indifferent things; what agreeance and conformitie he ought to keepe betwixt his outward behaviour in these things, and the vertuous qualities of his minde'.[13] Much of it is autobiographical and contains sound advice which James himself would have done well to have followed. 'Onlie remember', he told his son, 'that as Parliaments have been ordained for making of lawes, so ye abuse their institution, in holding them new for any mens particulars.'[14]

It is worth attempting to discern how far James's childhood experiences and education affected his subsequent kingship. He experienced at first hand from an early age the horrors of murders, intrigue and the permanent loss of his mother. His carefully planned education did little to obliterate the effect of these experiences. It might be argued that James's rigorous academic education, based on the Calvinistic principle of hard work, was an artificial one which over-emphasised the importance of scholarship rather than helping him to form judgements or provide training for his role as monarch. He was starved of affection as a boy and was surrounded mainly by men. His tutor, John Buchanan, held women in contempt and influenced James in his opinion of the superiority of the male.[15] Buchanan was also the author of *Detectio Mariae Reginae Scotorum*, a book which rehearsed all the adverse gossip concerning Mary Queen of

54

Scots; during his tutorship, he attempted to poison his pupil's mind and ensured that James's questions about her were answered in the worst possible light.[16] James's marriage to Anne of Denmark did not prove to be a happy one, marred by his attitude towards her as well as by his homosexuality; they ceased to live together from about 1606 or 1607. As he grew up, it was to men that he looked for companionship and assurance, often with unfortunate results. As an early biographer of James wrote, 'One of the earliest propensities which he discovered was an excessive attachment to favourites; and this weakness which ought to have been abandoned with other characteristics of childhood, continued to retain its ascendancy during every stage of his life.'[17] It was not surprising that he displayed open jealousy towards his eldest son Prince Henry from infancy, regarding him as a possible future threat to his own monarchy in the same way as he himself had been used against his mother. The Venetian ambassador reported in 1607 when Henry was 7 that the King was not 'overpleased to see his son so beloved and of such promise that his subjects place all their hopes in him'. Indeed, Roy Strong is of the opinion that the early death of Henry came almost as a relief to James.[18]

James overestimated his own abilities and acted in an overconfident manner in the conduct of business, keeping his own counsel in affairs of state, especially after he became king of England following the death of Elizabeth in 1603.[19] He became easily bored with routine affairs of government. As J. P. Kenyon has stated, 'He was lazy, never realising the wealthier the kingdom the more complex it was, and the more time was required to govern it. He spent far too much time reading and talking instead of doing; he had not time for the day-to-day chores of government – he even retreated to Royston or Newmarket at the height of the Parliamentary session.'[20]

Part of the problem was that the role of the King was very different in the two countries. James was welcomed to England in 1603, but the early goodwill soon ran out. His education had not fully prepared him for the English Court, and he made the mistake of trying to conduct the English Parliament in the same way as the Scottish estates. At the beginning of his reign, Puritan hopes were high because James had been brought up in Scotland by Calvinists. When he arrived in England he was presented with the Millenary Petition setting out a list of Puritan grievances. In 1604 James called a conference at Hampton Court, but he had no intention of moving the Church in the Puritan direction. The phrase 'no bishop, no king', summed up his attitude, although he appeared to listen sympathetically to some aspects of the Puritan cause. Nevertheless, the Archbishop of Canterbury, Richard Bancroft, encouraged Convocation in 1604 to draw up *Constitutions and Canons* against the Nonconformists. James also antagonised Puritans by ordering that his *Book of Sports* be read in every church, listing recreations which were and were not permitted on Sundays. In 1607 the emigration of Puritans began to increase, first to Holland and in 1620 the *Mayflower* took the celebrated group to Plymouth, Massachusetts.

James resented the English Parliament and did without it as much as he could; no parliaments sat between the years 1611 and 1621. However he was astute enough to realise that he could not behave in quite the same manner in England as he had done in Scotland. Despite his theory of absolute monarchy and divine right, in practice he did not attempt to change the English view of the authority of 'King in Parliament' when the issue was debated in 1610. He knew enough of English history to be only too well aware of such precedents as King John and Magna Carta, or what happened when kings ignored 'advice'. James's complex character, a mixture of insecurity (he feared assassination all his life), overwhelming vanity, high intelligence, a pleasure seeker rather than a ruler and a poor judge of men, hardly equipped him for the burdensome task of monarchy.

## CHARLES I (1600–49)

Charles, the youngest of the three surviving children of James and Anne of Denmark, was born at Dunfermline Castle on 19 November 1600. Three other children had already died in infancy, and Charles himself was a sickly child, thought unlikely to live. On the death of Queen Elizabeth three years later, James left Scotland with Charles's elder brother, Prince Henry, and his sister, Elizabeth, to become King of England and Scotland. Charles was left behind in the care of Lord and Lady Fyvie. On 30 May 1603, Lord Fyvie wrote to the King, 'Duke Charles continewis (praisit be God) in guid health, guid courage, and loftie minde, although weake in bodie, is beginning to speik sum wordis far better as yet off his minde and tongue nor off his bodie and feite.'[21]

It was not until April 1604 that a doctor and an apothecary were sent to Scotland from London to examine Charles to see if he was capable of undertaking the long journey south. By the summer, it was considered safe for the young prince to travel and he was reunited with his mother in Northamptonshire. This reunion was short-lived as he was immediately put under the charge of Sir Robert Carey and his wife, Elizabeth. Initially, there had been keen competition amongst the great ladies at Court for this post, but apparently 'when they did see how weak a child he was, and not likely to live, their hearts were down and none of them desired to take charge of him'.

The Careys were a well-suited couple for the care of Charles. Sir Robert had gained the King's favour by riding to London and bringing back the first news of the death of Queen Elizabeth. His wife was given responsibility for Charles, and Carey became governor of the household. In his *Memoirs*, Carey describes how his wife stood ground against the King's wishes:

> Many a battle my wife had with the King, but she still prevailed. The King was desirous that the string under his tongue should be cut, for he was so long beginning to speak, as he thought he would never have spoke. Then he would have put him in iron boots to strengthen the sinews and joints; but my wife protested so much against them both as she got the victory, and the King was fain to yield.[22]

Charles never overcame a bad stammer, which was perhaps one of the main reasons for his later shyness and reserve.

Although a delicate child, Charles was expected to participate in the ceremonies connected with the Court. He was made Duke of York on Twelfth Night, 1605. On the same occasion, the King created 11 Knights of the Bath. The centrepiece of the three-day ceremony was when the 4-year-old boy was brought in, accompanied by his knights, carried out again and brought back, this time by earls in their robes of the Garter. The patent for the dukedom was then read out in Latin and a large public dinner followed, where there was one table for the Duke and the Garter Earls and another his fellow Knights of the Bath.

Lady Carey firmly believed that Charles would benefit from living in the countryside away from the Court. The household accordingly moved from one royal palace to another, first Greenwich, then Oatlands, Kew and Richmond, and Charles slowly gained confidence both in his walking and in his speech. Thomas Murray, a learned Scottish wit who had no university degree and was not in holy orders, was appointed as his tutor. Murray was the uncle of William Murray, 1st Earl of Dysart, whom he introduced at Court. Dysart was the same age as Charles and was subsequently educated along with him. This was to be the start of a friendship which lasted throughout Charles's life and Dysart became one of Charles's closest advisers. Charles also had great respect for Murray and rewarded him in 1622 by appointing him as Provost of Eton, a post which he enjoyed until his death the following year.[23]

Charles's relationship with his father was a delicate one. Whereas James was an extrovert and often uncouth person, his son was more withdrawn, temperate and serious. Charles could hardly have failed to notice the contrast between the behaviour of his father and the ideals which he tried to instil into himself. One of James's actions which had disastrous consequences for Charles was to make him study closely the precepts of the *Basilikon Doran*. God, James told his son, 'made you a little God to sit on his throne and rule over other men'.[24]

By contrast, Charles held his mother in great affection, though it was only returned in full after the death of his elder brother, Prince Henry. Anne of Denmark was 15 years old when she married James. She loved clothes and jewellery, was extravagant with money and had a fine collection of pictures. She was a great patron of the arts. Inigo Jones was commissioned by her in 1604 to design the scenery for a masque and later staged three royal weddings. Charles took part in one, appearing as Zephyr attended by 12 little girls of his own age, to celebrate his brother's creation as Prince of Wales. Jones, as Surveyor of the King's Works, was also the architect of the Queen's House at Greenwich and the Banqueting House in Whitehall, where masques were performed. Anne also employed Thomas Campion to provide suitable music for these entertainments in collaboration with the poet Ben Jonson. Though living apart from her husband from the time Charles was 7 years old – James was 'ever best when furthest from her' – Anne continued to see her sons. There is little doubt that Anne's artistic tastes had an important influence on her children.[25]

Charles was emotionally attached to his sister Elizabeth, who was four years older than him. He admired her high spirits, charm and quick wit and though her main affection was for her other brother, Prince Henry, Charles greatly valued her company. Charles's relations with his brother, who was six years older, were more complex. Henry, like his father, was of an equally extrovert temperament and had the bearing and charm of a model prince. He preferred hunting and sports to studying, was a connoisseur of a wide range of arts and seemed mature well beyond his years. Charles not only admired Henry but began to model himself upon him. Through physical exercise he developed from his crippled state to become sufficiently adept at horsemanship to 'make war on the King's deer' like his brother.[26]

Charles wrote to Henry:

> Good Brother,
> I hope you are in good health and merry, as I am, God be thanked. In your absence I visit sometimes your stable and ride your great horses, that at your return I may wait on you in that noble exercise. So committing you to God, I rest,
> Your loving and dutiful brother,
> YORK.

Another earlier and rather touching letter indicates a brotherly love bordering on hero worship:

> Sweet, sweet Brother,
> I thank you for your letter. I will keep it better than all my graith; and I will send my pistols by Master Newton [Adam Newton, Prince Henry's tutor]. I will give anything that I have to you; both my horses, and my books, and my pieces, and my cross-bows, or anything that you would have. Good brother, love me, and I shall ever love and serve you.
> Your loving brother to be commanded,
> YORK[27]

Occasionally, though, there could be tension between the two brothers. When Charles was a teenager, he and Henry had met George Abbot, the Archbishop of Canterbury, who was waiting for an audience with the King. Afterwards, Henry, alluding to Charles's praise from his father for his proficiency with his studies, jocularly placed the archbishop's black cap on Charles's head, saying 'that if he continued a good boy, and followed his books, when he was King, he would make him one day Archbishop of Canterbury'. Charles felt humiliated by this quip, furiously flung the cap on the floor and trampled on it and 'not without much difficulty and some force being taken off from that eagerness'.[28]

Charles's life changed dramatically and tragically shortly after this event. In October 1612, Prince Henry was taken ill with typhoid fever and within a month he had died at the early age of 18. Only a short time after this, Charles's sister Elizabeth fell in love and was married to Frederick, the Elector Palatine. Charles was never to see her again. He was now alone as well as being heir to the throne.

Shortly before his brother's death, Charles, at the age of 11, was taken away from Lady Carey's household and established his own at St James's Palace. As Sir Robert Carey stated, 'Now my wife was to leave her charge, and the Duke to have none but men to attend upon him.' Murray remained as his tutor and supervised Charles's studies. Not a great deal of detail is known about his education. Charles had, from the beginning, been an intelligent and co-operative student. Murray himself taught Latin, and there were lessons in French, Spanish and Italian. Charles wrote eagerly to the King:

> Sweet, sweet Father,
> I learn to decline substantives and adjectives. Give
> me your blessing.
> I thank you for my best man.
> Your loving son,
> YORK.[29]

Charles had shown early promise with his studies. At the age of 8 he was reading the Colloquies of Erasmus, 'from which I trust to learn both the purity of the Latin language and elegance of manners'. Other tutors taught him arithmetic, John Beauchesne was his master for Italic writing, and John Norton supervised the library. Charles conscientiously studied theology, copying passages from Anglican divines such as Lancelot Andrewes and Thomas Hooker into commonplace books.[30] He remained throughout his life deeply religious and was devoted to the Anglican Church; later he was to delight in participating in theological disputations. He was the first monarch to be brought up from childhood in the doctrines of the Church of England, and was sympathetic to the High Church wing. Physical activities were not neglected. Through long and hard practice he had become a good horseman, an excellent shot and had strengthened his legs by running round the grounds of St James's Palace each morning; he also received coaching in royal tennis from John Webb and in fencing from Charles Guerolt. Within a decade he had transformed himself from being a hopeless cripple to a fine athletic youth. However, his shyness persisted and his natural reserve was enhanced by his persistent stammer, which he vainly tried to overcome by talking to himself with his mouth full of pebbles.[31]

James from the beginning took a close interest in his children's education and probably approved of his son's conscious balance between academic and physical activities. Charles wrote at the age of 8 to his father:

> Please your Majesty,
> The next Weeke I mean to use the benefit of your Majesty's gratious favour of hunting in Waltham forrest, the place appointed as fittest for the sport being Wansted. In the mean whyle, and after, I will employ my tyme at my booke the best I can to your Majesty's satisfaction, whereof hoping your Majesty will rest assured I kisse most humbly your hands as
> Your Most dutifull and obedient sonne,
> YORK[32]

Charles, like his parents and his brother, showed a great interest in the arts. He had inherited the extensive collection of paintings belonging to Prince Henry and his mother after their deaths.[33] A further stimulus to add to it followed a visit with George Villiers, Duke of Buckingham, to Spain in search of a bride. There they saw the collection of the young Philip IV, and Charles determined to form a collection to rival it. Altogether, he subsequently acquired some 1,500 pictures to build the finest collection of paintings ever assembled in Britain. It was, for the most part, sold off by Cromwell after Charles's execution in 1649. Charles commissioned Rubens to paint the ceiling of the Banqueting House and Van Dyck produced many Royal portraits; as a reward, both of the artists were knighted by Charles. Rubens described Charles as 'the greatest amateur of painting among the Princes of the world'.[34] Charles was also generous to his poet laureate, Ben Jonson, and his successor, Sir William Davenant.[35] In 1640, Charles and his wife took part in Davenant's masque *Salmacida Spolia*, elaborately dressed in fanciful costumes designed by Inigo Jones.[36]

In every sense of the word, Charles could be said to have received a satisfactory education: yet it hardly prepared him for the role of King of England. Although we have evidence that when he was later in captivity he read the Italian poets Ariosto and Tasso (in English) and Shakespeare's plays, he did not carry his learning into his everyday deliberations. Lord Clarendon remarked in his memoirs of the King that 'there were few gentlemen in the world that knew more of useful or necessary learning than this prince did: and yet his proportion of books was but small, having, like Francis I of France, learnt more by the ear than by study.'[37]

It is strange that despite his strong religious convictions, the word often used in connection with his character is 'duplicity'. For example, when he married Henrietta Maria, sister of Louis XIII, the settlement included a promise by Charles to give English Catholics considerable freedom; but at the same time he was telling Parliament that he would follow a policy of persecution. Another example of his duplicity was that he retained the idea of intervening in European politics to restore the Palatinate to his brother-in-law, but he sought to do this by intrigue rather than by open negotiation or war. Charles also treated very badly his closest adviser, Thomas Wentworth, Earl of Strafford, repaying the latter's loyalty by signing his death warrant. He felt guilty about Strafford, but nevertheless still claimed that he had a clear conscience in the matter. Charles often gave his word of honour as king, though on many occasions he wove secret plots, promising quite different and incompatible things to different people, yet he was often able to convince himself that he was being perfectly honest. As one historian has written:

> Charles carried belief in his own righteousness to an extreme. He could always justify his actions to himself, and he could not see how they seemed to be dishonest to other people, putting such accusations down to malicious and self-interested cavilling. The end result was that true statesmanship completely escaped his grasp.[38]

In many ways, Charles's outlook can be attributed to the events which occurred during his formative period, particularly the loneliness resulting from the virtual separation of his parents, the death of his brother Prince Henry and the marriage of his only sister Elizabeth, all by the age of 13. Charles's craving for love, which found expression in his close and widely unpopular friendship with the Duke of Buckingham, who was as politically inept as he was charming personally, led to headlong clashes with Parliament. Charles suffered from bad judgement, made worse by an arrogance which overrode common sense, such as the dismissal of Parliament only three years after his reign began. To make matters worse, he was hesitant in making decisions, and when a decision was made, he was slow in acting upon it. Charles had an unoriginal power of mind which shaped reality to his own personal ends.[39]

It may also be argued that Charles's preparation for kingship was hardly encouraged by his father. As a friend of Charles observed, 'Old Princes do not love to have their sons too active and tread too close upon their heels.' This may explain the four-year delay after the death of Prince Henry in making Charles Prince of Wales. Account must also be taken of Charles's physical condition. As we have seen, he was weak from early childhood and small in stature, being only 5 feet 4 inches in height as an adult. Charles hid his stammer behind an appearance of gravity and with a brevity of conversation which tended to make his audience unsure of his intentions. The French ambassador reported after being received by the King, 'To me he appeared extremely reserved, and this induces me to judge that he is either an extraordinary man, or one of very middling capacity.'[40]

These many paradoxes and inconsistencies in Charles's character, largely uninfluenced by his education, proved disastrous after he ascended the throne in 1625, leading to civil war and ultimately to his execution in Whitehall in 1649.

## CHARLES II (1630–85)

The birth of Charles at Oatlands Palace on 29 May 1630 was widely celebrated throughout the country. Almost a year before, his mother, Henrietta Maria, had lost her first child, Charles James, at birth. Her husband, Charles I, was also delighted that he now had an heir to the throne. Both parents were small in stature but the new baby was quite different. The Queen wrote to a friend shortly afterwards, 'He is so fat and so tall that he is taken for a year old and he is only four months. His teeth are already beginning to come. I will send you his portrait as soon as he is a little fairer, for at present he is so dark that I am ashamed of him.'[41] His sallow features were to remain with him for life. As an adult, on looking at himself in a mirror, he remarked, 'Odds fish, what an ugly fellow I am.'[42] Eventually he grew to be 6 feet 2 inches in height.

Charles's early childhood is not recorded in detail. We know that his parents had one of the happier of royal marriages and that the young Prince of Wales enjoyed the company of the children of the two sons of the Duke of Buckingham and later his brothers and sisters, Mary, James, Elizabeth, Anne and Henry. Although Charles was fond of his father, he had little real love for Henrietta Maria, a French princess who was slow in learning to speak English. Charles's greatest affection was reserved for one of his nurses, Christabel Wyndham; when he was 15, this relationship turned into a brief but passionate affair.

It is often difficult to assess the importance or otherwise of royal governors on their charges, but the appointment of William Cavendish, Duke of Newcastle, as Charles's governor when he was 8 years old had a profound effect on the Prince's philosophy and future actions. Newcastle, who had been educated at St John's College, Cambridge, had lavishly entertained King Charles and Henrietta Maria at his home at Welbeck Abbey and later anxiously sought a post in the royal household as a means of meeting his mounting debts. He was pleased, therefore, to be appointed as the Prince's governor in 1638 and the five years during which he was responsible for the upbringing of the Prince proved congenial to the young boy.

Newcastle had not displayed any great love of learning whilst at Cambridge, preferring action, in the form of riding, fencing and dancing, to bookish occupations. At the same time, he believed that education should prepare his charge for kingship and to become a gentleman. In a *Letter of Instructions to Prince Charles for his Studies, Conduct and Behaviour*, Newcastle wrote:

> For your education, Sir, It is fitt you should have some languages, tho' I confess I would rather have you study things than words, matter than language; for seldom a Critick in many languages hath time to study sense, for words; and at best he is or can be but a living dictionary. Besides I would not have you too studious, for too much contemplation spoils action, and Virtue consists in that. What you read, I would have it History and the best chosen Histories, that so you might compare the dead with the living; for the same humors is now as was then, there is no alteration but in names, and tho' you meet not with a Caesar for Emperor of the whole world, yet he may have the same passions in him; and you are not to compare fortunes, so much as humors, witt, and judgement; and thus you shall see the excellency and errors both of Kings and subjects, and tho' you are young in years, yet living by your wading in all those times, be older in wisdom and judgement than Nature can afford any man to be without this help.[43]

He considered that the arts should be studied provided they were of some practical use. Learning for learning's sake was not to be encouraged. 'Whenever you are too studious', Newcastle observed, 'your contemplation will spoil your government, for you cannot be a good contemplative man and a good common-wealth's man; therefore take heed of too much book.' Newcastle later in the *Letter* returns to this topic: 'The greatest captains were not the greatest scholars; neither have I known book-worms great statesmen; some have here to fore and some are now, but they study men more now than books, or else they would prove but silly statesmen.'[44]

The question of religious education was a sensitive one, as Charles's father was a devout Anglican, while Henrietta Maria was an equally devout Roman Catholic, a matter which had caused much anxiety both in Parliament and in the country. Newcastle advised a middle course of moderation, eschewing religious extremism:

4. *Children of Charles I*, Anthony Van Dyck, 1637. From left to right: Mary, Princess Royal, James, Duke of York (James II), Charles, Prince of Wales (Charles II), Princess Elizabeth and Princess Anne.

If you have no reverence at prayers, what will the people have, think you? They go according to the example of the Prince; if they have none, then they have no obedience to God; then they will easily have none to your Highness; no obedience, no subjects; no subjects – then your power is off that side ... Of the other side, if any be bible mad, over much burn't with fiery zeal, they may think it a service to God to destroy you and say the Spirit moved them and bring some example of a King with a hard name in the old Testament. Thus one way you may have a civil war, the other a private treason.[45]

To be a gentleman was of supreme importance: the Prince should be courteous and civil to everybody, especially women, and should speak no evil of people. 'Even there sometimes a hat or a smile in the right place will advantage you, but at other times you may do more, and civil speeches to people and short doth much win of them.' Dignity and bearing were also important in order to emphasise the authority of kingship: 'the King must know at what time to play the King and when to qualify it, but never to put it off'.[46]

Newcastle was happy to leave the day-to-day instruction to Charles's tutor, Brian Duppa, Bishop of Chichester and former Dean of Christ Church, Oxford, who was appointed at the same time as the Duke. The latter forecast that Charles would find Duppa pleasing 'since he hath no pedantry in him'. This proved to be the case and Charles had great admiration for Duppa throughout his life. As Duppa lay dying in his bed at Richmond in 1662, Charles, now King, visited him and on his knees begged his blessing.[47]

When the Prince was 9, Duppa reported favourably on his progress. 'He hastens apace out of his childhood', he wrote, 'and is likely to be a man betimes, and an excellent man if my presage deceives me not, and flattering and humoring him, the bane of Princes, do not spoil him. But I will hope for the best and do my best as long as I am here.'[48] In fact, Charles proved to be an idle though not unintelligent student. He was poor at both Latin and Greek and it was only when he was in exile that he learnt to speak fluent French and to understand Spanish and Italian.[49]

Whereas in later years he was to follow Newcastle's advice closely, as we shall see, as a young boy Charles adopted a different attitude to his mother's entreaties on safeguarding his own health. She wrote a letter 'To my dear Sone the Prince', saying:

> Charles, I am sore that I must begin my first Letter with chiding you because I heere that you will not take phisike. I hope it was onlei for this day and that tomorrowe you will do it, for if you will not I must come to you, and make you take it, for it is for your healthe. I have given order to my lord Newcastle to send me worde tonight whether you will or not, therefore I hope you will not give me the paines to goe, and so I rest
> Your affectionate mother
> Henriette Marie, R.

Charles's impish sense of humour shows through in his note to Newcastle, probably written soon after the Queen's:

> My Lord
>
> I would not have you take too much Phisick: for it doth alwaies make me worse and I think it will do the like with you.
>
> Charles P. [50]

The Prince's happy childhood was being increasingly over-shadowed by national events. Charles I's attempt to rule without Parliament, the resentment engendered by his support for the High Church party and the bungled attempt to force an English-based prayer book on the Scots, and the Queen's continuing adherence to Catholicism proved disastrous. The King was obliged to recall Parliament in 1640, which was dissolved within three weeks, but later the same year a new and more determined Parliament, labelled the 'Long Parliament', assembled. As a direct challenge to the King, it condemned to death his close adviser, the Earl of Strafford. Both father and son witnessed the debate on the Bill of Attainder in the House of Lords. Then followed an astonishing episode. The King, after reluctantly giving the royal assent to the bill, sent a letter to the Lords pleading for Strafford's life. The Prince of Wales, who was not yet 11 years of age, was chosen as the messenger. He delivered it to the Lord Keeper of the Great Seal in a crowded and silent House of Lords. On the following day, 12 May 1641, Strafford was beheaded on Tower Hill. The Prince's reactions to these happenings are not recorded. On a happier note, two months before this, the King had taken Charles to Cambridge, accompanied by Duppa, to receive an honorary master of arts degree from the vice-chancellor.[51]

Later in the same year, both Newcastle and Duppa resigned their respective posts, Newcastle to retire to the country and later fight in the civil war for the King and Duppa to become Bishop of Salisbury. Newcastle was replaced by William Seymour, Marquis of Hertford, an appointment which the King hoped would be more to the liking of Parliament. This proved not to be the case and the Commons voted in August 1641 to nominate two Puritan peers to be joint governors with the marquis. A later plan devised by the Commons was to seize the Prince at Greenwich after Henrietta Maria had fled abroad, but the King arrived just in time to thwart these plans.[52] Charles was to remain with his father for the next three years.

Hertford proved to be a poor appointment. He had married James I's cousin, Arabella Stuart, in secret in 1610, much to the King's fury, and had been put in the Tower and then exiled, but he had now been restored to favour. Clarendon considered it a misfortune that the quick-witted and vigorous boy should have fallen into the hands of a governor 'of an age not fit for much duty and fatigue, who loved, and was even so much wedded to, his ease, that he loved his books above all exercises'.[53] Nevertheless, Charles I saw Hertford as a useful man of action in the approaching struggle. He joined the King at York in April 1642 and became lieutenant-general for the western counties. Although Hertford continued as the Prince's tutor until 1643, it is doubtful if he played any significant part in advancing his education.

He was replaced by Thomas Howard, Earl of Berkshire, who had been Master of the Horse to Charles I when he was Prince of Wales. Berkshire was something of a nonentity, of poor intellect and equally poor judgement. He was imprisoned in the Tower by the Parliamentary party but released in 1643 as 'a man that could do them no harm anywhere'.[54] Berkshire remained the Prince's governor until Charles's escape from England three years later. By the time of the outbreak of the Civil War in August 1642, Charles was still only 12 years of age. Together with his brother James, he witnessed at close quarters the battle of Edgehill while under the charge of Dr William Harvey, the physician, and he subsequently spent much of his time with the King at Oxford or with the various armies. After the success of the Ironsides under Oliver Cromwell, the Prince, who was now 15, was sent to the West Country to take command of all the royal forces in that part of England. The tide was turning against the King, and Charles I ordered his son to escape to the Continent. On 2 March 1646, the Prince and his party boarded ship for the Scillies, eventually settling in France after a short stay in Jersey. It was to be another 14 years before his exile was ended.

Charles's position in France was a difficult one. Although still an adolescent, he had experienced four years of war and had begun the first of his many amorous affairs. Now, at Henrietta Maria's insistence, he once more became a schoolboy. Together with the sons of the Duke of Buckingham, Charles received instruction once more from Brian Duppa and reading for an hour a day with John Earle, though he tried to avoid these sessions.[55] Perhaps the most interesting of Charles's tutors at this time was Thomas Hobbes. He had left England in the week that Strafford had been impeached, convinced that his homeland was no longer a place for a philosopher of his bent. Hobbes had previously been tutor and a good friend of William Cavendish, 2nd Earl of Devonshire, for over 20 years until the latter's death in 1628. Hobbes entered into correspondence with Devonshire's cousin, William Cavendish, Marquis of Newcastle, and found that they were of like minds. Newcastle subsequently became Hobbes's patron and offered him residence at Welbeck, which Hobbes accepted. Hobbes dedicated his first political work *The Elements of Law* to Newcastle in 1640 and later expanded it into the treatise *De Cive* ('On the Citizen').

Newcastle left England in 1644 after the Royalist defeat at Marston Moor for Paris where he once more met Hobbes. The intellectual life of the city at the time was a rich one. Newcastle's wife records the conversation at a dinner given by Newcastle attended by three philosophers, Hobbes, Descartes and Pierre Gassendi, and the poet Edmund Waller:

> They began, amongst the rest, to argue upon this subject, namely,
> Whether it were possible to make man by art fly as birds do; and

when some of the company had delivered their opinion, viz., That they thought it probable to be done by the help of artificial wings; my Lord declared, that he deemed it altogether impossible, and demonstrated it by this following reason. Man's arms, said he, are not set on his shoulders in the same manner as bird's wings are; for that part of the arm which joins to the shoulder is in man placed inward, as towards the breast, but in birds outward, as toward the back; which difference and contrary position or shape hinders that man cannot have the same flying action with his arms, as birds have with their wings. Which argument Mr Hobbes liked so well, that he was pleased to make use of it in one of his books called *Leviathan*, if I remember well.[56]

The arrival of Charles in Paris in the summer of 1646 induced Hobbes to remain there, where he was employed as a mathematics tutor for the Prince and Buckingham for the next two years.

The close philosophical and intellectual agreement between Newcastle and Hobbes is reflected in the guidance on the role of the monarch which Newcastle gave to the young prince. The supremacy of the monarchy and its detailed control of the instruments of state, were, in his view, essential to the well-being of the nation. Furthermore, much of this Hobbesian advice, as set out in Newcastle's lengthy *Advice to the Prince*, written on the eve of The Restoration, was acted upon after Charles became king in 1660. Parliament agreed to forfeit its claim to constitutional supremacy, placing the sole power over the armed forces in the hands of the King; the Church of England was re-established under the government of its bishops; and freedom of speech and the uncontrolled presses were limited by Acts of Parliament along the lines advocated by Newcastle.

Education was another area which came under close scrutiny. Newcastle's suspicion of too much book learning and study were now openly displayed. The power of the legal profession, which he disliked, could be curtailed in the following way: 'If you cut off much reading and writing, there must be fewer lawyers and clerks.' Newcastle complained that there were far too many grammar schools. There were also too many students at the universities and he recommended that if 'each university should have one half the number [of students] they would be better fed and taught'. Subsequently, the universities were purged, numbers fell sharply and colleges were kept under strict control.[57]

One of the more positive outcomes of Hobbes's tuition was that the Prince acquired an appreciation of mathematics and science. Charles's life-long interest in the practical applications of science led to the formation of the Royal Society under his patronage and the building of the Royal Observatory at Greenwich in 1675. He had a private laboratory built in Whitehall and a telescope constructed for his own use and he became deeply interested in the science of navigation.[58]

Charles was subsequently well-disposed towards Hobbes, even though his clergy had advised him not to meet the philosopher after being presented with a copy of *Leviathan* on its publication in 1651.[59] However, this phase soon passed and John Aubrey wrote that 'his Majestie had a good opinion of him and said openly that he thought Mr Hobbes never meant him hurt'. Charles awarded the philosopher a pension of £100 a year and was always glad to see him at Court, where he 'very much delighted in his witt and smart repartee: the witts at Court were wont to bayte him; he would make his part good and feared none of them. The King would call him the Beare. "Here comes the Beare to be bayted."'[60]


Charles's 25 years as king was a mixture of achievement and failure. With his encouragement, the arts, especially music, architecture, the stage and painting, flourished in a new golden age. His foreign policy gained him much unpopularity. He had married Catherine of Braganza, a Portuguese princess and a Catholic, in return for a large dowry paid in instalments. Charles also agreed secretly, under the Treaty of Dover, to receive a large subsidy from the French in return for help in fighting the Dutch. He was to declare himself a Catholic and use French troops to convert his countrymen. However, it was not until Charles was dying that he became a Catholic.[61]

Charles was unfortunate in having two ineffectual governors at the most receptive time in a boy's life, though the advice he received from the Duke of Newcastle prepared him in many ways for his role as king. He became a man of wide interests and curiosity, mixed well with people of all ranks and displayed courtesy and politeness at all times. On the other hand, Charles was apt to be lazy, concealing and disguising many of his real thoughts behind a facade of cynicism. This may partly be accounted for by his experience of 18 years in exile and the need to survive, bearing in mind the fate of his own father. His attitude to people was often surprisingly hard; for example, he reduced his mother's pension at the end of her life when she was most in need.[62] His disposition towards women is particularly well known. A contemporary, the Marquis of Halifax wrote of him:

> It may be said that his inclinations to love were the effects of health and a good constitution, with as little mixture of the *seraphic* part as ever man had, and though from that foundation men often raise their passions, I am apt to think his stayed as much as any man's ever did in the *lower region.*[63]

He was averse to his mistresses exercising political influence, for, as his minister Clarendon observed, 'The King did not in his nature love a busy woman, and had an aversion from speaking with any woman, or hearing her speak, of any business but to that purpose he thought them all made for.' Although he is reputed to have fathered at least 14 illegitimate children, Charles and his wife had none of their own. He did, however, show some compassion for his favourite mistress; one of his last messages on his deathbed was 'And let not poor Nelly [Gwynn] starve.' He died shortly afterwards on 6 February 1685 in his fifty-fifth year.

A man of commanding presence who had a good intellect and was also an incessant talker, Charles II was something of a paradox. His character was well summed up in a contemporary epigram:

> We have a pritty King
> Whose word no man relies on,
> Who never said a foolish thing
> Nor ever did a wise one.

## JAMES II (1633–1701, ABDICATED 1688)

Although, as we have seen, the childhood experiences of James, Duke of York, and his elder brother, Charles, were similar, the outcomes of their reigns were very different. James, the third of

the six children of Charles I and Henrietta Maria, was born on 14
October 1633 at St James's Palace. Whereas his brother Charles
was dark skinned and not immediately attractive, James was fair
and with handsome features. He lacked his brother's sense of wit
and humour, and was somewhat dour and from an early age
showed that he could be obstinate. In many ways he was also less
intelligent and was less able to manoeuvre himself out of difficult
situations.[64] As the Duke of Buckingham later said of them, 'The
King [Charles II] could see things if he would and the Duke [of
York] would see things if he could.'[65]

James's christening ceremony was in the best of Protestant
traditions. Archbishop Laud, a champion of the Anglican church,
officiated and his godparents were Elizabeth, Queen of Bohemia,
and the Prince of Orange, who was to succeed James to the
throne. Before he was 3 years old, James was given the title of
Lord High Admiral and was formally appointed to that office 18
months later. His formal education was even more abbreviated
than that of his brother, who was some three years older. Mary,
Countess of Dorset, was governess to the two boys but at the age
when he would normally have been put into the hands of tutors,
these plans were disrupted, for by the beginning of 1642, Charles
I's position in London had become intolerable. James was taken
with his parents first to Hampton Court and when the King went
to York in the spring to establish his headquarters there, he was
left with his newly appointed governor, the Marquis of Hertford,
at Richmond. Charles soon sent for his son to join him and
although Parliament had expressly forbidden such a move,
Hertford reunited father and son at York. At a ceremony shortly
afterwards, James was made a Knight of the Garter. From now
on, the Civil War was to take priority over education in the young
prince's everyday life.

Evidence of this change was soon forthcoming. Charles sent his
8-year-old son, accompanied by his tutors and equerries, from
York to Hull. The seaport contained a large store of ammunition
which the King much needed for his troops. James, who was
ostensibly on a sightseeing tour, spent the night in Hull and was
invited to lunch on the following day with the governor, Sir John
Hotham. Meanwhile, the King had sent a message to Hotham

stating that he intended to join them. When the King arrived at the city gates, escorted by 300 horsemen, he was refused entry and after a furious exchange, he was obliged to withdraw to nearby Beverley. Meanwhile, James was still within the city, and it was with some difficulty that he was eventually released. The effect on the boy is not known but in later life, when he became a military man, he was always an advocate of swift action against a potential enemy in order to achieve surprise.[66] James was at Nottingham when the royal standard was raised to mark the beginning of the Civil War and, as has already been mentioned, he witnessed at close quarters the battle of Edgehill. Charles, accompanied by his two sons, thereafter set up his headquarters at Oxford in October. It was to be James's home during the next four years, the most formative period of his life.

The atmosphere in wartime Oxford was not conducive to study. The colleges housed members of the Court and their families, and the presence of the Cavalier army provided much distraction. The university was also put on a war footing, with both tutors and scholars helping to dig defence fortifications round the city.[67] James's formal education was continued under the supervision of three tutors who were fellows of their colleges, Brian Duppa, Broughton and Coucher. He was taught French and writing by a sub-tutor named Massonett, a versatile man who also acted later as physician to James's household. It is clear from perusing the many letters which James wrote throughout his life that his style was pedestrian with much repetition, no doubt a legacy of his less than perfect tuition. On the other hand, unlike his elder brother, he became a fluent speaker of French. He was not, it seems, a natural scholar. King Charles at one stage implored him to 'ply his book more and his gun less'. One contemporary summed up the Prince's attitude as follows:

> His ingenious towardliness was not ignorant how much learning adds to nature, which made him eager after that accomplishment, though I cannot say he ever minded to make study his business, being so averse from prying upon his book, that he cared not to plod upon his games; for his active soul was more delighted with quick and nimble recreations, as running, leaping, riding.[68]

Apart from his interest in the guitar, on which he performed with some skill, James took no part in patronising the arts or sciences as his brother later did. Physical activities were more to his taste. Writing to his niece, the Countess of Litchfield, from Scotland, James stated:

> Now we have very good weather which I make use on by being abroad every day and playing at Goffe, which is the only divertion I can have without doors, this not being a good hunting country; within doors we have plays, Bassett [a card game] and Billiards, and do not pas our tyme so ill here as may be you thinke.

On another occasion he wrote:

> Cockfighting has been almost the only thing one could do here, and that for the most part we have twise a day. I have been a fox hunting thrise ... to morrow I am to go to it againe.[69]

Except for a brief visit to Oxford in 1644 by his mother, and occasional times spent with his father, James saw little of his parents between the ages of 9 and 12. In any case the King was not a competent instructor in statecraft, and the young prince grew up unimpressed with his father's indecisiveness in his dealings with Parliament and his enemies. The tide of war was turning against Charles I and he began to make plans for the safety of his family. Henrietta Maria was already in her native country, France; James's elder brother, Charles, had left for the Continent and the King himself departed from Oxford in April 1646 shortly before the parliamentary army besieged the city. Of the royal household only James was left in the city, in the charge of his governor, Sir George Radcliffe, a lawyer by training and a former friend of Strafford.

After the fall of Oxford to the parliamentary forces in June, Radcliffe escorted the Prince to London and handed him over to Algernon Percy, Duke of Northumberland, a moderate politician who had attempted to act as mediator between the King and Parliament. For the next two years James was virtually a prisoner at St James's Palace, together with his younger brother, Henry, and his little sister, Elizabeth. They were well treated. Northumberland received £7,500 a year from Parliament for James's maintenance and provided him with an elaborately decorated coach to go driving in Hyde Park.[70] However, the Prince lost his Oxford retinue, including his favourite dwarf, and a new household was established. He was also allowed from time to time to see his father, now a prisoner, at Hampton Court, where Charles secretly urged his son to escape to France to join his mother and elder brother.

It was not until April 1648 that James, dressed as a girl, boarded a barge in London after evading parliamentary vigilance and sailed to Holland. He resided there for a while with his sister Mary and her husband, William III, and joined his mother in Paris early in the following year. Henrietta Maria appointed a new governor, Sir John Berkeley, a former military commander and a domineering man who deliberately provoked arguments between the two brothers, James and Charles. James's unhappiness was not helped by frequent clashes with his mother, stemming partly from his obstinate nature. The situation was exacerbated by Henrietta Maria, who openly made unfavourable comparisons between Charles and James to her ladies at Court.

There is no doubt that James became more interested in military matters than in book learning. In 1652, when he was 19, he became apprenticed to the great army commander, Henry, Vicomte de Turennne, Marshal of France, and they became good friends. James proved to be a courageous and enterprising cavalry commander. His *Memoirs*, covering the campaigns in which he fought over the next eight years and written in the third person, present a full picture of his adventures, but typically are illuminated only by a few dry comments.[71] James was obliged to resign from the French army in 1656 after a treaty was signed between France and Cromwell, forcing the royal party to leave for the Spanish Netherlands; there he briefly served in the Spanish army against his former ally, France. After the Restoration, as Lord High Admiral, he commanded the British Fleet in two naval engagements against the Dutch with great success and took an active part in bringing about much-needed naval reforms. At the time, he won the admiration of the nation for his exploits. After the capture of New Amsterdam from the Dutch in 1664, it was renamed New York in his honour.

James's later errors of judgement after the Restoration and throughout his own short reign (it lasted only three years) can be largely attributed to his character rather than to his education. His adoption between 1660 and 1671 of the Roman Catholic faith, which contributed to his eventual downfall, is one such example. He also lacked discretion. In November 1687, during a dispute with the Privy Council, he told the assembled company, 'He that is not with me is against me.'[72] James disapproved of Charles II's acquiescence with his Parliaments on several matters. Shortly after his accession in 1685, James, in an interview with the French ambassador, told him:

> I know into what difficulties the deceased King my brother was thrown, when he suffered himself to waver with regard to France: I will take good care to hinder parliament from meddling in foreign affairs, and will put an end to the session as soon as I see the members shew any ill will.[73]

Not surprisingly, his relationship with Parliament deteriorated during his reign, leading to its formal dissolution in 1687.

It might be surmised that much of the bitterness and ruthlessness of his outlook stemmed from his boyhood experiences. Shortly before his accession, James's character was described by Gilbert Burnet, Bishop of Salisbury, who knew the Prince well:

> He has a strange notion of government, that everything is to be carried on in a high way and that no regard is to be had to the pleasing the people; and he has an ill opinion of any that proposes soft methods, and thinks that is popularity; but at the same time he always talks of law and justice.[74]

On the other hand, his stubbornness was a considerable asset in war if not in the handling of national affairs. At the battle of the Dunes near Dunkirk in 1658, when James commanded the right wing against Cromwell's New Model Army, Pepys recorded, 'Contrary to the advice all about him, his counsel carried himself and the rest through them safe.'[75]

Like his brother, James possessed a strong sexual appetite, though unlike Charles he was not attracted to great beauty. The Count of Grammont remarked, 'He was perpetually in one amour or other, without being very nice in his choice: upon which the King [Charles] once said, he believed his brother had his mistress given him by his priests for penance.'[76] James believed he had offended God by his love of women. In a letter of advice to his son, Prince James Francis Edward Stuart, the Old

Pretender, he confessed:

> I have always an aversion to prophane and Atheisticall men, yet I
> must owne with shame and confusion, I let my self go too much
> to the love of Women, which but for too long gott the better of me,
> by ill Example, and my not being enough on my gard at the first
> attaques of so dangerous an enemy.[77]

James married twice. His first wife was Anne Hyde, daughter of
Edward Hyde, Earl of Clarendon, his Lord Chancellor. They
married publicly in September 1660; seven weeks later a son was
born, but he lived for only a short time. This was followed by the
birth of two daughters, Mary and Anne. His second marriage in
1671, two years after his wife's death, was to a Catholic princess,
Mary of Modena. The birth of a son in June 1688, who would
possibly be a Catholic monarch, was unwelcome in a country
where the tide of political Anglicanism was rising. In July of that
year, an invitation to William of Orange was extended by leading
Whig opponents of the King. William landed at Torbay on 5
November and James eventually fled the country, landing in
France on Christmas Day. He was to live on in exile, full of vigour
but with a senile mind, until 17 September 1701,when he was
buried in the Church at St Germain-en-Laye, near Paris.

## MARY II (1662–94)

Mary's character was clearly moulded by the circumstances of
her childhood. She was born on 30 April 1662 at St James's Palace,
the eldest daughter of James Duke of York and his first wife, Anne
Hyde. They were an ill-matched couple: she was neither witty
nor charming and quickly grew fat whilst James, who had been
briefly infatuated with her, soon resumed his affairs with other
women. Anne bore him eight children in all, only two of whom
survived, Mary and her sister Anne, born three years later in
1665.

Both children suffered from poor eyesight, probably inherited
from their sickly mother. Mary was good-looking, tall and slight
with a quick intelligence and amiable disposition which she
retained throughout her life. During her early childhood the
nursery moved from place to place, including St James's Palace,
Twickenham, Richmond and Deptford, where her father

transacted naval business.[78] As both James and his wife had secretly converted to Catholicism, their uncle King Charles considered that the greatest priority was to give Mary and Anne a thorough religious education which would free them from any taint of the old religion. The Bishop of London, Dr Henry Compton, the second son of the Earl of Northampton and a former soldier, was appointed as their preceptor. Compton was a committed Protestant, and he impressed on his charges the teachings of the Church of England with some success. Mary's lifelong religious convictions were due to Compton's instruction. She regarded him with affection and he later officiated at her wedding. He was assisted in the teaching by a sub-preceptor, Dr Edward Lake, Prebendary of Exeter Cathedral, who was also chaplain to the Princesses, and Dr Thomas Doughty, Canon of Windsor. Lake wrote a text especially for Mary, the *Officium Eucharisticum*, which became a popular manual.[79]

In 1671 when Mary was 9 years old, her mother, now grossly fat through overeating, died of cancer. Mary was her father's favourite and she had been neglected by Anne Hyde. It was a measure of James's indifference to his wife that he did not attend the funeral nor did Mary or the other three children.[80] Shortly after this, the Princesses were installed in Richmond Palace under the care of Colonel Edward Villiers, Keeper of the Park, and his wife Frances. The young girls were not lacking in company. They were brought up together with the Villiers' six daughters, Elizabeth, Katherine, Barbara, Anne, Henrietta and Mary, and were from time to time joined by others such as Anne Trelawney and Sarah Jennings. Mary flourished with such friendly companions who also shared their lessons with her. She particularly loved dancing, and as Pepys described seeing her, 'a little child in hanging sleeves, dance most finely so as almost to ravish me, her airs were so good'.[81] Her education, which was not to a high standard, consisted of what was regarded as desirable female accomplishments. French was taught by Peter de Laine, and in later life she was sufficiently accomplished to be able to keep a secret diary in that language.[82] Although she enjoyed English lessons, she was a poor speller all her life. Drawing and painting instruction was given by Richard Gibson, a dwarf who was a gifted painter of miniatures, and his wife, who was also a dwarf. For dancing, she had Mr Gorey, an elderly dancing master.

It was probably soon after entering the Villiers' household that Mary began her 14-year correspondence with her new friend, Frances Apsley. Her father, Sir Allen Apsley, was Treasurer of the Household to Charles II and Receiver-General to Mary's father at St James's Palace. Frances, who was some nine years older than Mary and was very beautiful, became the object of a romantic attachment by Mary as her letters to Frances strongly indicate. Mary's passionate outpourings might have been a seeking for the motherly love she never received; on the other hand, there is evidence that Anne Hyde herself had, when young, indulged in an amorous correspondence with her cousin, Barbara Aylesbury.[83]

Mary began her first letter to Frances with the salutation 'Dear Husband' and ended with 'Your loving Wife', and the correspondence continued in this vein throughout the years. Mary signed herself as Mary, Marie, Clorin or Clorine (in Beaumont and Fletcher's play *An Evening's Love*, Clorin is the name of the Faithful Shepherdess) and Frances was Aurelia, the 'cruel, fair blest husband'.

> What more can I say more to perswade you that I love you with more zeal then any lover can [Mary once wrote]. You are loved more than can be exprest by your ever obedient wife, vere afectionate friand, humbel sarvent to kis the ground where one you go, to be your fish in a net, your bird cage, your humbel trout.[84]

The correspondence, which was carried on in secrecy and conveyed between the couple mainly by Richard Gibson, contained typical examples of lovers' tiffs and misunder-standings. However, it continued even after the marriage of Frances in June 1682, when Mary wrote, 'Adieu, dear friand, I shall never change nor hope you wont.'[85]

Within two years of her mother's death, Mary's father had married again. Mary of Modena, his bride, was only 15 years of age. James broke the news to his daughters with the sentence, 'I have brought you a playfellow.' The new queen was different from Anne Hyde and she became a good friend of her step-daughter. In 1677, on learning of Mary's impending wedding to William of Orange, she wrote, 'I am much grieved to lose her, because I hold her in much affection and she really is a Princess of great merit.'[86]

Part of Mary and Anne's education was their participation in masques at Court. In 1674 the two princesses were involved in a performance of *Calisto or the Chaste Nymph,* based on the second book of Ovid's *Metamorphoses* and written by a minor dramatist, John Crowne. Both Mary and Anne represented young nymphs together with five other girls, an early example of women performing on the English stage.

Within three years, after much hard bargaining between King Charles, James, Duke of York, and William of Orange over questions of the balance of power between European nations, Mary, the 15-year-old princess, was offered to William as his wife. William, who was also her cousin, was a serious-minded soldier with a slightly hunched back, a hooked nose and an asthmatic wheeze, standing some four inches shorter than Mary, and he was a reluctant bridegroom. When Mary was told the news, she broke down and wept for a day and half,[87] but there was little time for speculation: the wedding took place in London, in Mary's bedroom, a fortnight later. Mary left England and settled in Holland with her new husband, and despite her earlier misgivings, she became a devoted wife and a firm defender of William's actions as Stadtholder of Holland.[88]

In 1688, when her father, now James II, provoked the hostility of the English public, Mary was offered the throne alone, but loyally refused, telling the ministers, 'I am the Prince's wife and would never be any other than what should be in conjunction with him.' A joint sovereignty was eventually agreed upon. John Evelyn in his diary at the time commented, 'It was believ'd that both, especially the princess, would have show'd some seeming reluctance at least of assuming her father's crown ... [instead] she came into Whitehall laughing and jolly, as at a wedding, so as to seem quite transported.'[89] However, such apparent lack of filial respect had its roots in the recent past when the religious differences between them had grown greater. James, who had opposed Mary's confirmation, had renounced all authority over her, and because of her education in Church of England doctrines, called her 'a child of the State'.[90]

William instructed Christopher Wren to rebuild much of Hampton Court Palace and enlarge Kensington Palace, the latter of which reminded Mary of her Dutch homes. Mary played little part in carrying out royal duties except when William was abroad, presiding at meetings of her cabinet and the Privy Council. That she never showed much interest or understanding of political happenings is not surprising in the light of the lack of preparation for monarchy in her sketchy education. As one historian has noted, 'She remains from first to last a creature unexplained, silent, almost invisible.'[91] Mary, who had two miscarriages, died childless on 28 December 1694 aged 32, with William surviving her for another eight years until his own death in 1702.

### ANNE (1665–1714)

A modern biographer of Anne has claimed that 'No one has been less tutored in queenship nor any more determined to serve well.'[92] Some of the reasons for this must be sought in an account of her childhood and education.

Anne, the second daughter of James Duke of York and Anne Hyde, was born at St James's Palace on 6 February 1665. She was rapidly removed to the nursery at Richmond Palace where she was placed in the hands of a wet nurse and a governess, Lady Frances Villiers, whom she shared with her sister Mary. Anne inherited the poor health of her parents, especially an eye complaint which was to dominate her early life. When she was three, Anne was sent to France to seek the help of eye specialists and resided with her grandmother, Henrietta Maria, at Colombes near Paris. The condition, then called defluxion of the eyes, was never fully cured and left her with a permanent squint. It also affected her character and may have accounted for her 'tincture of sourness', stubbornness and a wish to confine her friendships to a small circle of friends so that her disability would not be widely known.[93] The consequences for Anne's education were important; she avoided reading books whenever possible and later was not interested in the visual arts, never going to the theatre and seldom holding dramatic performances at Court. [94]

A story relating to Anne's childhood and recounted by Sarah Churchill gives a glimpse of the effect of Anne's disability on her behaviour. One day when she was walking with Mary in Richmond Park, a dispute arose between them as to whether an object they saw at a distance was a man or a tree. Mary, who was long-sighted, believed that it was the former whilst Anne, who

5. *James, Duke of York (James II) and Anne Hyde, Duchess of York, with their children, Princess Mary (Mary II) and Princess Anne (Queen Anne)*, Peter Lely and Benedette Gennari, *c.* 1670–80.

was short-sighted, insisted that it was the latter. When they came nearer, it became obvious that Mary had been correct. 'Now, Anne,' she asked, 'are you satisfied that it is a man?' In reply, Anne turned away and persisting in what she had originally stated, said, 'No, sister, I still think it is a tree.'[95]

Whilst staying in France, Anne became well acquainted with the language. Henrietta Maria died in 1669 whilst Anne was in her care and for the next year Anne joined the nursery of the children of her aunt, Henrietta Duchess of Orleans. Anne enjoyed her new companions but her stay was not to last for long. In June 1670 she was brought back to England by Lady Frances Villiers. Within two weeks Anne learnt of the sudden and mysterious death of her French aunt. Seven months later Anne's own mother died.

Anne provided a striking contrast in appearance and abilities to her sister. Whereas Mary was tall, slender, intelligent and articulate, and had inherited the handsome features of the Stuarts, Anne had the characteristics of her mother's family, the Hydes. She had plain looks and a more rounded figure, and was unintelligent and self-centred. In adulthood she became corpulent and suffered from chronic ill-health; at her Coronation she had to be carried in a sedan chair to the ceremony at Westminster Abbey. Anne's bad habits had started in infancy when her mother had encouraged her to drink chocolate with her and eat to excess.[96]

At Richmond Palace she shared governors and tutors with Mary. Anne was no better than Mary in mastering the rudiments of English, and her spelling was equally capricious. Little attention was given in their lessons to history, geography or aspects of the constitution; the classics did not feature in their curriculum as they had so prominently for Mary Tudor and Elizabeth a century before. Anne's French proved to be excellent and she could write it fluently and could converse with French ambassadors in their own language. She also had a surprisingly sweet voice which so pleased her uncle, Charles II, that he engaged Mrs Barry, a well-known actress of the day, to give her elocution lessons. Like Mary, she was also proficient at dancing. Anne was a good musician and learnt the guitar and harpsichord under the tuition of a music master, Anthony Robart.[97] She retained a life-long interest in music, and she attended concerts at

Court. However, Anne's chief recreations were physical ones, especially hunting, which she continued until adulthood, and she was a keen gardener. Anne also became an enthusiastic card player, at one time incurring debts which her father was obliged to meet.[98]

Religious instruction in the tenets of the Church of England was as happily received by Anne as her sister. Dr Henry Compton had no difficulty in winning her over to his deeply felt anti-Catholic views. When she was 13, Anne expressed her own religious convictions in a letter to her sister:

> I hope you don't doubt but that I will be ever firm to my religion whatever happens. However, since you desire me to write freely on this subject, I must tell you that I abhor the principles of the Church of Rome as much as is possible for any to do, and I as much value the doctrine of the Church of England. And certainly there is the greatest reason in the world to do so, for the doctrine of the Church of Rome is wicked and dangerous, and directly contrary to the Scriptures, and their ceremonies – most of them – plain, downright idolatry.[99]

It was partly due to his influence that when Anne came to the throne, she instituted Queen Anne's Bounty, which from 1704 remitted all arrears of first fruits and tenths to poor clergymen in debt; she also used the funds to increase inadequate stipends.[100]

Anne's childhood, carefully supervised by her clerical superiors, was a solemn one. On the King's orders she was confirmed in January 1676 on the same day as Mary. Later, at her first communion, her chaplain, Edward Lake, reported, 'Her Highness was not (through negligence) instructed how much of the wine to drink, but drank of it twice or thrice, whereat I was much concern'd, lest the duke should have notice of it.'[101] Anne's friends were carefully vetted for their religious allegiances: it was for this reason that one of her earliest intimate friends, Cicely Cornwallis, a Roman Catholic, was banished from the Court. In such a closed society, the two sisters found an outlet in writing letters to their special friends. It was earlier noted that Mary carried on a long and passionate correspondence with Frances Apsley; Anne joined her sister in this activity. Frances was 12 years older than Anne and whereas Mary addressed Frances as 'husband', Frances adopted the role of 'wife' with Anne.

When Mary married William of Orange in 1677, Anne was too ill in bed with smallpox to attend the ceremony. Anne recovered, but shortly afterwards her governess, Lady Frances Villiers, died of the same disease, thus removing an important mother figure from her life. In her place was appointed her aunt, Lady Clarendon who, according to Sarah Jennings 'looked like a madman and talked like a scholar, which the princess thought agreed very well together'. Anne quickly grew to dislike her and dismissed her last governess at the first available opportunity.

Of overwhelming importance in Anne's life (and for the future history of this country) was her friendship with Sarah Jennings, later Duchess of Marlborough. They had first met when Anne was 5 and Sarah was 10; there is a record that at an early age the Princess visited Sarah's widowed mother at her home at Sandridge, near St Albans.[102] Anne recognised that Sarah possessed all the qualities which she herself lacked – self-confidence, beauty, a quick mind and an outspokenness which impressed her. Within a few years, Sarah had married the soldier, John Churchill, later to become the first Duke of Marlborough and the hero of Blenheim. By contrast, Anne's insecurity had been increased after the embarrassment caused by a probable affair in 1682 with Lord Mulgrave, an opportunist who was subsequently exiled. The friendship between the two women developed as Anne's emotional dependence grew. Now Anne flung caution to the wind. According to Sarah:

> She [Anne] grew uneasy to be treated by me with the form and ceremony due to her rank; nor could she bear from me the sound of words which implied in them distance and superiority. It was this turn of mind which made her one day propose to me, that whenever I should happen to be absent from her, we might in our letters write ourselves by feigned names, such as would import nothing of distinction between us. MORLEY and FREEMAN were the names her fancy hit upon, and she left me to choose by which of them I would be called. My frank, open temper led me to pitch upon FREEMAN, and so the Princess took the other; and from this time Mrs Morley and Mrs Freeman began to converse together as equals, made so by affection and friendship.[103]

Sarah's influence on Anne had unfortunate consequences. She was instrumental in persuading the Princess to treat William of Orange with disrespect. Politically, matters were exacerbated when Churchill, then Earl of Marlborough, intrigued against William, and Anne still sided with Sarah. The situation caused a rift between Mary and Anne which was never resolved. Sarah also attempted to impose her strongly Whig views on Anne, who was a Tory sympathiser.[104] It was not until 1710 that Anne summoned the courage to dismiss both her and the Duke of Marlborough from her service.

Anne's private life had had its tragedies. In 1683 she had married Prince George of Denmark, a vacuous but amiable Protestant and a man of few words who predeceased her by six years. Charles II once said of him, 'I have tried him drunk and I have tried him sober, and there is nothing to him.' Nevertheless, Anne was devastated by his death in 1708 and kept the Court in mourning for two years.[105] She had 17 pregnancies in all: five of her children survived but only one, the Duke of Gloucester, reached the age of 11. Anne had succeeded to the throne on the death of William of Orange in 1702. Though her reign saw many splendid military success in Europe and the laying of the foundations of the British Empire, Anne's own contribution is difficult to assess. Her religious beliefs, formed in childhood, tended to govern many of her actions – for example, the revival of the touch for the King's Evil and her attempt to restore newspaper censorship as a method of dealing with 'the false and scandalous libels, such as are a reproach to any government'.[106] However, although in the main obstinate, she was often dependent on others and showed little evidence of an independent mind during her reign, apart from asserting her right to choose her ministers.

Towards the end of her life, Anne was wearied by the political crisis of the nation which was being divided between the Whigs and the Tories. She fell ill in July 1714 and, when she was dying, passed on the White Staff of the Treasurership to the Earl of Shrewsbury, a leading Whig, who supported the Hanoverian succession. Queen Anne, the last of the Stuarts, died at Kensington Palace on 1 August 1714 at the age of 49. Her doctor said, 'I believe sleep was never more welcome to a weary traveller than death was to her.'

The difference between the crown that James I willingly accepted and the much more limited monarchical authority of Queen Anne is so great that some historians have suggested that if we use a strict definition of monarchy, it ceased to exist in England after 1688.[107] On the other hand, we can see the Stuart period as the time when almost absolute authority was transformed into the beginnings of limited monarchy of a constitutional kind. The divine right of kings was gone forever in England, and the Hanoverians reigned by Act of Parliament.

As power passed from sovereigns to politicians, the education of future monarchs became less crucial, in some respects. Nevertheless, the almost complete loss of the Renaissance ideal of education without its being replaced by any adequate alternative model was a tragedy for the individuals involved. Almost nothing of the intellectual excitement of seventeenth-century science or the educational ideas of Comenius and Harltib found their way into Stuart education.

The Stuart era also witnessed the development of political philosophy, especially that of Hobbes and Locke. There is little evidence that these ideas made much of an impact on royal minds, either. But the later Stuarts were forced to deal with the practical politics of the new parties, the Whigs and the Tories. The need for education was greater than the awareness of the need of the monarchs themselves. A dangerous situation existed and the fact that it did not result in a republic probably owes more to the politicians than to the royal family.

## NOTES

1. M. Kishlansky, *A Monarchy Transformed: Britain, 1603–1714* (Allen Lane, 1996), p. 2.
2. J. Melville, *The Memoirs of Sir James Melville* (D. Wilson, 1752 edn), p. 139.
3. D. M. Bergeron, *Royal Families, Royal Lovers: King James of England and Scotland* (Columbia, MO: University of Missouri Press, 1991), p. 22.
4. G. P. V. Akrigg (ed.), *Letters of King James VI and I* (Berkeley, CA: University of California Press, 1984), p. 46.
5. C. and H. Steeholm, *James I of England: The Wisest Fool in Christendom* (Michael Joseph, 1938), p. 36.
6. Melville, *Memoirs*, p. 250.
7. I. D. McFarlane, *Buchanan* (Duckworth, 1981), p. 449.
8. D. Irving, *Memoirs of the Life and Writings of George Buchanan* (Edinburgh: Blackwood, 1817), p. 162.
9. W. McElwee, *The Wisest Fool in Christendom: The Reign of King James I and VI* (Faber & Faber, 1958), p. 42.
10. L. Aikin, *Memoirs of the Court of King James the First*, vol. I (Longman, Hurst, Rees, Orme & Brown, 1822), p. 6.

11. D. H. Willson, *King James VI and I* (Cape, 1956), p. 23.
12. D. Mathew, *James I* (Eyre & Spottiswoode, 1967), p. 28.
13. J. Craigie (ed.), *The Basilikon Doron of King James VI* (Edinburgh: Scottish Text Society, 1944), pp. 14–15.
14. Ibid., p. 59.
15. C. Bingham, *The Making of a King* (Collins, 1969), p. 53.
16. B. Bevan, *King James VI of Scotland and I of England* (Rubicon Press, 1996), p. 15.
17. Irving, *George Buchanan*, p. 165.
18. R. Strong, *Henry, Prince of Wales* (Thames & Hudson, 1986), pp. 14–15.
19. A. Fraser, *King James VI of Scotland and I of England* (Weidenfeld & Nicolson, 1974), p. 35.
20. J. P. Kenyon, *Stuart England* (Allen Lane, 1978), pp. 50–1.
21. Maitland Club, *Letters to King James the Sixth*, 35 (1835), p. xxxiii.
22. Robert Carey, Earl of Monmouth, *Memoirs* (Edinburgh: Constable, 1808), pp. 140–1.
23. W. Sterry, *Annals of The King's College of Our Lady Beside Windsor* (Methuen, 1898), p. 113.
24. M. Ashley, *Charles I and Oliver Cromwell: A Study in Contrasts and Comparisons* (Methuen, 1987), p. 21.
25. J. Bowle, *Charles I: A Biography* (Weidenfeld & Nicolson, 1975), p. 21.
26. F. M. G. Higham, *Charles I: A Study* (Hamish Hamilton, 1932), p. 15.
27. H. Ellis, *Original Letters, Illustrative of English History*, ser. 1, vol. III (Harding, Triphook & Lepard, 1825), pp. 92–3.
28. I. Disraeli, *Commentaries on the Life and Reign of Charles the First*, ed. B. Disraeli, vol. I (Henry Colburn, 1851), p. 9.
29. C. Petrie (ed.), *The Letters, Speeches and Proclamations of King Charles I* (Cassell, 1935), p. 3.
30. C. Carlton, *Charles I: The Personal Monarch* (Routledge & Kegan Paul, 1983), p. 16.
31. C. Hibbert, *Charles I* (Weidenfeld & Nicolson, 1968), p. 24.
32. Ellis, *Original Letters*, p. 94.
33. O. Millar, *The Age of Charles I* (Tate Gallery, 1972), p. 10.
34. C. Lloyd, *The Queen's Pictures* (Royal Collection Enterprises, 1994), p. 16.
35. M. Chute, *Ben Jonson of Westminster* (Hale, 1954), p. 306.
36. J. A. Gotch, *Inigo Jones* (Methuen, 1928), p. 211.
37. Lord Clarendon, *Memoirs of King Charles I* (I. Herbert, 1795 edn), p. 8.
38. D. R. Watson, *The Life and Times of Charles I* (Weidenfeld & Nicolson, 1972), p. 210.
39. I. J. Reeve, *Charles I and the Road to Personal Rule* (Cambridge University Press, 1989), p. 296.
40. Disraeli, *Commentaries*, p. 11.
41. C. Falkus, *The Life and Times of Charles II* (Weidenfeld & Nicolson, 1972), p. 13.
42. R. Ollard, *The Image of the King: Charles I and Charles II* (Hodder & Stoughton, 1979), p. 63.
43. Ellis, *Original Letters*, p. 288.
44. Ibid., p. 289.
45. Ibid., p. 289.
46. Ibid., p. 290.
47. N. Pocock, 'Brian Duppa', in L. Stephen (ed.), *Dictionary of National Biography* (Smith Elder, 1888), p. 242.
48. *Calendar of State Papers*, Charles I 1639, Domestic (HMSO, 1873), p. 509.
49. J. Miller, *Charles I* (Weidenfeld & Nicolson, 1991), p. 3.
50. Bowle, *Charles I*, pp. 163–4.
51. A. Fraser, *King Charles II* (Weidenfeld & Nicolson, 1979), p. 22.
52. R. Hutton, *Charles the Second: King of England, Scotland and Ireland* (Oxford: Clarendon Press, 1989), p. 52.
53. O. Airy, *Charles II* (Goupil & Co., 1901), p. 9.
54. G. E. C. Cokayne, *The Complete Peerage*, ed. V. Gibbs, vol. II (St Catherine Press, 1912), p. 150.

55. E. Scott, *The King in Exile: The Wanderings of Charles II from June 1646 to July 1654* (Constable, 1905), p. 27.
56. Margaret, Duchess of Newcastle, *The Life of William Cavendish, Duke of Newcastle*, ed. C. H. Firth (John C. Nimmo, 1886), p. 197
57. T. R. Slaughter, *Ideology and Politics on the Eve of Restoration: Newcastle's Advice to Charles II* (Philadelphia: American Philosophical Society, 1984), pp. xv, xxxi.
58. A. C. A. Brett, *Charles II and His Court* (Methuen, 1910), p. 170.
59. D. D. Raphael, *Hobbes, Morals and Politics* (Allen & Unwin, 1977), p. 13.
60. D. Tylden-Wright, *John Aubrey* (HarperCollins, 1991), p. 131.
61. H. Elsna, *Catherine of Braganza* (Hale, 1967), p. 164.
62. C. Oman, *Henrietta Maria* (Hodder & Stoughton, 1936), p. 327.
63. H. C. Foxcroft (ed.), *Life and Letters of Sir George Savile, Bart, First Marquis of Halifax*, vol. II (Longman, Green, 1898), p. 348.
64. P. Earle, *The Life and Times of James II* (Weidenfeld & Nicolson, 1972), p. 19.
65. O. Airy (ed.), *Burnet's History of My Own Time*, vol. I (Oxford: Clarendon Press, 1897), p. 295.
66. J. Haswell, *James II: Soldier and Sailor* (Hamish Hamilton, 1972), p. 8.
67. C. E. Malet, *A History of the University of Oxford*, vol. II (Methuen, 1924), pp. 354–5.
68. F. C. Turner, *James II* (Eyre & Spottiswoode, 1948), p. 13.
69. Viscount Dillon, 'Some Familiar Letters of Charles II and James, Duke of York, Addressed to their Daughter and Niece, the Countess of Litchfield', *Archaeologia*, 58 (1902), pp. 164, 177.
70. M. Ashley, *James II* (Dent, 1977), p. 22.
71. A. L. Sells (ed.), *The Memoirs of James II* (Chatto & Windus, 1962), p. 36.
72. C. E. Whiting, *Nathaniel Lord Crewe, Bishop of Durham, 1641–1721, and his Diocese* (SPCK, 1940), p. 167.
73. J. Dalrymple, *Memoirs of Great Britain and Ireland*, vol. II (A. Strachan & T. Cadell, 1790), p. 2.
74. H. C. Foxcroft, *A Supplement to Burnet's History of My Own Time* (Oxford: Clarendon Press, 1902), p. 51.
75. R. Latham and W. Matthews (eds), *The Diary of Samuel Pepys*, vol. V (Bell, 1971), p. 170.
76. W. Scott (ed.), *Memoirs of Count Grammont by Anthony Hamilton*, vol. I (John C. Nimmo, 1885), p. 90.
77. J. S. Clarke, *The Life of James the Second, King of England*, vol. II (Page & Foss, Budd & Calker, 1816), p. 623.
78. H. W. Chapman, *Mary II Queen of England* (Cape, 1953), p. 20.
79. G. Godwin, 'Edward Lake', in S. Lee (ed.), *Dictionary of National Biography* (Smith, Elder, 1892), p. 410.
80. E. Hamilton, *William's Mary: A Biography of Mary II* (Hamish Hamilton, 1972), p. 17.
81. Latham and Matthews, *Diary of Samuel Pepys*, vol. IX (1976 edn), p. 507.
82. N. M. Waterstone, *Mary II Queen of England* (Durham, NC: Duke University Press, 1928), p. 29.
83. Chapman, *Mary II*, p. 30.
84. B. Bathurst (ed.), *Letters of the Two Queens* (Robert Holden, 1924), pp. 60–1.
85. M. Haile, *Queen Mary of Modena: Her Life and Letters* (Dent, 1905), p. 64.
86. Bathurst, *Letters*, p. 148.
87. G. P. Elliot (ed.), 'The Diary of Dr Edward Lake, 1677–8', *Camden Society Miscellany*, 1 (1847), p. 5.
88. H. and B. van der Zee, *William and Mary* (Macmillan, 1973), p. 144.
89. W. Bray (ed.), *The Diary of John Evelyn* (Bickers & Son, 1906), p. 69.
90. M. F. Sandars, *Princess and Queen of England: Life of Mary II* (Stanley Paul, 1913), p. 28.
91. M. Bowen, *The Third Mary Stuart* (The Bodley Head, 1929), p. 281.
92. D. Green, *Queen Anne* (Collins, 1970), p. 11.
93. E. Gregg, *Queen Anne* (Routledge & Kegan Paul, 1980), p. 7.
94. J. Ashton, *Social Life in the Reign of Queen Anne*, vol. II (Chatto & Windus, 1882), p. 10.
95. A. Strickland, *Lives of the Queens of England*, vol. VII (Longman, Green, Reader &

Dyer, 1875), p. 13.
96. Ibid., p. 5.
97. N. Connell, *Anne: The Last Stuart Monarch* (Thornton Butterworth, 1937), p. 25.
98. G. M. Trevelyan, *England under Queen Anne: Blenheim* (Longman, 1936), p. 35.
99. B. C. Brown (ed.), *The Letters and Diplomatic Instructions of Queen Anne* (Cassell, 1935), p. 16.
100. E. F. Carpenter, *The Protestant Bishop: Being the Life of Henry Compton, Bishop of London* (Longman, Green, 1956), p. 35.
101. Elliot, 'The Diary of Dr Edward Lake', p. 29.
102. A. Colville, *Duchess Sarah* (Longman, Green, 1904), p. 37.
103. S. Churchill, *An Account of the Conduct of the Dowager Duchess of Marlborough* (George Hawkins, 1742), p. 15.
104. F. Harris, *A Passion for Government: The Life of Sarah, Duchess of Marlborough* (Oxford: Clarendon Press, 1991), pp. 2–3.
105. A. W. Speck, *The Birth of Britain: A New Nation, 1700–1710* (Oxford: Blackwell, 1994), p. 13.
106. M. Foot, *The Pen and the Sword* (McGibbon & Kee, 1957), p. 79.
107. J. A. Cannon, 'The Survival of the British Monarchy', *Transactions of the Royal Historical Society*, 5th ser., 36 (1986), p. 146.

# 4 The Education of the Hanoverian Kings in the Age of Reason:
## From George I to William IV

IN 1714 QUEEN ANNE died without an heir, although she had produced no fewer than 17 offspring, if we include her numerous miscarriages. This meant the end of the Stuart dynasty, and according to the Act of Settlement, the crown passed to the Protestant descendants of the Electress of Hanover (grand-daughter of James I).

The Hanoverian period may conveniently be divided into two parts: an age of tranquillity during the reigns of George I and George II (1714–60), then the beginnings of various kinds of turbulence from the reign of George III onwards.

The dominant feature of life under George I and George II was stability: in politics there was the rise of the Whig Party under Walpole, while in religion and social life in general there was calm almost to the point of dullness. From the beginning of the reign of George III however, there was much less stability: the expansion of the colonies was counterbalanced by the loss of America, while at home there was the rapid development of industry and consequent social unrest. Throughout the period social disorder was feared both domestically and internationally, with the Napoleonic wars following the French Revolution; and there was the sporadic threat of revolution in England.

There were also momentous changes in the intellectual climate of the period, often referred to as the Enlightenment or the Age of Reason. This was essentially a movement by intellectuals to apply to social life lessons learned from advances made in the physical sciences. In France, Diderot and D'Alembert channelled much of Enlightenment thinking into their great project the *Encyclopédie* (1751–76) – an attempt to revolutionise knowledge, replacing religion by science, and faith by reason.

England was less affected by this movement than other parts of Europe but was not totally isolated: here 'progress' was transformed into the more practical 'improvement'. Perhaps the strangest feature of this intellectual development was that it had so little influence on the education of royal offspring.


To understand the education of the Hanoverian royal children it is necessary first to look at the situation prevailing in comparable households on mainland Europe at the time.

A universal feature was their separation from their parents shortly after birth, the child being given his or her own establishment of nurses and governesses. At the age of about 7, a royal prince was placed in the hands of a new governor, usually a nobleman or a senior soldier. The post of governor was a much-coveted position as the holder was in close contact with the monarch and was thus well placed for social and political advancement.

The day-to-day lessons were the responsibility of the preceptor or tutor, almost certainly a leading churchman, which indicated the importance of religion in the Princes' curriculum (princesses were kept in separate households). The preceptor was expected to be with his charges throughout most of the day, a remit which extended beyond merely teaching. As John Bettam, the tutor to James Francis Edward Stuart, the Old Pretender, wrote in his *Brief Treatise on Education* for the Prince's use:

> The quality most essential to a Tutor fit to Educate a Prince, is a Quality without a Name, and which is not fixt to any certain Profession. It is not simply to be skill'd in History, in Mathematics, Languages, Politicks, Philosophy, in the Ceremonies and Interests of Princes, all of which may be supply'd. 'Tis not necessary that he who has the care of instructing the Prince should teach him all; 'tis sufficient he teach him the use of all.

Every possible occasion, Bettam suggested, was to be used for preparing the Prince for his future role:

> Ordinary Tutors think themselves only oblig'd to instruct Princes at certain hours, to whit, when they teach them what they call

92

their Lesson. But the Man we speak of, has no set hour of teaching, or rather, he reaches him at every hour: For, he often instructs him as much in his Play, in his Visits, in his Conversation, and Table talk with those present, as when he makes him read Books; because, having for principal aim to frame his Judgement right, for this he finds the various objects, that offer themselves often more available, than premeditated Discourses: Since nothing sinks less into the Mind, than what enters there under the unpleasant shape of a Lesson or Instruction.[1]

It is little wonder, then, that conflict often occurred between the preceptor and a wilful or resentful prince, as will be seen with some of the Hanoverian children.

In the Continental courts. French was taught as the universal language, with as much Latin as was necessary to read international treaties.[2] A lack of fluent English was to prove a handicap to the early Georges. Paramount in a royal education, however, was the need to equip the Prince for his future position, with little reference to his physical or emotional needs.

A conservative view of religion was inculcated which tended to colour his view of politics. Accomplishments in the arts, particularly dancing, elocution and music, formed an essential part of the curriculum to add stature to the royal persona. No better example is afforded than the court of Louis XIV at Versailles, where the King himself would appear at the climax of the ballets and operas written by one of his composers, Lully. History provided a useful guide to dynastic knowledge as well as emphasising the achievements of past monarchs. When Louis XV was only 7 years old, he asked the Papal Nuncio, 'M. le Nonce, how many popes have there been up till now?' While the Nuncio hesitated in his reply, the young king went on, 'You do not know the number of popes? But I know how many kings there have been in France right down to myself, and I am only a child.'[3] Similarly, geography was seen as a good way of introducing tales of leaders and warriors in far-off lands at a time when royal travel was strictly limited. The military arts were considered of great importance, as they contributed to royal bearing – the image of Charles I on horseback, for instance, is a very striking one – and provided insights into strategy in conducting warfare. As has been mentioned, the Prince's household invariably included military men in one post or another and who could readily introduce the Prince to such training.

Sex education was not overlooked, as one of the duties of the Prince was to ensure the continuity of the dynasty. Initiation was provided at the onset of puberty. It is recorded that a Madame d'Elitz of the family of Schulenburg was mistress of George I, became a paramour of his son, George II, and was employed in the seduction of Frederick, Prince of Wales, George I's grandson.[4]

This instrumental view of education contrasted sharply with the philosophy postulated by the French Encyclopedists. Voltaire, too, in his writings urged intellectual, religious and political freedom. Rousseau's educational theories, contained in his influential book *Emile*, published in 1762, the year which saw the birth of the future George IV, were seen as deeply radical, namely that the child was essentially born good, that knowledge needed by an adult should not form the basis of schooling, and that the aim of education was to liberate the individual rather than be regarded as a preparation for fitting into society. It is little wonder that such ideas were wholly unacceptable as a basis for royal education.

Indeed, as an anonymous French 'Royal Author' wrote in 1777, 'The education of the nobility is certainly reprehensible from one end of Europe to the other.'[5] It was unlikely that Enlightenment views on education would be adopted for royal children, since the Enlightenment was potentially subversive, casting doubt on traditional beliefs, including those of authority and religion.

## GEORGE I (1660–1727)

It has been well stated that 'the first four Georges ruled for a little over a hundred years, yet they witnessed far profounder changes in economic, social and cultural life than any previous monarchs'.[6] But there seemed to be little promise with the arrival of the first Hanoverian king.

George Louis, born at Osnabrück on 28 May 1660, succeeded to the English throne in 1714 at the age of 54 on the death of Queen Anne. His father, Duke Ernest Augustus, Elector of Hanover, was interested in astronomy and alchemy and had a passion for building, constructing among others a new palace at Osnabrück. He had few intellectual pursuits but loved music.

Ernest was a soldier and took an active part in the campaigns against the French in the Netherlands.

George's mother was Sophia, Electress of Hanover, the granddaughter of James I of England and daughter of Elizabeth, the Winter Queen, widow of Frederick V, King of Bohemia. Sophia, whose intellectual curiosity greatly outshone her husband's, had as a child undergone a strict regime of study. At an early age she had been sent to Leiden by her mother, who according to Sophia 'preferred the sight of her monkeys and dogs to that of her 12 children';[7] she was accompanied by her governess, who had been her father's tutor. The regime, apart from inculcating Palatine etiquette, consisted of a diet of learning several languages, including French, German, English, Dutch, Greek and Latin as well as theology, law, mathematics and dancing. By the age of 9 or 10, Sophia had given it all up. 'They believed', she wrote, 'that I should turn out a prodigy of learning because I was so quick, but my only object in applying myself was to give up study when I had acquired all that was necessary, and be no longer forced to endure the weariness of learning.'[8]

However, she remained deeply interested in intellectual pursuits. She was, for instance, delighted to inherit from her late brother-in-law his Court Councillor, Gottfried Wilhelm von Leibnitz, the mathematician (who invented the calculating machine) and philosopher, whose responsibilities included those of acting as librarian, political adviser, international correspondent and technological consultant. Their correspondence over many years reveals a meeting of minds; Leibnitz called her 'the learned Electress' and declared her 'the oasis in the intellectual desert of Hanover'.[9]

Perhaps one important consequence of Sophia's relative neglect by her mother was her alleged indifference to her eldest son, George. This lack of affection might help to account for his reserved and phlegmatic personality, his pathological hatred of his own eldest son, the future George II, and his own disastrous marriage to Sophia Dorothea of Zell. Her presumed relationship with the Swedish Count Philipp von Königsmark led to her trial and divorce in 1694; she was subsequently incarcerated in a castle at Ahlden, northern Germany, for 32 years. Sophia's place was filled by a number of mistresses. John Toland, a leading Dissenting minister and commentator on the political scene of his day, wrote of the future king from Hanover in 1702:

> The fire of his temper appeared in every look and gesture; which, being unhappily under the direction of a small misunderstanding, was every day throwing him upon some indiscretion. He was naturally sincere, and his pride told him that he was placed above constraint; not reflecting that a high rank carries along with it a necessity of a more decent and regular behaviour than is expected from those who are not set in so conspicuous a light. He was so far from being of that opinion, that he looked on all the men and women he saw as creatures he might kick or kiss for his diversion; and, whenever he met with any opposition in those designs, he thought his opposers insolent rebels to the will of God, who created them for his use, and judged of the merit of all people by their ready submission to his orders, or the relation they had to his power.[10]

Ernest had planned a military career for his eldest son and little emphasis was placed on formal education. George greatly pleased his father when at the age of 7 he drilled a company of 60 'soldiers', formed from the young sons of his uncle's ministers and officials.[11] Nevertheless, when his father became Elector of Hanover, George was sent to France on an educational tour in the hope that it would help him acquire an appetite for elegance and culture. At the age of 15, he first accompanied his father into battle against Louis XIV, fighting in campaigns in Hungary, Germany and Flanders.

George enjoyed gambling, hunting and the company of women. Lord Chesterfield observed, 'No woman came amiss to him ... if they were very willing and very fat ... the standard of His Majesty's taste made all those ladies who aspired to his favour, and who were near the statutable size, strain and swell themselves like the frogs in the fable to rival the bulk and dignity of the ox. Some succeeded, and other burst.'[12] Like his father, he had little time for the visual arts, preferring in his spare time to cut out paper figures. Genealogy was one of his abiding interests, and he granted Leibnitz an allowance in order to carry out research on the recent family history of the House of Brunswick.[13] George did, however, inherit his parents' love of music. In June 1710, while he was Elector of Hanover, George Frederick Handel was appointed Kapellmeister to the court, with the concession that the composer would have 12 months' leave immediately in

London in order to pursue his career. In fact, Handel, on arrival, soon settled in the household of Lord Burlington in Piccadilly. The story is told that when George became King of England in 1714, Handel was naturally concerned about his position. The situation was saved and a reconciliation was effected when the King and his court took an excursion by barge on the Thames, followed by another barge containing 50 musicians conducted by Handel. The *Water Music*, specially written for the occasion, was apparently so liked by George that it was repeated three times, each performance lasting an hour. As a result, Handel was restored to favour. Although there are a number of inaccuracies in this version – for example, the *Water Music* was not written until two years later, and the King had begun to patronise Handel within two months of the sovereign's arrival in England – the story illustrates the King's enthusiasm for music. Indeed, it was Handel who was asked to teach the King's two youngest daughters.

One interesting consequence of the Hanoverian succession was that for the first time for many centuries the sovereign barely understood the English language and only occasionally spoke it. The Whigs and Tories were burgeoning as political parties and, since the reign of William III, the Cabinet had been functioning largely without the King's presence. George spoke and understood French better than English and all State papers were issued in both languages; however, it is likely that Cabinet discussions took place in English.

George's eldest son, the Prince of Wales, who was English-speaking, at first attended Cabinet meetings with his father, but such was the hatred of the King towards his son that the latter was subsequently forbidden to participate in the proceedings. George himself attended infrequently, seeing his ministers instead privately in his closet after meetings. This marked the beginning of the rise of more powerful king's ministers who were now more responsible to Parliament.

Political considerations led George to decree, upon his accession to the British throne, that his grandson, Frederick Louis, then aged 7, should be educated in Hanover and be brought up as a German prince, whereas the boys' parents, the Prince and Princess of Wales, were ordered to live in London.

An interesting insight into the relationship between father and son is afforded in a dispute between them, some three years later, which required the counsel of 12 judges. When in 1717 the Prince of Wales christened his fifth child, who died in infancy, George William, without first consulting the King as to the proposed godparents, he was initially imprisoned and his remaining children taken away from him. The Prince wrote afterwards to his father:

> Your Majesty has for some time detained our children from us, in which we have patiently acquiesced, being desirous above all things to avoid the appearance of any thing like a dispute with Your Majesty, and we humbly hop'd that our submission in so tender an instance would be convincing proof of our duty, and soon procure us to be restored both to them and to Your Majesty.
>
> But instead of this happy event, we have the mortification to see by Your Majesty's late commands the whole care of their education taken from us as well as the comfort of their presence, and a wound thereby given to those two branches which are the tenderest and most essential in every man's property, the education of my Children and the disposition of my Revenue.
>
> I must therefore beg leave humbly to represent Your Majesty that the Care of our Children in their tender years, and the sole power to make use and dispose of my property, are inestimable rights and privileges, given to me by the Law of Nature, and preserved to me by the Laws of this Realm, which I have done nothing to forfeit, I cannot depart from without becoming the most contemptible of Men.
>
> ... I have always been at a loss to know the cause of Your Majesty's taking the Children from us: That no want of care, no failure, or neglect in any part of their Education, can be imputed to the Princess, I am confident your Majesty will do the justice to confess.

After lengthy deliberation, although the view was expressed that 'the right to custody and care of the nurture and Education of Children till the age of 14 at least belongs to the Father', the majority of the judges supported the King.[14] The children were not returned, and the Prince did not recover his parental rights until after his father's death almost ten years later.

This affair made a deep impression on his contemporaries. In

1728, the year after the Prince of Wales became George II, Daniel Defoe began his unfinished treatise *Of Royal Educacion*, a brief history of kingship from William the Conqueror to Elizabeth. While describing the upbringing of future monarchs, including references to the 'want of care taken in the education of young princes and how fatall the effects of it have been in their future conduct', Defoe was understandably anxious not to appear to be referring directly to the incident. He felt obliged to deny at the end of his work 'that it threatens a pointed satyr at our own times, and that I am preparing to fall upon the particular conduct of familyes and persons who ought not to be mark't out by the undutifull hints of any hand without doors'.[15]

Although his own education had been of the scantiest, George I was not indifferent to the advancement of learning. In 1715 he had presented to the University of Cambridge the valuable library of Dr John Moore, Bishop of Ely, which consisted of some 30,000 precious books, together with £2,000 for housing them. Oxford, with its Tory loyalties, on the other hand, was snubbed by him. This gift gave rise to versification by the rival universities. From Oxford, Dr Joseph Trapp wrote:

> The King, observing with judicious eyes,
> The state of both his universities,
> To Oxford sent a troop of horse; and why?
> That learned body wanted loyalty;
> To Cambridge books he sent, as well discerning
> How much that loyal body wanted learning.

This drew a response from a Cambridge don, Sir William Browne:

> The King to Oxford sent a troop of horse,
> For Tories own no argument but force;
> With equal skill to Cambridge books he sent,
> For Whigs admit no force but argument.[16]

George I was, not surprisingly, more comfortable in Hanover than in England and he returned to Germany whenever possible. One consequence of this was that the renaissance of the arts which occurred under Queen Anne continued without interference, especially in literature as well as in the fields of mathematics and science. Indeed, the achievements in the latter field in both countries could lead George, on being congratulated on becoming King of England, to reply, 'Rather congratulate me on having Newton for a subject in one country and Leibnitz in the other.'

The period of the first Hanoverian king, with its dissensions at court, the rise of rival political parties and their complex manoeuvrings, led to much outspoken public criticism and cynicism. This was made more vociferous with the failure of the South Sea Company, which promised great wealth for investors from trading with South America. The bubble burst in 1720, when thousands of speculators lost their money. Both Walpole and the King were involved in the speculation, and the event gave birth to the political cartoon. William Hogarth's first two cartoons were inspired by the South Sea Bubble,[17] and in the same year, 1721, George's mistresses became the subject of attack.

Satire on politics and the court in Georgian England found embodiment in Jonathan Swift's *Gulliver's Travels*, published in 1726. English society is held to a mirror in the four countries visited by Lemuel Gulliver – Lilliput, Brobdingnag, Laputa and the land of the Houyhnhnms. The book became an instant success, being widely read, as it was claimed, 'from the Cabinet council to the nursery'.

The death in 1727 of George I on his way home to Hanover, where he was buried, was comparatively unmourned in England. During his short reign, moves had been made towards strengthening the powers of Parliament: he was the first monarch under whom it had the right to determine the succession to the throne and the conditions under which it was to be held.[18] But the modest education received by the monarch combined with his dullness and indolence contributed little to contemporary English society.

## GEORGE II (1683–1760)

Although he reigned two decades longer than his father, George II is hardly remembered by historians, with few biographies to commemorate his name. Born in 1683 at Hanover, he was educated by his grandmother, Sophia, the talented wife of the Elector Ernest Augustus. Like his father, George was no scholar but developed a great love for history, especially in memorising

100

dates and studying the genealogy of European royal families. He studied military affairs, learnt Latin and French, and picked up English, though spoken with a heavy German accent. He did little intelligent reading and considered both 'boetry and bainting' a bore.[19] George never forgot the fate of his mother, Sophia Dorothea, whom he did not see again after the age of 11. Indeed, Lord Hervey, a close observer of the court, could write in his *Memoirs* (1737) that the King would freely expound on a wide range of topics 'excepting what related to his mother, when on no occasion I ever heard him mention, not even advertently or indirectly, any more than if such a person had never had a being'.[20]

As a person, again like his father, he was stupid and coarse, but somewhat redeemed by his love of music. His patronage of Handel encouraged the composer to remain in England. We have already seen that his command of English placed him in a favourable position in political matters, and though still essentially a Hanoverian by disposition, he enjoyed the company of the Court. Mary, Countess Cowper, a Lady of the Bedchamber to the Princess of Wales, recorded in her diary for 22 March 1716:

> Dined with Mrs Clayton … Mrs Clayton in Raptures at all the kind Things the Prince had been saying of the English, – that he thought them the best, the handsomest, the best shaped, the best natured, and lovingest People in the World, and that if Anybody would make their Court to him, it must be by telling him he was like an Englishman.[21]

His main prowess, however, was as a military man. Starting at an early age under the tutelage of an army officer, George was prepared as a soldier, learning drill and military strategy. He achieved distinction at the battle of Oudenarde in 1708 and was in nominal command of the combined British, Hanoverian and Hessian forces against the French at the battle of Dettingen in 1743, the last English king to lead his troops into battle. On his return to England, the King was treated as a popular hero, Handel composing a *Te Deum* in his honour. George died on his commode in 1760.

## GEORGE III (1738–1820)

In strong contrast to his grandfather, the future George III's education was a broad and liberal one. This was due to his father, Frederick Louis, Prince of Wales, the eldest son of George II. Frederick, like his other Hanoverian predecessors, was perpetually at odds with his father, being called by the latter 'the greatest ass, and the greatest liar, and the greatest *canaille*, and the greatest beast in the whole world, and I heartily wish that he was out of it'. It was not until December 1728 that the King could be persuaded to let Frederick come to England from Hanover. Frederick also endured the hatred of his mother, Queen Caroline of Ansbach, because he sided with the opposition to undermine the authority of Robert Walpole. From a reading of contemporary diaries, however, a picture emerges of a man of great affability who attracted a wide circle of friends, with a streak of childishness as witnessed by his love of practical jokes which led him into trouble, and with low moral standards typical of his age. Constantly in debt through his extravagance and generous with his money – he demanded an allowance of £100,000 in 1737 – his popularity with the English people only fuelled the dislike of his parents.

Frederick married the 18-year-old Princess Augusta of Saxe-Gotha in 1736 and immediately set about teaching her English. Within a year she could speak the language fluently. A crucial incident in Frederick's relationship with King George and Queen Caroline was the furore following the birth of their first child in 1737. Informing his parents of the forthcoming event from their house at Kew, known as Kew House or the White House, Frederick was in return ordered to ensure that the baby should be born at nearby Hampton Court, where the Queen was in residence. However, while the Princess was in labour, the couple drove secretly to St James's Palace, where the birth of a daughter, Augusta, was greeted by a cheering mob. As a result, Frederick and his wife were formally expelled from the palace by the King, thus repeating the pattern of George's own experience with his father 20 years before. Further, all peers, peeresses and privy councillors were informed that if they went to the Prince's court, they would no longer be received by the monarch. Two months later, when the Queen was dying, she refused to see Frederick, purportedly saying, 'At least, I shall have one comfort in having my eyes eternally closed. I shall never see that monster again.' Reconciliation with his father had to wait another four years until after the downfall of Walpole.

Frederick and his wife rented Cliveden House, in Buckinghamshire, and the palatial Norfolk House in London. It was there that George William Frederick, the future George III, was born on 24 May 1738. The second of nine children – five boys and four girls – George was brought up in a stimulating and enlightened environment by parents who put a high premium on education. Frederick, by the 1740s, had become more mature and was also completely anglicised. He composed poetry and songs, and took a lively interest in drama. He commissioned the engraver and antiquary, George Vertue, to compile a catalogue of the paintings at Kensington Palace, Hampton Court and Windsor, and collected pictures on his own account. He delighted in his gardens at Kew and Cliveden, taking an active part in planning and planting, and allocated plots of land for his children to cultivate. His collection of foreign plants and trees formed the basis for Kew Gardens as we know it.[22] He also became interested in astronomy.

An amateur cellist – there is a portrait of him playing music with two of his sisters in the garden at Kew in the National Portrait Gallery – he inherited the Hanoverian love of music. In 1740, Thomas Arne was commissioned by Frederick to write the music for the patriotic masque, *Alfred*, to celebrate his daughter Augusta's third birthday. Performed in the open-air theatre at Cliveden, it soon became a popular success, with its rousing final chorus, 'Rule Britannia'. He was also responsible, with friends in starting some seven years earlier, the Lincoln's Inn Theatre, London, staging Italian opera under the direction of the composer Giovanni Bononcini.

He was fond of sports, especially cricket, of which he was something of a pioneer. Although the rules of the ancient game were not codified until 1744, Frederick had played with a Surrey group as early as 1735 and was later patron of a match between Kent and an All-England team.[23] He would join the children and their friends in a game of cricket and when it was too wet to play outside at Cliveden, they would play what they called 'baseball' in a large, bare room.

George inherited from his father much of his interests and

tastes. Frederick, who favoured the adoption of modern educational ideas, based the curriculum for his eldest two sons, George and Edward, largely on that of contemporary public schools. As the first Hanoverians to be brought up exclusively in England, George and Edward were the recipients of an arduous programme which was set down in writing in 1749 by Frederick for the information of his sons' tutors. The boys were to be woken at 7 a.m., to read mathematics with a sub-tutor from 8 to 9 and were then to be passed to another tutor until 11 for Latin and history. A Mr Fung taught them music until midday, followed by a Mr Ruperti for fencing for half an hour. From 12.30 until 3 p.m., the boys were allowed to play, after which dinner followed. Mr Desnoyer, the dancing master, came three days a week to give half an hour's instruction, then Mr Fung taught them once more from 5 to 6.30 p.m. After two more hours of lessons, supper was served at 8 p.m. and the Princes retired to bed between 9 and 10 p.m.[24]

This routine of classroom work for about eight hours a day, six days a week would have been taxing even if the Princes were intellectually able, but there is little evidence of this. Edward's high-spirited behaviour required constant watching, whereas George tended to be apathetic and indolent. As his father chided, 'This is your great fault, Dear George, that *nom challance* you have, of not caring enough to please.' The reasons for George's approach to learning were complex. We know that his mother favoured his more self-assured brother in contrast to George, who was comparatively silent and easily abashed. Even when he ventured an opinion, he was greeted with scorn, Augusta saying, 'Do hold your tongue, George; don't talk like a fool.'[25] Nor was his confidence enhanced, as we shall see, by the frequent changes in the personnel of those responsible for his tuition.

Frederick, who took a close interest in the boys' progress, wrote anxiously to his eldest son:

Clifden
Friday morning

Dear George
Thank God you are all well, we are so too. How do you advance in the English History and in what Reign are you and why don't you write me what you have learnt with Ayscough and Funge? As

you and Edward are both in Town, I think one might speak of ev'ry bodys health, and th'other acquaint me with Progresses you make with your Masters, but Edward has forgot me, and has giv'n me no signs of life this fortnight, which hurts me. For the Future I beg both may take it by Turns, to tell me in writing once a Week, what you have read, it will imprint it better on your mind, and convince me that you both aply, which will make me happy, as nothing can do that more, than a Prospect, to say my Children turn out an Honour to me, and a Blessing to my Country.

Frederick P[26]

Frederick, who was frequently absent from home, plaintively wrote on another occasion, 'I think you might have spar'd a quarter of an hour of your Employments to please me in hearing from you, which would have been no great Trouble to either of you.'

A somewhat different aspect of their education arose out of Frederick's enthusiasm for theatricals, which they shared. He employed a professional actor to train them and in 1749 at Leicester House before an invited audience, the royal children and their friends acted Addison's *Cato*, a dramatic play in praise of constitutional freedom. George, now aged 11, delivered the prologue which contained the following passage:

> Should this superior to my years be thought,
> Know 'tis the first great lesson I was taught.
> What, though a boy! it may with pride be said,
> A boy in *England* born – in England bred;
> Where freedom well becomes the earliest state,
> For there the love of liberty's innate.

It was probably no coincidence that George was given these lines to deliver as their patriotic ring was seen as part of his preparation for the monarchy. Frederick in a memorandum written shortly after this event 'according to the ideas of my Grand Father and best friend, George I' for his eldest son, proffered some sound advance for the day when he would be king:

> Flatterers, Courtiers or Ministers are easy to be got, but a true Friend is difficult to be found. The only rule I can give You to try them by is, if they will tell You the truth, and will venture for Your

sake ... to risk Some moments of disagreeable Contradictions to Your Passions through which they may lose Your Favour, if you are a Weak Prince; but will Settle themselves firmer in it, if You turn out that man. which I hope to God will make You.

Frederick's lesson on the national economy has a timeless quality:

Whenever the Crown comes into Your hands employ all Your hands, all Your power, to live with Oeconomy, and try never to Spend more in the Year, than the Malt and two Shillings in the Land Tax.

If you can do so, You will be able to reduce the National Debt, which, if not done, will Surely one time or another, create Such disaffection, and despair, that I dread the consequences for You, My Dear Son.

The sooner You have an opportunity to lower the interest, for Gods Sake, do it.

Let Your Treasury Speak with firmness to the Companies and Monied Men. Let it be Shewn to them that it is Your earnest desire, to Support the Credit of the Nation, but that for so doing, You expect their assistance and Support, to ease the Land of the vast Burthen it is loaded with, which can only be done by reducing the National interest.[27]

How meaningful such a statement was to an 11-year-old is open to speculation. George himself hardly lived frugally, later spending, for instance, some £10,000 a year on candles alone.[28]

He also inherited his father's skills in architectural drawing, as the many examples of his efforts preserved at Windsor clearly demonstrate. William Chambers, the architect, had worked at Kew on the building of 30 temples under the patronage of Frederick and in 1757 dedicated a book to him entitled *Designs for Chinese Buildings*. Subsequently, Chambers was appointed to teach the Prince and his mother, the Dowager Princess Augusta, architectural drawing for three mornings a week.[29]

Frederick had urged his son 'to convince this Nation that You are not only an Englishman born and bred, but that You are also this by inclination'. In order to achieve this, it was important to choose carefully those who were to be responsible for his education. George's first tutor was the inefficient Reverend

6. *Francis Ayscough with the Prince of Wales (George III) and Edward, Duke of York*, Richard Wilson, 1749.

Francis Ayscough, who obtained the post through his brother-in-law, George Lyttelton, a follower of Frederick in the Commons. One of Ayscough's tasks was to teach George Christian beliefs. Frederick decided to make new arrangements for the boy's education in 1749. Ayscough was given an assistant, George Lewis Scott. A Fellow of the Royal Society and a mathematician, Scott was born in Hanover and had been recommended by the statesman Viscount Bolingbroke, but he was loyal to the Crown. An enlightened and sympathetic person to whom George responded, Scott taught him history and some elementary physics and chemistry, thus making him the first British monarch to study science as part of his education.[30] A governor was also appointed, Francis, Lord North, 1st Earl of Guilford, the father of the future Prime Minister, described by Horace Walpole as 'an amiable, worthy man of no great genius'.

Frederick died suddenly, probably as the result of a chill, in March 1751. George, now heir to the throne, when informed of the news, put his hand on his heart and said, 'I feel here as I did when I saw a workman fall from the scaffold at Kew.' the King, ever unrelenting, wrote at the end of the year, 'I have lost my eldest son, but I was glad of it.' Earlier, he had ordered that the original funeral expenses should be reduced and as a result the ceremony was 'without either anthem or organ'.[31] A supposedly Jacobite jingle at the time captured well the general reaction of the British public:

> Here lies poor Fred, who was alive and is dead.
> We had rather it had been his Father,
> Had it been his brother (Cumberland), better'n any other.
> Had it been his sister, no one would have missed her.
> Had it been the whole generation, all the better for the nation.
> But as it's just poor Fred, who was alive and is dead,
> There's nothing more to be said.

The death of Frederick was the occasion for a further upheaval in the new Prince's household, more concerned with a political power struggle than his future education. North and Ayscough were dismissed by the Whigs. Simon, 1st Earl Harcourt, a former army colonel, took over from North, and Ayscough was replaced by Thomas Hayter, Bishop of Norwich, a pedant who, Princess Augusta told Bubb Dodington, the political diarist, was 'a mighty learned and able man: but he did not seem to her very proper to convey knowledge to children; he had not that clearness she thought necessary'. Also, 'Lord Harcourt and the Prince agreed very well, but she thought that he could not learn very much from my Lord.'[32] Scott was threatened with dismissal, but at the insistence of the young Prince he was retained. A fourth member was added to the team, Andrew Stone, MP for Hastings and holder of several offices under the crown, as sub-governor.

For their education, George and his brother Edward had in 1751 been settled, together with their household, in Savile House, Leicester Square, next door to their parents. There was great upheaval in the Princes' household in the following year when in May 1752, Harcourt and Hayter had an audience with the King. They alleged that their subordinates, Scott and Stone, were teaching their young charges on Jacobite principles. It was claimed, for instance, that one of the Princes had been caught reading a Jacobite history of the 1688 Revolution. The King did not believe these allegations, and Harcourt and Hayter were dismissed. The cause of this affair was more likely to have arisen out of the jealousy of governor and preceptor of their subordinates who were responsible for the day-to-day education of the Princes.

The new governor was James, second Earl of Waldegrave, and the preceptor was John Thomas, Bishop of Peterborough. Though a Roman Catholic, Waldegrave was one of the King's favourites. In view of the recent upheavals in the staff concerned with the Princes' education, he reluctantly accepted the post. The new team's impact, especially upon George, was limited. Writing in his *Memoirs* of this period, Waldegrave stated that although Thomas, Stone and Scott were 'men of sense, men of learning, and worthy, good men, they had but little weight and influence. The mother and the nursery always prevailed'.[33] Augusta's determination to have a large say in the education of her children is thus clearly shown.

She had earlier complained to Hayter on the grounds that 'he insisted upon teaching the Princes logic, which, as she was told, was a very old study for children of their age, not to say of their condition'.[34] There was some truth in the Princess's complaint: neither Hayter nor Harcourt added much to the Princes' education, the former being more of a politician than a prelate and the latter lacking in character. Harcourt was supposed to have urged Josiah Tucker, Dean of Gloucester, who was an economist as well as a priest, to compose for George a 'treatise on national commerce' in order to enlighten him on economic affairs, but, as a nineteenth-century writer put it, 'the Prince remained to the end of his days as unenlightened on this important subject as his Chancellor of the Exchequer'.[35]

The adolescent George, a solitary, shy youth, now found inspiration in his new tutor, John Stuart, third Earl of Bute, who was appointed in 1755. Bute had shared Frederick's love of dramatics and had been made a Lord of the Household shortly before his master's death. George, in need of someone in whom he could confide, was immediately attracted to this witty and cultivated Scottish nobleman, though at 42, Bute was some 25 years older than himself. When the Prince came of age in 1756 and was given his own household, Waldegrave expected to be made Groom of the Stole, but to his chagrin, on George's insistence, the post was reluctantly granted by the King to Bute. Bute now virtually became both his governor and his preceptor, and later rose to become Prime Minister.

George poured out his heart over the next six years in a long series of letters to his friend. In one of his earliest surviving letters to Bute, he wrote, concerning the negotiations with Waldegrave and the King over the appointment to Groom of the Stole, 'I long for tomorrow or at farthest for Friday to see you again, without you, Kew even tires me.' Later, in July 1756, in a lengthy letter, George affirmed that

> I have had the pleasure of your friendship during the space of a year, by which I have reap'd great advantage, but not the improvement I should if I had follow'd your advice; but you shall find me make such a progress in this summer, that shall give you hopes, that with the continuation of your advice, I may turn out as you wish ... I do in the same solemn manner declare, that I will defend my Friend and will never use evasive answers, but will always tell him whatever is said against him, and will more and more show to the world the great friendship I have for him, and all the malice that can be invented against him shall only bind me the stronger to him. I do further promiss, that all the allurements

my enemies can think of, or the threats that they may make pour out upon me, shall never make me in the least change from what I so solemnly promiss in this paper. I will take upon me the man in every thing, and will not shew that indefference which I have as yet too often done. As I have chosen the vigorous part, I will throw off that indolence which if I don't soon get the better of will be my ruin, and will never grow weary of this, tho' [the King] should live many years ... I hope, my dear Lord, you will conduct me through this difficult road and will bring me to the gole [*sic*]. I will exactly follow your advice, without which I shall inevitably sink.[36]

Not only did Bute have an eager and receptive pupil; progress was facilitated by his use of enlightened teaching methods. In history, for example, Bute would have the Prince read up the topic in question; this was followed by an essay which was corrected, then discussed, and then a revised essay was written. The syllabus covered many aspects of modern British and European history, at a time when the public schools paid scant regard to this subject. The curriculum also included geography, agriculture, commerce and mathematics.[37] Bute had a great interest in natural philosophy and had his own cabinet of apparatus. George and his brother were given a course of lectures which fired the future king's enthusiasm for the subject. The constitution, including the history of the monarchy, was studied. The *Commentaries* of Blackstone, with particular emphasis on the freedom of the judicature, was carefully scrutinised, the author lending Bute a manuscript copy of the work for the Prince's use.

That the young prince, dazzled by his affection for Bute, failed to observe that his mentor regarded the tuition as a means to achieving the fulfilment of his own political ambitions is not important in the present context. George was certainly the best educated of the Hanoverians, growing up to be an amiable, country-loving king, fond of exercise and outdoor sports and a devoted husband. He was very well read and a patron of the arts. In 1762, two years after his accession, George acquired the important collection of paintings from Joseph Smith, consul in Venice, for £20,000, which included the largest single collection of Canalettos in the world. In the same year, he assisted in the founding of the Royal Academy, paying the initial expenses of the institution at Somerset House. George inherited his father's love of astronomy, building an observatory at Kew, taking a personal

7. *John Stuart, 3rd Earl of Bute, governor to Prince George (George III),* Joshua Reynolds, 1773.

interest in new advances in the subject by keeping in touch with leading figures, including William Herschel. In 1782, Herschel discovered a new star and named it after the King, *Georgius Sidus*.[38] George's magnificent collection of over 1,000 pieces of scientific apparatus are now housed in the Science Museum, in London. Perhaps his finest achievement, though, was in the field of book collecting at a time when bibliophily was at its peak. From his earliest purchases, George had in mind the establishment of a national library. At his death in 1820, he had amassed some 65,000 books and 450 manuscripts. These were presented to the British Museum in 1823 by his successor and the gift commemorated in the title, the King's Library; they are now in the British Library. He admired writers, such as Samuel Johnson and Sheridan, and was well acquainted with the plays of Shakespeare.

Much of his reign was clouded by the royal malady, porphyria, which resulted in spells of insanity; his last attack was in 1810 and from which he never recovered. Of the greatest importance, however, was the fact that he was the first Hanoverian to be recognised as a British sovereign, thanks largely to his education. 'Born and educated in this country', he proclaimed in the opening speech of his reign to Parliament, 'I glory in the name of Briton [*sic*], and I hold civil and religious rights of my people equally dear to me to be the most valuable prerogatives of my crown.' The 60 years of his reign well bore out this contention. George had been taught to exercise his royal authority over ministers and hoped to keep this historic authority rather than, like his predecessors, be ruled by them. As a young and vigorous man, he was the embodiment of a patriotic king.[39]

## GEORGE IV (1762–1830)

The author of a memoir of George III, written a decade after his death, acutely observed that 'the British nation, so jealous almost in everything that regards its princes, has been singularly and culpably inattentive to whatever concerns their education. Parliament, which limits the settlement of the crown, which points out the religion of the reigning family, which takes cognizance of the marriages of the Princes of the blood, and confers on them revenues and establishments, leaves the education of our British princes wholly to the discretion of the reigning sovereign'.[40]

The education of the Hanoverian kings is a good case in point, none more so than that of George III's eldest son, George Augustus Frederick, born in St James's Palace on 12 August 1762, some two years after his father had become monarch. From the beginning, it was clear that the King insisted that his children should receive intensive tuition, of a higher standard than his own, from tutors known for their high moral character and attainments.

In fact, the mode adopted was a mixture of a liberal education, in the spirit of a broad approach to learning, coupled with child-rearing based on the absolute principles of German aristocracy. The latter was soon evident. Five days after his birth, George was created Prince of Wales and a week later, 'for the gratification of the public', the child was on display at St James's Palace between the hours of one and three every afternoon. People of fashion flocked to the palace to see the baby, being cautioned not to touch him, and consumed wine and cake estimated at a cost of £40 per day.

Queen Charlotte, the daughter of the Duke of Mecklenburg-Strelitz, had come to England the previous September, 1761, when her marriage to George III took place. She was then a young girl of 17, unfamiliar with the English customs of the time, and soon attracted criticism for her indelicacy in appearing in public, at the installation of the Knights of the Garter at Windsor, only four weeks after George's birth. The Prince's inoculation against smallpox was also the subject of adverse comment. Charlotte took little or no interest in affairs of state or politics and the Prince was never close to his mother. Indeed, it would have been surprising if this had been so, as the Queen bore 14 more children between 1763 and 1783. There is a well-known story of how Zoffany, the artist, who then resided at Kew, was asked to paint a large picture of the family, which consisted of the King and Queen and nine children. After having made a number of preliminary sketches, Zoffany was informed that another prince, Adolphus, Duke of Cambridge, had been born and that he must be introduced into the group. Various circumstances delayed the completion of the work, and a second messenger in due course brought the news of the birth of Princess Mary. This required the obliteration of one-and-a-half figures to accommodate the newcomer. Shortly before the portrait was completed, a letter came from a maid of honour announcing yet another baby, the Princess Sophia. In despair at ever seeing the end to his endeavours, Zoffany rapidly completed the assignment.[41]

George's first official engagement took place in March 1765, when, not yet 3 years of age, he made a carefully rehearsed speech to a deputation of the Society of Ancient Britons, who were requesting support for an institution providing education and maintenance for necessitous Welsh children. The King and Queen also decided, following German fashion, that their four eldest children should hold a joint 'infantine' Drawing Room in 1769: George, aged 7, Frederick, 6, who was elected as Bishop of Osnabrück when he was six months old, William Henry, who was 4, and the Princess Royal, not yet 3. The occasion provided a field day for the caricaturists of the time, and the experiment was not repeated.

Shortly after he was born, the Prince was handed over to an establishment headed by a governess, Lady Charlotte Finch, wife of the sixth Earl of Winchilsea, with a deputy governess, wet and dry nurses and other staff. The child was soon joined by his brother, Frederick, Duke of York, and they became life-long friends. In April 1771, the boys' proper education began, with a new household of their own. While the rest of the growing family remained in the larger White House at Kew, George and Frederick were transferred to the nearby Dutch House. A contemporary witness of the routine of the royal household at Kew has left this description:

> At six in the morning their majesties rise, and enjoy the two succeeding hours in a manner which they call their OWN. At eight, the Prince of Wales, the Bishop of Osnabrug, the Princess-royal, and the Princes William and Edward, are brought from their respective apartments, to breakfast with their illustrious parents. At nine, the younger children then attend, to lisp or smile their good morrows; and whilst the five eldest are closely applying to their tasks, the little ones and their nurses pass the morning in the garden.
>
> The King and Queen frequently amuse themselves with sitting in the room while the children dine; and once a week, attended by

the whole offspring in pairs, make the delightful tour of Richmond Gardens, where Her Majesty has erected a cottage after a design of her own, in a chaste style, and ornamented it with a large collection of the best English prints. In the afternoon, while the Queen works at her needle, the King reads Shakespeare, or some other favourite author; and whatever charms ambition or folly may conceive to avail so exalted a station, it is neither on the throne nor in the drawing-room, in the splendour or the toys of sovereignty, that they place their felicity: it is in social and domestic gratifications, in breathing the free air, admiring the works of nature, tasting and encouraging the elegancies of art, and in living without dissipation. In the evening, all the children pay their duty at Kew House, before they retire to bed; after which, the King reads to Her Majesty; and having closed the day with a joint act of devotion, they retire to rest. This is the order of each revolving day, with such exceptions as are unavoidable in their high station. The sovereign is the father of his family: not a grievance reaches his knowledge that remains unredressed, nor a character of merit or ingenuity disregarded: his private conduct, therefore, is as exemplary as it is amiable.[42]

Horace Walpole somewhat unkindly remarked about the Prince, 'Two points only were looked to in his education. The first was, that he should not be trusted to anything but a ductile cypher; the other, that he should be brought up with due affection for regal power; in other words, he was to be the slave of his father, and the tyrant of his people.'[43] Certainly, in true Hanoverian fashion, the Prince hated his father from an early age, claiming that the Duke of York was the King's favourite.

As we have seen, George III's notion of education was based on the inculcation of pride in the constitution, of religious belief, and of a sense of duty which would fit his son to become a king. Unlike his predecessors, however, he had been able to gain some insights into current educational practices through the close interest which he took in the nearby public school, Eton. A few months after the birth of the Prince of Wales, the royal couple visited the college, where they visited many of the buildings, after which the King inspected the assembled company of boys. George, at the end, asked for six holidays and the Queen for three. After the final speeches and ceremonies were over, the

King good-naturedly placed the sum of £230 in the hands of the Provost for distribution to the scholars.[44] Not since the reign of the founder of the college, Henry VI, had any subsequent monarch displayed such a genuine interest in it. 'I wish from time to time', he wrote, 'to show a regard for the education of youth, on which most essentially depend my hopes of an advantageous change in the manners of the nation.'[45] George frequently visited the school, following the academic progress of the pupils and he once invited 80 of them to a ball at the castle given by the young Princesses. The King was popular with both staff and pupils and his birthday, 4 June, is still celebrated at the school each year. Standing at one of the windows of the apartments in Windsor Castle with the Marquess of Wellesley, the King once called his guest's attention to the prospect. 'Look, my Lord', he said, with a tone of reverential affection, 'there is the noble school where we were all educated!' This was a reference to the fact that almost all the leading men who held office during his reign had been schoolboys at Eton.[46]

Queen Charlotte was also concerned with education, but at a rather different level. Mrs Sarah Trimmer, the author of children's primers, who was obsessed with the belief that followers of Voltaire intended to destroy Christianity, became interested in the education of the poor and in 1786 set up a Sunday school at Brentford, close to Kew. The Queen, wishing to establish similar schools at Windsor, had a two-hour interview with Mrs Trimmer which led to the publication in 1786 of a book, *The Oeconomy of Charity*, dealing with the promotion and management of Sunday schools.[47] George himself later took an interest in promoting elementary education, as did his eldest son. The fine facade of the Parochial Schools of St Martin, next to St Martin-in-the-Fields, London, bears a bold inscription stating that it was 'built upon the ground, the gift of His Majesty George the Fourth'. In 1805, Joseph Lancaster, who subsequently founded the British and Foreign School Society, explained his plans to provide a system of Christian education for the poor to the King, who with his family subsequently became subscribers.[48]

The King naturally took a great interest in the future education of the two princes and selected a team of tutors to carry out his plan. George III chose Robert Darcy, Earl of Holdernesse, a former Secretary of State and Lord Warden of the

Cinque Ports, as their governor. Described by Horace Walpole as 'that formal piece of dullness', Holdernesse was 53 at the time of his appointment and suffering from ill-health. The high-spirited boys were not easy to handle, and Holdernesse was obliged in 1774 to go on the Continent in order to recuperate. The governor was well aware of his own failings. In resigning from the post two years later, he admitted to the King that 'I have not obtained that share of the young princes' confidence which alone could enable me to be of use to them.'[49] However, some benefits were gained: both Holdernesse and his wife wrote frequently to the boys when on their travels and there survives a series of letters in excellent French which Frederick wrote to Lady Holdernesse.[50] A sub-governor, Captain Robert Smelt, Royal Engineers, a near neighbour in Yorkshire and an old friend of Holdernesse, was appointed in 1771. Smelt was described by Mrs Delany, the author and favourite of the royal family, as 'of the most noble and delicate kind, and deserved the pen of a Clarendon to do justice to it'.[51]

The first preceptor was Dr William Markham, who had been appointed headmaster of Westminster School in 1753 at the age of 33. During his 11 years there, he had made several organisational changes which had helped to improve the school.[52] Jeremy Bentham recalled that 'we stood prodigiously in awe of him ... He was no martinet; he was a tall, portly man and held his head high.'[53] Like the other posts in the household, Markham's had been gained through his connections: a former Dean of Christ Church, Oxford and chaplain to George II, he was appointed Bishop of Chester and as preceptor to the Princes in 1771 on the recommendation of his friend, Lord Mansfield. Markham chose as his sub-preceptor Cyril Jackson, one of his favourite pupils from Westminster and a good scholar. He too went on to become Dean of Christ Church. The household was completed by General Budé, an instructor of Swiss origin who had served in the Hanoverian army, and another Swiss, de Salzes, a good classical scholar of amiable disposition. The resignation of Holdernesse in 1776 – it was alleged that it was because of his wife taking advantage of his position as Lord Warden of the Cinque Ports to smuggle dresses in from France – led to a complete restructuring of the teaching staff in the Princes' household. In his anxiety to fill the vacant governor's post, the

King approached Thomas, Lord Bruce, Lord of the Bedchamber, to whom, as George later stated, 'I used every argument to compell him to step forth to my assistance'.[54] Bruce, who had little experience for such a position, accepted reluctantly, and only on condition that Markham was replaced by Richard Hurd, then Bishop of Lichfield, a moderate Tory and author of *Letters of Chivalry*. Markham's sub-preceptor, Cyril Jackson, was superseded by William Arnald, a Fellow of St John's College, Cambridge and Hurd's precentor at Lichfield. Arnald, an ambitious but thwarted man, taught the boys science, and was subject to bouts of madness, sometimes wearing a mitre, and died insane.

The changes did little to rouse the enthusiasm of the two Princes. Whereas they had had some respect for Holdernesse, it was soon obvious that Bruce's ignorance of classical learning placed him at a disadvantage. According to one nineteenth-century writer:

> The Prince of Wales, who was very quickly at odds with his new governor, had, in the prescence of other members of the Household, cunningly asked him [Bruce] awkward questions about Greek and Latin which he was totally unable to answer. The Prince, it was averred, had proved himself a better classical scholar than Lord Bruce, who became the butt of the whole Court.[55]

Whatever the substance of this story, Bruce immediately resigned his post, allegedly on account of his wife's illness. Surprisingly, in the circumstances, the King created him Earl of Ailesbury, an act which Horace Walpole called 'the reward of ignorance'. 'I have met with some severe blows', wrote the King, 'but this is perhaps the strongest I have ever received.' To fill the gap, he appointed Bruce's elder brother, George Brudenell, Duke of Montagu, the Constable of Windsor Castle, at the same time giving him the additional title of Earl of Montagu. A deputy-governor, Lieutenant-Colonel George Hotham, who proved later to be an invaluable member of the household, was also appointed.

In later years, the Prince would, in conversation, consider that Markham had been a wiser man and a better teacher than Hurd, though he had little time for either. Markham was dismissed as 'a pompous schoolmaster' and Hurd as 'a stiff, old, but correct gentleman'. Hurd, who was a shrewd judge of character, was asked one day by his cousin, 'How do you think your pupil His Highness the Prince of Wales will turn out?' 'My dear cousin', the bishop replied, laying his peculiarly small white hand upon her arm, 'I can hardly tell; either the most polished gentleman, or the most accomplished blackguard in Europe; possibly an admixture of both'.[56]

The Prince was now ready to undertake a royal education, in accordance with Tory principles as interpreted by the King. 'Something like a plan of studies is projecting', wrote Hurd in 1776, 'and will be wanted in long time.' George became fluent in French, German and Italian and made some progress with the classics, becoming familiar with Virgil, Horace and Tacitus. The Prince cultivated a great liking for reading, and enjoyed literature and poems, especially those of Thomas Gray, a friend of Hurd's since their Cambridge days. However, he was never able to spell correctly, a characteristic which he shared with both his father and his tutors. In order to prevent the boys getting up to any mischief, the King ordered that they should be occupied in their studies for eight hours a day. Extra subjects were added to the curriculum, such as scripture, elocution, music, dancing, fencing, drawing and husbandry, which including growing wheat and then making bread from it.

The Princes' household was moved to Kew Palace, where they were much nearer to the King and Queen. Princes William and Edward were in another house and Princes Ernest, Augustus and Adolphus were in a third. It seems likely that George III approved of the use of corporal punishment for his sons to curb their exuberant behaviour. The Prince of Wales was subject to outbursts of temper, and it is not surprising, given his nature, that his education was not a success. Like most parents, the King had been anxious to protect his children from bad influences, but in so doing he had been unduly restrictive. Unlike other schoolboys, they were necessarily educated apart from their peers and their daily routine allowed for little leisure. The situation was not helped by the changes in teaching staff and their differing levels of competency.

When the Prince reached his eighteenth birthday in 1780, his father wrote a lengthy letter to him, expressing disappointment at the outcome of his education:

> Windsor Castle, 14 Aug. 1780
>
> No one feels with more pleasure than I do your nearer approach to manhood, but the parent's joy must be mixed with the anxiety that this period may not be ill spent, as the hour is now come when whatever foundation has been laid must be by application brought to maturity, or every past labour of your instructors will prove abortive.
>
> This has made me think it my duty to state on paper what I trust the goodness of your heart and no want of penetration will make you thoroughly weigh ... Your own good sense must make you feel that you have not made that progress in your studies which, from the ability and assiduity of those placed for that purpose about you, I might have had reason to expect; whilst you have been out of the sight of the world that has been kept under a veil by all those who have cirrounded you, nay your foibles have less been perceived than I could have expected; yet your love of dissipation has for some months been with enough ill nature trumpeted in the public papers, and there are those ready to wound me in the severest place by ripping up every error they may be able to find in you ...
>
> I fear your religious duties are not viewed through that happiest of mediums, a gratitude to the Great Creator, and a resolution to the utmost of your power implicitly to obey His will as conveighed to us in the Scriptures. It is this alone that gives man a well-grounded superiority in merit to the brute creation. No one can entirely escape errors, but those shields will prevent their degenerating into habitual vices.
>
> ... Latin and French you have learned, and with a moderate degree of attention those languages may be kept up; as to German your proficiency is certainly very moderate, yet in Germany you will have possessions that will place you in one of the superior stations in that great Empire. You cannot do your duty unless more master of that language; besides, you must acquire a knowledge of its Constitution and more particularly of that of your future dominions, whose prosperity must chiefly depend on the fatherly hand of its Sovereign, and the conduct of those subjects but too well deserve every attention, from their unalterable attachment to their Princes.

You have read cursorily some historians, by which you may have acquired a general view of the principal facts in Antient and Modern History but as yet no insight into the springs which caused them, or any comprehensive knowledge of the Constitution, laws, finances. commerce, etc. of these Kingdoms, and of the relative situation as to these points of our rival neighbours, and of the other European States ...

Believe me, I wish to make you happy, but the father must, with that object in view, not forget that it is his duty to guide his child to the best of his ability through the rocks that cannot but naturally arise in the outset of youth, and the misfortune is that in other countries national pride makes the inhabitants wish to paint their Princes in the most favourable light, and consequently be silent on any indiscretion; but here most persons, if not concerned in laying ungrounded blame, are ready to trumpet any speck they can find out.[57]

Even though the Prince was now 18 and with his own modest establishment, he was not given an independent income. Until he came fully of age he was obliged to live with his parents in Buckingham House, a red brick building situated at the end of St James's Park which George III had purchased in 1762. Permission had to be given by the King for attending the theatre, and he was not allowed to accept invitations to parties and balls in private houses. The Prince was also expected to attend church every Sunday. Further isolation resulted from the monarch's decision to send Frederick, his closest friend, to Hanover to begin his military career.

Before this, and unbeknown to his parents, the Prince had begun an affair with the actress Mary Darby, better remembered as the great beauty, Perdita Robinson. In 1779 the Prince, seeing her in *The Winter's Tale* at Drury Lane, fell hopelessly in love with her and by the following spring was secretly meeting her at Kew. The liaison became public knowledge in June – hence his father's reference in his letter to 'your love of dissipation has been trumpeted in the public papers' – and the Prince gave her a promissory note for £20,000, to be paid on his coming of age. By the end of August 1781 the affair had ended and Perdita threatened to publish his love letters. Hotham was sent to sort matters out by means of a £5,000 payment and an annuity of £600 for the recovery of the letters and the promissory note, paid from the secret service account.[58]

This was only the first of several publicly known affairs of the Prince which culminated in the farce of his unsuitable marriage to the eccentric Caroline, Princess of Brunswick, and his earlier relationship with the notorious twice-married Mrs Fitzherbert. In 1784, after feigning suicide, he contracted a marriage with her, though under the Royal Marriages Act, it was declared void without the King's permission. Ten children were eventually born of the union.

It was well known that for ladies, low necklines were virtually compulsory whenever he entertained.[59] He had taken to drink, and the grossness of his body soon became a ready target for the caricaturists: at his death, George IV weighed 23 stones.

An interesting insight into George's character is provided by a conversation he had, while regent, with Lady Spencer when he stated, 'You know, I don't speak the truth, and my brothers don't, and I find it a great defect, from which I would have my daughter free. We have always been brought up badly; the Queen having taught us to equivocate.'[60] Like previous Georges, the Prince was continually at loggerheads with his father. This is not surprising given that the Prince, who was full of animal spirits, was deliberately kept as a child as long as possible. It has been claimed that he had only to know his father's wishes in order to disobey them. This is borne out in such incidents as when he was a youth beating on the door of his father's bedroom and shouting, 'Wilkes forever – Number 45 for ever!', a reference to the issue of the *North Briton* in which the radical had criticised the King's speech to Parliament, commemorating the Peace of Paris of 1763.[61] Later, he sided with the Foxite Whigs and deliberately filled Buckingham House with an assortment of moneylenders, women of doubtful virtue and even more doubtful cronies, much to his father's displeasure.

In his years as Prince Regent from 1811, during his father's madness, and his decade as king, 1820–30, although intellectually able, he had a meagre understanding of politics. Indeed, Roger Fulford once wrote that 'He was one of the very few [English sovereigns] to whom it was possible to attribute no political objects except the avoidance of trouble and the indulgence of their own whims and fancies.'[62] But if his education had not equipped him adequately for his role as monarch, George IV's good taste in architecture and related arts has perhaps been his enduring legacy. For example, although his father had decided to accommodate his family at Windsor from 1779, it was his son who employed Wyatt to restore the castle, which under the Hanoverians had been abandoned for the first time in its history, and he made it a suitable residence for succeeding monarchs.[63] Buckingham House was virtually rebuilt to become Buckingham Palace, though he never lived to see it completed. George also rebuilt Carlton House in Pall Mall, which, with its sumptuous fittings, furniture and china, became a centre for royal entertaining.

Two other projects are closely linked with the Prince Regent – the Royal Pavilion at Brighton and the incomplete Nash replanning of the terraces of Regent's Park and Regent Street. In 1834, when he was king, he helped to persuade the government to buy 38 valuable pictures from John Julius Angerstein to form the nucleus of what was to become the National Gallery. His love of literature remained, especially the works of Walter Scott and Jane Austen. On one of her visits to London in 1815, Jane Austen visited the library at Carlton House and subsequently dedicated her novel *Emma* to the Prince.[64] But it was typical of the man that his extravagance in erecting buildings and in furnishing them outran his purse, and that their flamboyance well matched his character.

## WILLIAM IV (1765–1837)

One of the problems facing any parents is the time taken up with their children's education. No sooner had George III made the necessary arrangements for his two elder sons, George Prince of Wales and Frederick Duke of York, than it was time to turn his attention to the next two boys, William, later Duke of Clarence and then William IV, and Edward, later Duke of Kent. Only two years separated them in age, William having been born in 1765 and Edward in 1767. Born in Buckingham House, William had fair hair and prominent blue eyes and showed early signs of high spirits and aggressiveness but, unlike his eldest brother, presented no real problems to his parents. Mrs Chapone, a niece of Bishop Thomas of Peterborough, Salisbury and Winchester, reported a meeting which she had witnessed between the royal family and the bishop on his eighty-second birthday, when William was 12. 'I was pleased with all the Princes', she wrote afterwards, 'but particularly with Prince William, who is little for his age, but so sensible and engaging, that he won the Bishop's heart, to whom he particularly attached himself, and would stay with him, while all the rest ran about the house. His conversation was surprisingly manly and clever for his age.'[65]

Whereas his two eldest brothers quickly forged a close friendship, William did not find a ready companion in Edward, a moody, truculent and not always dependable youth. Edward's character changed in adulthood and he became an indulgent parent to his only daughter, the future Queen Victoria. William instead looked to his sisters, the Princesses Charlotte and Augusta, for friendship. But it was his eldest brother, George Prince of Wales, whom he most admired, particularly for his sophistication and recklessness and his position as future monarch. This attitude was to influence the King in deciding on William's future.

As with the Prince of Wales and the Duke of York, the King entrusted the bulk of his sons' education to clergymen. Dr John Fisher, a firm Tory but mild-mannered man, was appointed preceptor in 1780 on the recommendation of a former holder of the post, Bishop Hurd. He remained in the post for five years, though two decades later, when he was Bishop of Exeter, he undertook the supervision of the education of Princess Charlotte, using his tedious *Hints towards the forming of Character of a young Princess* as a textbook for the lessons.[66] He went on to become Bishop of Salisbury.

The other tutor was an elderly cleric, John James Majendie, of Huguenot descent, a canon at Windsor and the author of many religious works in French and English. Majendie had been responsible for teaching Queen Charlotte to speak perfect English when she had first arrived in England. Initially he was involved in tutoring the two elder Princes, but after a short spell, considered himself too old to undertake the education of the two younger and livelier brothers. Instead, he gave this task to his son, the Reverend Henry William Majendie. Henry had a lively social conscience, later opening a Sunday school when the movement was in its infancy, and he retained William's affection until his death two weeks before his former pupil ascended the throne.

General Budé, who was tutor to the two elder princes, also taught William and Edward. The curriculum which they followed differed little from that in the other household. The overburdened timetable presented few joys, though William acquired a liking for mathematics. How much progress the Prince would have made in this setting is open to speculation, for the scheme came to a sudden end when he was 13 years of age.

The King had come to the conclusion that his sons should be usefully occupied in their adult life. As the Prince of Wales was destined to be the King, then Frederick should be a soldier and William a sailor. This plan would also have the advantage of geographically separating William and Frederick from the possible bad influence of their elder brother. Nevertheless, it may seem a surprising choice that a member of the royal family should join the Navy. Previous precedents had been unfortunate. Two of William's uncles had also been sailors, and there was much public criticism over their unduly accelerated promotions. Edward Duke of York rose in four years from midshipman to vice-admiral, attaining the latter rank at the age of 23. Henry Duke of Cumberland quickly became Admiral of the White at a similar age.

William, later to be known as the 'Sailor King', was the first monarch to have served in the Royal Navy, but it was not considered likely at the time that he would become king. One of the reasons for joining at such a tender age was that the rules of the Navy prescribed the age beyond which an individual would not be admitted to the service, so it was imperative to enter William before he reached his fourteenth birthday. On a visit to Portsmouth in 1778, the King had consulted with Sir Samuel Hood, the Commissioner of the Dockyard, and Rear-Admiral Robert Digby, in charge of the battleship *Prince George*. Digby agreed to take William as a midshipman and, accordingly, the Prince arrived at Spithead on 15 June 1779 to board ship and start his new career.

As a contemporary chronicler noted, 'The quarter-deck of a man of war, or the "middy" cabin, is not the place to advance a youth in the attainment of those branches of learning without which no education can be considered complete.'[67] Such accommodation would be the home for youths and for older men who had been promoted from the lower deck and perhaps their wives (and in ports, prostitutes). There would also be a surgeon and, for the younger members, even a schoolmaster. The Prince was advised by Hood to bring with him '2 uniforms, a short blue coat of the jacket make, with uniform buttons and waistcoat and breeches, 3 dozen of shirts, 3 dozen pairs of stockings, 2 Hatts and 2 round ones – Hatts are liable to be lost overboard! Pocket handkerchiefs, night caps and netts, Basons, washballs, brushes, combs, etc.' He was also requested to bring navigational instruments, various text books, *The Mariner's New Calendar*, mathematical tables, the latest *Nautical Almanack*, pens, slate and pencils, with powder, paper and books for keeping his log journal.[68]

To ensure that William did not fall prey to the temptations which would surround him, the King arranged that the Prince would be accompanied on board by his tutor, the Reverend Henry Majendie, who was given the rank of honorary midshipman. George III outlined to Majendie the nature of his duties. He 'should take every proper opportunity of instructing my Dearly Beloved Son Prince William in the Christian Religion, to inculcate the habitual reading of the Holy Scriptures and to accompany these with Moral Reflections that may counteract the evil he may have but too many Opportunities of hearing'. Latin was to be continued with so that 'he should not only read it with ease but taste its beauties'. English and writing were to be taught and the Prince's letters home corrected for grammar, but not for their content. History was considered useful, though Majendie was 'merely to teach him the Facts and omit much Political Reasoning'. French conversation was to be encouraged, and 'all Books of Recreation ought to be in that language, and at the same time, there are more Books of that kind void of evil than in his native tongue'.

William continued conscientiously with his studies at sea, claiming that on his first tour of duty he had worked through the first six books of Euclid three times, mastered some algebra and trigonometry, written a short account of the history of England from the Reformation to the Revolution of 1688 and was now reading Sully's *Mémoires*. He admitted to his father that drawing had rather been neglected but that he intended to devote more time to it in the immediate future. The Prince was anxious at this stage to secure the approval of his father; in return, the King's letters often contained discouraging and painful remarks:

> You are now launching into a scene of Life [he wrote] where You may either prove an Honour or a Disgrace to Your Family. It would be very unbecoming of the love I have for my Children if I did not at this serious moment give You advice how to conduct yourself ... Though when at home a Prince, on board the Prince *George* You are only a Boy learning the Naval Profession; but the Prince so far accompanies You that what other Boys might do, You must not. It must never be out of Your thoughts that more Obedience is necessary from You to Your Superiours in the Navy, more Politeness to Your Equals and more good nature to Your Inferiors, than from those who have not been told that these are essential to a Gentleman.[69]

Although William continued to try and please his father, he was met with constant discouragement. He soon determined to demonstrate that he was no different from the other midshipmen. He asked to be called, not Prince William Henry, but simply William Guelph. He was already self-confident, but there was now much more opportunity for outspokenness, fighting, swearing and practical jokes, for which he later became notorious.

William's first year at sea was his most successful one. The American War of Independence was still in progress and France and Spain were now at war with Britain. He was present in January 1780 when a Spanish flagship was captured; it was renamed the Prince *William* in his honour. A few days later, when Admiral Rodney defeated the Spanish at Cape St Vincent, the Prince took part in the battle. When he returned to London, William found himself hailed as a hero and he was at the height of his popularity. For a youth of 16, such adulation was not easy to cope with and his behaviour increasingly incurred the disapproval of his parents. At sea again, William received a letter from Queen Charlotte saying, 'I love You so well, that I cannot bear the idea of You being only Mediocre. Reflection is the thing you should aim at.'

William's affair with his first love, Julia Fortescue, alarmed his parents and it was decided that a spell overseas would be salutary. He went with his ship to New York and it was there that he first met Captain Horatio Nelson, whom he instantly admired. 'There was something irresistibly pleasing in his address and conversation,' William later reported, 'and an enthusiasm, when speaking on professional subjects, that shewed he was no common being.'[70] The Prince attributed his lifelong interest in the Navy to Nelson. The two young officers enjoyed each other's company and frequently dined together. William insisted on being Nelson's best man at his wedding and kept the letters from his hero until his death.[71]

School lessons, during the heady times of the American War, seemed more of an irrelevance than ever. Majendie wrote to the King from New York in March 1782, 'Prince William's aversion to Latin, which was always pretty much marked, has become unconquerable; and I have thought it at his age better to give up the point without telling him so than by persevering with little or no profit to see him discontented day after day. The violent dislike young people conceive for Latin is generally owing to their having been over-fatigued with it when children.[72] For his pains, Majendie was, like his father, made a canon at Windsor and eventually Bishop of Chester.

William's boisterousness, often overspilling into violence, became more prominent. He quarrelled with his captain and when given command of a ship equally fell out with his subordinates. His foul language was legendary. In an attempt to help matters, the King sent him to Hanover for two years, where he linked up once more with his brother, Frederick Duke of York, but he led a dissolute existence, becoming entangled in affairs with women, and got heavily into debt. Although he went to sea again, William had lost the confidence of the Admiralty and left the Navy in 1789 with the rank of post-captain. His father now created him Duke of Clarence.

With little to occupy his time Clarence, like his brother before him, fell in love with an actress, the celebrated Dorothea Jordan; she had already had two children by previous lovers. While continuing with her acting career, Dorothea and Clarence lived as man and wife at their residences in St James's Palace and Clarence Lodge, indulging in elaborate entertaining. To help clear his son's growing debts, George gave him £6,000 and the notional office of Ranger of Bushy Park, near Hampton Court, which became their new residence. Between 1794 and 1807 ten children were born – five boys and five girls. Although he showed great affection for Dorothea, after they had been together for 20 years Clarence met a young heiress whom he hoped to marry, and so ended the liaison only a few months after his brother had terminated his own long-standing arrangement with Mrs Fitzherbert.[73] He was promoted to admiral in 1799 and married Adelaide of Saxe-Meiningen, living with her at Bushy. The Duke of York died in 1827, leaving Clarence as heir to the throne. He succeeded three years later as William IV.

During William's short reign the Reform Bill of 1832 was passed. Until then he had left most of the conduct of political affairs in the hands of his ministers, but he was appalled at the prospect of creating an unlimited number of peers who would support the bill. In 1834 William dismissed Melbourne only a few months after he succeeded Earl Grey as Whig Prime Minister, replacing him with Peel. However, in the ensuing general election the Tories were defeated and Melbourne was reinstated. Reluctantly, the King was obliged to consent, though he refused to speak to his ministers except on business for their first few months in office. 'I would rather have the devil than a Whig in the house', he is reported to have said.[74] Since then, no monarch has been responsible for the dismissal of a Prime Minister. His straightforwardness of manner never left him and the soubriquet of 'Sailor King' fitted his bluffness and natural bonhomie. Within seven years of becoming King, William died without a legitimate heir on 24 May 1837.

The Hanoverian period had witnessed great changes in British society. For one thing, the Industrial Revolution had transformed the towns and the countryside and witnessed the rise of a prosperous middle class. The growth of private and charity schools, the latter of which under the first two Georges were identified with Jacobite sympathies, encouraged the spread of literacy which in turn led to a demand for newspapers. From then on, the activities of royalty were widely but discreetly reported. Communications, especially road systems, were becoming more efficient, and the new railways revolutionised travel. The demand for franchise reform and the growing powers of Parliament in its dealings with the monarch inevitably affected the nation's views of its rulers.

These events had remarkably little influence on the upbringing and education of the royal children. Their isolation from others was further compounded by the exercise, by George I, for example, of the right of the King not only to separate children from their parents and be responsible for their education but also to intervene in the upbringing of their grandchildren. It is not surprising that the Hanoverian princes developed antisocial behaviour, cynicism and frequently a life-long hatred of their fathers, which was hardly helped by an over-rigid regime. The nature and content of their education, consisting of a heavily overloaded curriculum, only added to these difficulties.

It is true that George III took a keen interest in the life of nearby Eton, but, as with the majority of other noble families of the time, it would not been have been expected that the royal children would attend what we would now call a public school. During the eighteenth century, open rebellion by the boys at Harrow, Rugby and Westminster hardly enhanced the standing of the schools; even George III's beloved Eton suffered three such outbreaks during his reign. Instead, the aristocrat, in raising his sons to be gentlemen, would have completed their education by sending them on the Grand Tour of France and Italy, an experience denied to the Princes. The newly reformed public schools, under such headmasters as Dr Thomas Arnold at Rugby (1828–42), came too late in this period to have any effect on princely education.

On the more positive side, it might be argued that the breadth of their education developed their sensibilities in a number of fields. A flowering in architecture during the reigns of George III and George IV was brought about in part by their commissions, and the styles of the period are immediately identifiable by the adjectives 'Georgian' and 'Regency'. Royal patronage of the fine arts and literature was another benefit. We have also seen that monarchs developed a life-long interest in one or other subjects, ranging from literature to mathematics. It is a fitting ending to an account of the period, perhaps, to observe that at William IV's last public appearance, in May 1837, at a celebration of the anniversary of the battle of La Hogue, when a combined English and

Dutch fleet defeated a French force, the King made a lengthy speech recounting England's naval wars and its history.[75]

Perhaps the most surprising aspect of the education of the Hanoverians is the lack, or at least the low level, of connection between Enlightenment ideas and royal educational practice. The Age of Reason is certainly in the background, but it made much less direct impact on the education of the future kings than might have been expected.

What we tend to notice about the education of George I, for example, are more practical issues such as his speaking English so imperfectly that it limited his participation in government business, and the fact that he had not been schooled in the complexity of English political life. It was only with George III that the Hanoverians became 'British' and were reasonably well educated and prepared for sovereignty. Even so, the progress towards greater limitations on royal power moved on relentlessly, and the Hanoverians only occasionally needed to be reminded of their status as kings by Act of Parliament. It was during the Hanoverian period that the political parties, rather than the King, began to exercise the power of appointing ministers, although officially it remained part of the royal prerogative. From this time onward part of the task of royal education was to prepare future monarchs for a constitutional position which was not only continually evolving but was not written down.

Some of the Hanoverians found this difficult and, as we shall see in the next chapter, Queen Victoria sometimes found it possible to choose to ignore the unwritten constitution.

NOTES

1. J. Bettam, *A Brief Treatise on Education with a Particular Respect to the Children of Great Personages for the Use of His Royal Highness the Prince* (Paris: P. Lauren, 1693), pp. 6–7.
2. E. Gregg, 'The Education of Princes: Queen Anne and Her Contemporaries', in J. D. Browning (ed.), *Education in the Eighteenth Century* (Garland Publishing, 1979), p. 91.
3. Prince Chulua Chakrabongse of Siam, *The Education of Enlightened Despots* (Eyre & Spottiswoode, 1948), p. 33.
4. J. Walters, *The Royal Griffin: Frederick, Prince of Wales* (Jarrolds, 1972), pp. 32–3.
5. Anon., *A Letter upon Education: Translated from the French of a Royal Author*, 2nd edn (J. Nourse, 1777), p. 9.
6. J. H. Plumb, *The First Four Georges* (Batsford, 1957), p. 34.
7. H. Forester (trans.), *Memoirs of Sophia, Electress of Hanover, 1630–1680* (Bentley & Son, 1888), p. 3.
8. Ibid., pp. 6–7.

9. M. Kroll, *Sophia, Electress of Hanover: A Personal Portait* (Gollancz, 1973) p. 144.
10. L. Melville, *The First George in Hanover and England*, vol. 1 (Pitman, 1908), pp. 194–5.
11. R. Hatton, *George the First: Elector and King* (Thames & Hudson, 1978), p. 30.
12. S. Petrie, *The Four Georges* (Eyre & Spottiswoode, 1931), p. 68.
13. G. M. Ross, *Leibnitz* (Oxford University Press, 1984), pp. 18–19.
14. H. B. Ray, 'Eyre Papers', *Miscellanies of the Philobiblon Society*, vol. 2 (1855–56), p. 68.
15. D. Defoe, *Of Royall Educacion*, ed. K. D. Bülbring (David Nutt, 1895), p. xii.
16. L. and H. Fowler (eds), *Cambridge Commemorated* (Cambridge University Press, 1984), p. 126.
17. M. Wynn Jones, *The Cartoon History of Britain* (Stacey, 1977), p. 17.
18. V. Bogdanor, *The Monarchy and the Constitution* (Oxford University Press, 1995), p. 8.
19. C. Chevenix Trench, *George II* (Allen Lane, 1973), p. 7.
20. R. Sedgwick (ed.), *Lord Hervey's Memoirs* (William Kimber, 1952), p. 353.
21. Mary Countess Cowper, *Diary of Mary, Countess Cowper, Lady of the Bedchamber to the Princess of Wales, 1714–20* (Murray, 1864), p. 99.
22. M. Marples, *Poor Fred and the Butcher* (Michael Joseph, 1970), p. 85.
23. Walters, *Royal Griffin*, p. 204.
24. J. H. Jesse, *Memoirs of the Life and Reign of King George the Third*, vol. 1 (Tinsley Brothers, 1867), p. 11.
25. J. A. Home (ed.), *The Letter and Journals of Lady Mary Coke*, vol. 1 (Bath: Kingswood Reprints, 1970), p. lxxvi.
26. A. Edwards, *Frederick Louis, Prince of Wales, 1707–51* (Staples Press, 1947), pp. 176–7.
27. G. Young, *Poor Fred: The People's Prince* (Oxford University Press, 1937), p. 173.
28. M. De-La-Noy, *the King Who Never Was: The Story of Frederick, Prince of Wales* (Peter Owen, 1996), p. 214.
29. J. Harris, *Sir William Chambers* (Zwemmer, 1970), p. 9.
30. J. Brooke, *King George the Third* (Constable, 1972), pp. 42–3.
31. Young, *Poor Fred*, p. 221.
32. J. Carswell and L. A. Dralle (eds), *The Political Journal of George Bubb Dodington* (Oxford University Press, 1965), p. 178.
33. Earl J. Waldegrave, *Memoirs: From 1754 to 1758* (John Murray, 1821), p. 10.
34. J. Timbs, *School-Days of Eminent Men* (Kent & Co., 1858), p. 138.
35. W. B. Donne, *The Correspondence of King George the Third to Lord North, 1768–1783*, vol. 1 (Murray, 1867), p. xix.
36. R. Sedgwick (ed.), *Letters from George the Third to Lord Bute, 1756–1766* (Macmillan, 1939), pp. 2–3.
37. Brooke, *George the Third*, p. 57.
38. A. Q. Morton, *Science in the Eighteenth Century: the King George III Collection* (Science Museum, 1993), p. 42.
39. S. Ayling, *George the Third* (Collins, 1972), p. 58.
40. R. Huish, *Memoirs of George the Fourth* (T. Kelly, 1830), p. 18.
41. G. N. Wright, *The Life and Reign of William the Fourth*, vol. 2 (Fisher, Son & Jackson, 1837), pp. 21–2.
42. J. Watkins, *Memoirs of Sophia Charlotte, Queen of Great Britain* (Henry Colburn, 1819), pp. 252–4.
43. H. Walpole, *Memoirs of the Reign of King George the Third*, ed. G. F. R. Barker, vol. 4 (Lawrence & Bullen, 1894), p. 206.
44. *Annual Register for 1762* (R. & J. Dodsley, 1762), p. 105.
45. L. Hollis, *Eton: A History* (Hollis & Carter, 1960), p.179.
46. Jesse, *George the Third*, vol. 1, p. 131.
47. E. Lee, 'Mrs Sarah Trimmer', in S. Lee (ed.), *Dictionary of National Biography* (Smith, Elder, 1899), p. 232.
48. J. W. Adamson, *A Short History of Education* (Cambridge University Press, 1919), p. 252.
49. Brooke, *George the Third*, p. 252.
50. A. H. Burne, *The Noble Duke of York* (Staples Press, 1949), p. 18.
51. D. Fitzgerald, *The Life of George the Fourth*, vol. 1 (Tinsley Brothers, 1881), p. 9.
52. J. Sargeaunt, *Annals of Westminster School* (Methuen, 1898), p. 190.
53. J. Bowring, *Collected Works of Jeremy Bentham*, vol. X (Edinburgh: William Tait, 1843), p. 30.

54. Donne, *Correspondence,* vol. II, p. 25.
55. Huish, *George the Fourth,* p. 340.
56. Revd F. Kilvert, *Memoirs of the Life and Writings of the Right Revd Richard Hurd* (Richard Bentley, 1860), p. 378.
57. A. Aspinall (ed.), *The Correspondence of George, Prince of Wales, 1770–1812,* vol. 1 (Cassell, 1963), pp. 33–5.
58. J. Ingamells, *Mrs Robinson and Her Portraits,* Monograph I, Wallace Collection (Wallace Collection, 1978), p. 14.
59. A. Somerset, *Ladies-in-Waiting* (Weidenfeld & Nicolson, 1984), p. 266.
60. W. M. Torrens, *Memoirs of the Second Viscount Melbourne,* vol. 1 (Macmillan, 1878), p. 157.
61. D. Creston, *The Regent and his Daughter* (Eyre & Spottiswoode, 1947), p. 23.
62. R. Fulford, *George the Fourth* (Duckworth, 1935), p. 224.
63. N. Williams, *The Royal Residences of Great Britain* (Barrie & Rockliff, 1960), p. 47.
64. J. Halpern, *The Life of Jane Austen* (Brighton: Harvester Press, 1984), pp. 282–4.
65. Huish, *George the Fourth,* p. 29.
66. Marples, *Poor Fred,* pp. 148–9.
67. Huish, *George the Fourth,* p. 38.
68. T. Pocock, *Sailor King: The Life of King William the Fourth* (Sinclair-Stevenson, 1991), p. 10.
69. P. Ziegler, *King William the Fourth* (Collins, 1971), pp. 30–1.
70. J. Watkins, *The Life and Times of William the Fourth* (Fisher, Son & Jackson, 1831), p. 81.
71. F. Bradford, *Nelson the Essential Hero* (Macmillan, 1977), p. 57.
72. Brooke, *George the Third,* pp. 354–5.
73. C. Tomalin, *Mrs Jordan's Profession* (Viking, 1994), pp. 241ff.
74. D. Cecil, *Lord M.* (Constable, 1954), p. 251.
75. F. Malloy, *The Sailor King: William the Fourth, His Court and His Subjects,* vol. II (Hutchinson, 1903), pp. 599–600.

# 5 Victoria, Edward VII and the Debate on Education

T HE EFFECTS OF THE Industrial Revolution on society were most clearly seen during the course of the nineteenth century. Technological changes, with increased productive power, gave rise to a demand for a workforce which had received at least some form of education. This had been accompanied by a population explosion. In 1801 the population of England and Wales was 8.8 million: by 1881 it was almost 26 million. With the growth of towns from what were formerly villages, such as Birmingham, there were fears for maintaining a civilised society; campaigns against the use of alcohol and widespread crime were witnesses to this. Indeed, there was a public debate as to whether more schools or more prisons should be provided. There was also a revival in religion by means of which the Churches sought to influence and improve the morality of the working classes. Added to these changes was the slow growth of democracy with the successive Reform Acts. By the middle of the nineteenth century, the personal power exercised by George III and George IV had disappeared, to be replaced in the House of Commons by members with party labels.[1]

The zeal for reform which characterised this period is nowhere more clearly seen than in the field of education. As early as 1853 in a speech to the House of Commons, J. A. Roebuck proposed a compulsory scheme of education for 6- to 12-year-olds. He stated that if parents did not provide suitable education themselves, 'then the State should step in and supply this want by compelling the parent to send the child to the school of the State'. The appropriate providers of school accommodation for the population was a battleground for the rest of the century between the Church and those who wished to introduce local or state secular education. Politicians were an important factor in the outcome: many, such as Victoria's first Prime Minister, Lord Melbourne, held decided views on the matter, as the next section demonstrates.

State intervention in the education of the poor was inevitable. Landmarks in its progress were the establishment of the Committee of the Privy Council on Education in 1839 and the formation of the Education Department 17 years later, though there continued to be many unsatisfactory features of the system. Perhaps one of the first royal expressions of concern at the state of mass education was voiced by Prince Albert in June 1857 as President of the Conference on National Education, which was convened to devise strategies for keeping children at school long enough to benefit from their education. Steering clear of the state versus voluntary school controversy, the Prince noted that out of almost 5 million children in England and Wales between the ages of 3 and 13, only 2.8 million received education lasting more than two years, while in addition something over 1.5 million were at school for two years or less.

How to deal with the problem required delicate handling. For the working man, the Prince declared,

> His children are not only his offspring, to be reared for a future independent position, but they constitute part of his productive power, and work with him for the staff of life; the daughters especially are the handmaids of the house, the assistants of the mother, the nurses of the younger children, the aged and the sick. To deprive the labouring family of their help would be almost to paralyse its domestic existence.

Nevertheless, the Prince urged parents not to neglect their children's education which it was 'not only their most sacred duty, but also their highest privilege' to secure for them.[2]

Another worrying feature was the educational provision for the rising middle classes and for sons of the elite. The Clarendon Commission, set up in 1864 to investigate the nine leading public schools, reported glaring deficiencies, especially their concentration on the classics to the exclusion of 'modern' subjects, such as mathematics and natural sciences. Four years later, another Royal Commission, headed by Lord Taunton, examined the condition of 800 endowed schools and painted an equally gloomy picture. One late inclusion in its terms of reference was the provision of 'middle-class female education'. In the light of Victoria's own education, the evidence heard before the Commission is of interest. James Bryce, then an Assistant Commissioner for Lancashire, found that on average a girl attending one of the few endowed schools which provided for them spent a quarter of her time on music and only one-thirteenth on arithmetic, a subject in which she was supposed to have some ability. Again, as with Victoria, the emphasis was very much on accomplishments, with other subjects taught mechanically by the question-and-answer methods advocated by teaching manuals, what Bryce called 'the noxious brood of catechisms'.

Victoria, as we shall see, held decided views on school education, no doubt stemming from her own experiences. Later, when she was queen, one of her maids of honour, Amelia Murray, became the chief mover in a plan to improve the educational standards of governesses. Murray, the authoress of *Remarks on Education*, in which she expressed many enlightened views on girls' education, persuaded Victoria to lend her name in 1848 to the founding of Queen's College, Harley Street, London, the first institution in Britain to offer an enlightened and advanced education for women.[3]

Both Albert and Victoria were determined that their own children should receive a truly English education, drawing on tutors of proven worth. However, despite the widespread public discussion on the most appropriate form of that education, which favoured a more secular and broad-minded approach in keeping with the times, the Queen and her Consort refused to break down the comparative isolation of the royal children from their contemporaries.

## VICTORIA (1819–1901)

The lives of few monarchs have been recorded in such detail as that of Victoria. Unlike almost all her predecessors, she kept a journal throughout her life; several volumes of her correspondence have also been published, including that to her children, and her activities during her long reign were widely covered in the press. In spite of this and though several authors have dealt with her formative years, the effect of her own education on her developing character has not been fully explored. This, no doubt, is at least partly due to her complex family background which requires some explanation.

When she was born, on 24 May 1819 at Kensington Palace, her grandfather, George III, was insane, and his five daughters were either spinsters or childless. His eldest son, the Prince Regent, later George IV, had lost his only daughter, Charlotte, Princess of Wales, and her own baby boy in childbirth in 1817. The second son, Frederick Duke of York, was childless. With the likely demise of their father in mind, the three eligible princes, who were hardly in the first flush of youth – William Duke of Clarence was 52, Edward Duke of Kent was 50 and Adolphus Duke of Cambridge was 43 – turned their attention to making swift and suitable marriages. The marriage of the Duke of Cambridge was the first, to Augusta Wilhelmina of Hesse-Cassel, in June 1818, to be followed a month later by the Duke of Clarence, now free from Mrs Jordan and their large family, to another German princess, Adelaide of Saxe-Meiningen.

The third brother, Edward Duke of Kent, was perhaps the least enthusiastic at the prospect of marrying. A man of great extravagance, after an early army career he had in typical Hanoverian fashion sided politically with the radical wing of His Majesty's Opposition, much to the fury of George III. On religious matters, he favoured Dissent rather than Anglicanism and was the patron of numerous charities. Financial exigencies made it necessary for him to leave the country for Brussels in 1816. Edward had met Madame Julie de St Laurent, the wealthy daughter of a French civil engineer, in 1790 and the couple had lived happily together for over a quarter of a century, much to the disapproval of the English Court.

With the death of his niece the Princess of Wales within a year of his self-imposed exile, Edward realised that he needed to find a bride in order to establish his claim to the throne. Such a person was already waiting in the wings. The late Princess of Wales's husband, Prince Leopold of Saxe-Coburg-Saalfeld, had a widowed sister, Victoire, Princess of Leiningen, who was almost 20 years younger than Edward. The mother of two, Charles, born in 1804 and Feodore, born in 1807, Victoire had endured an

8. *Victoire, Duchess of Kent with Princess Victoria*, William Beechey, *c.* 1821.

unhappy marriage but, possessing a strong personality, was fiercely devoted to her children. After some diplomatic shuttling, Edward and Victoire were married in Coburg on 29 May 1818; to ensure the legitimacy of the claim of any future offspring of the union, a second marriage ceremony took place at Kew on 13 July. Although Edward spoke fluent German as well as English his bride was German-speaking only and English lessons had to be quickly arranged.

The Duke's debts, already high, increased after his marriage, and, like his younger brother, Adolphus Duke of Cambridge, he decided to settle in Germany. But on learning in November that Victoire was pregnant, Edward immediately decided that their child should be born in England. Approaches to Clarence, the Prince Regent, for financial assistance were rejected and it was only in March 1819 that a committee of supporters raised enough money to pay off the Prince's debts to enable him and his wife to return to his native country. In April, Edward and Victoire were settled in Kensington Palace; it was there on 24 May that a healthy baby girl was born, Alexandrina Victoria, subsequently known as Victoria. The baby princess was fifth in line to the throne.

Money worries continued to plague Edward. The £6,000 voted by Parliament in 1818, though augmented by his supporters, was still insufficient to enable the family to continue to live in London. A poorly maintained cottage was rented in Sidmouth, Devon, for the winter. The year 1820 opened with freezing cold weather and living conditions at the coastal resort were dire. All three members of the family were taken ill, particularly the Duke, who, after a gastric attack, was confined to his bed. His condition rapidly deteriorated and two of Edward's army friends, together with Prince Leopold and his adviser, a young Coburg doctor, Christian Stockmar, joined Victoire at the Duke's bedside. Edward died on 23 January 1820 at the age of 52.

Although Victoire and her daughter returned to Kensington Palace, where they remained for the next 17 years, there were a number of difficulties to be faced. George III had died just nine days after Edward, and Clarence, the Prince Regent, succeeded his father as George IV. No love had been lost between the new king and his brother Edward, and George soon made it clear that he wished Victoire and her daughter to return to Germany.

However, she was advised by her brother, Leopold, to stay in England and raise Victoria in the best English manner, should the situation arise where she might one day become queen. The new king also refused to increase Victoire's meagre allowance, pointing out that as Leopold received £50,000 a year from Parliament, he should be responsible for helping his sister. In the end, Leopold made an allowance of £3,000 to augment Victoire's existing sum of £6,000 per annum. Such was the monarch's animosity towards his sister-in-law that it was not until 1826 that Victoire and Victoria were invited to stay with the King at Windsor.

By then, it was obvious that George and his brother William, the future William IV, would have no surviving legitimate offspring and that the Princess Victoria was the likely successor to the throne. In May 1825, the King had sent a message to the Commons requesting Parliament to grant a further sum of £6,000 per annum each to Victoria and George Frederick, the son of the Duke of Cumberland, specifically for their education. Both children were 6 years old. Whereas the proposal for George Frederick was badly received on the grounds that he would be educated in Germany, that for Victoria met with little opposition. As one speaker stated, 'In England it was essential that all members of the royal family should be educated. If left in foreign countries, it was impossible that they should not, imperceptibly, get impressions not congenial with the free principles of the British constitution.'[4]

During the debate, the Duchess of Kent was praised for her upbringing of the little princess. In fact, the regime to which Victoria was subject was far from admirable in the circumstances. It must be remembered that Victoria was only 8 months old when her father died, and so was brought up in a one-parent family (the Duchess never remarried). It has been suggested, too, that part of her later life was occupied in searching for surrogate fathers to compensate for her loss.[5] Although on good terms with her step-brother and step-sister, Victoria was several years younger than them. Added to this was the chronic shortage of money in the household: the food was frugal, furnishings were rarely renewed and economy was emphasised on all occasions. Victoria's simple tastes in adulthood were a direct consequence of this regime.

The Duchess described her situation at the time: 'We stood alone, almost friendless and unknown in this country. I could not even speak the language of it. I did not hesitate to act. I gave up my home [in Germany], my kindred, and other duties, to devote myself to a duty which was to be the sole object of my future life.'[6] The upbringing of Victoria henceforth was her paramount concern.

Thus was started the so-called 'Kensington System' which would isolate her from the outside world. At no time was the young Princess allowed to be on her own. At nights she slept with her mother and during the day she was constantly and closely supervised. Even when she had lessons with her tutors, the Duchess would frequently be present and she was not permitted to talk to anyone unless in the presence of a third party. Victoria was not allowed to play with other children of her own age and was instead surrounded with adult company. Not surprisingly, she was a precocious child, subject to outbursts of tantrums, but from contemporary accounts, she was also cheerful, playful and well mannered, content to be on her own. Her greatest joy was her 132 adult dolls, which she kept in a box. Each one was given a name and character and were to be her closest companions until the age of 14.[7]

Other influences were at work to ensure that the Princess's isolation should continue. Sir John Conroy, formerly the Duke of Kent's equerry and comptroller of the Duchess's household, encouraged the Duchess to pursue the Kensington System, hoping in this way to gain more personal influence over the future monarch. Victoria was greatly in awe of her governess, Fraulein Louise Lehzen, who was appointed in 1824 when Victoria was five years old. Lehzen, who had been previously governess to Feodore, devoted herself entirely to the needs of her charge, complementing the Duchess in her role. Created a baroness in 1827, Lehzen was both a firm disciplinarian and a mother substitute. She found many ingenious ways of engaging Victoria's attention. Whilst dressing, the Princess would invent her own stories from which Lehzen could assess the state of mind of her charge. When the servants had gone and Victoria was having her hair brushed, Lehzen would read her little history stories, which were very much enjoyed. This tradition persisted and, as queen, Victoria was habitually read to as she prepared her toilet. As the centre of her mother's ambitious world, the little princess was well aware of her own importance. On the occasion of a rare visit by another 6 year old to Kensington Palace, Lady Jane Ellice, the visitor began to play with the toys in front of her. At this she was rebuked by Victoria, who said, 'You must not touch these, they are mine; and I may call you Jane, but you must not call me Victoria.' Temperamentally, she was stubborn and self-willed, refusing at times to accept rebukes from her instructors. When told by her piano teacher that she must practise the instrument like everyone else, she shut the piano lid with a bang and shouted, 'There! There is no *must* about it.'

Victoria's formal education began when she was 8 years old under the tuition of the Reverend George Davys, a Fellow of Christ's College, Cambridge and a former priest in a Lincolnshire parish. He had been responsible for teaching English to the Duchess after her marriage to Edward. Davys, who lived at the palace, was a Low Churchman. As both the Duchess and Lehzen were Lutherans, his views met with their approval. This did not affect his religious teaching with Victoria, which was strictly conventional but more open-minded than that experienced by previous royal children. Davys showed great affection for his pupil which she responded to and he remained as preceptor until her accession to the throne. He was also responsible for teaching her Latin, though she had little capacity or liking for it, as well as geography and history. Davys planned an unusually liberal curriculum, which contrasted sharply with his own educational writings. He had composed various pious works, such as *A Village Conversation on the Catechism of the Church of England* in the year of his appointment as Victoria's tutor. Davys was also the author of *A Plain and Short History of England For Children,* which took the form of letters from a father to his son, with questions for the pupil at the end of each letter. It was a great success, reaching a thirteenth edition by 1859.

The tone of the letters is flattering when dealing with the history of the monarchy, starting from Saxon times. It is only when Davys deals with recent events that his confidence falters. In the final letter of the book, he wrote briefly, 'I think I must now conclude my history, as you know what happened during George the Fourth's and the late King's reign as well as I do.'[8] Certainly, history captured Victoria's imagination. Uncle Leopold told her: 'history is what I think the most important study for you. It will be difficult for you to learn humankind's way and manners otherwise than from that important source of knowledge.' With Davys, she had read Russell's *Modern Europe* and Clarendon's *History of the Rebellion* and drew up tables of kings and queens 'as the history of my own country is one of my first duties'. Victoria replied to her uncle, therefore, that 'Reading History is one of my greatest delights'.[9] Davys's good work with his charge was rewarded in 1839 when he was appointed Bishop of Peterborough.

Victoria's education was based on the curriculum found in most schools for girls of middle-class families, with a heavy emphasis on 'accomplishments'. Modern languages occupied a large place in the timetable, especially French, which was taught by M. Grandineau, using both conversation and writing. Although German was her mother's first language, Victoria was forbidden to speak it outside the classroom, though she was adept at learning it through her tutor, the Reverend Henry Barez, a Lutheran clergyman. Music was a particular favourite of hers; in this she was particularly encouraged by the Duchess who was a talented musician.[10] She was taught the piano by Mrs Anderson, a pupil of Mendelssohn, and, possessing a good soprano voice, had singing lessons from John Sale, organist of St Margaret's, Westminster. Later, she was to have lessons with Luigi Lablache, the famous operatic bass. The Princess also showed a talent for drawing which flourished under the tuition of a royal academician, Richard Westall. She showed some promise at arithmetic as well as writing, both taught by Thomas Steward, writing master at Westminster School. Dancing was another great favourite, taught by Mlle Boudin, and her gracefulness and deportment, instilled in her by her mother and Fraulein Lehzen, were shown to good effect in this activity. English was taught less imaginatively, with Mrs Trimmer's volumes of moral tales providing a solid basis.

The weekly timetable was strictly adhered to. Weekday lessons were from 9.30 a.m. to 11.30 a.m. and 3 p.m. to 5 p.m., followed by an hour of either learning poetry or modern language conversation. A shortened version of this pattern was repeated on Saturdays. Unlike her Hanoverian predecessors, Victoria did not share her lessons with another royal pupil. It was one day in March 1830, when George IV was a dying man, that Victoria, alone with Lehzen in the classroom, opened her *Howlett's Tables of the Kings and Queens of England* to find that an extra sheet had been added to the book. On it were the names and dates of the death of each recent possible heir to the throne. Then she came to the names of her two uncles, George and William, followed by her own. Aware for the first time of the situation, after saying, 'I am nearer to the throne than I thought', Victoria burst into tears and, looking up, remarked solemnly, 'I will be good.'

The Duchess, hoping to be Regent during her daughter's minority, decided to strengthen her case by requesting the Bishop of London, Charles Blomfield, and the Bishop of Lincoln, John Kaye, to test the 'moral and intellectual progress' made by her daughter as a result of her education. The Duchess also asked the bishops to point out any defects which they found and the ways in which they could be remedied. The examination, conducted in March 1830, seemed to be a triumph for the Kensington System. The bishops wrote in their report:

> The result of the examination has been such as in our opinion amply to justify the plan of instruction which has been adopted. In answering a great variety of questions proposed to her, the Princess displayed an accurate knowledge of the most important features of Scripture, History, and of the leading truths and precepts of the Christian Religion as taught by the Church of England, as well as an acquaintance with the Chronology and principal facts of English History remarkable in so young a person. To questions in Geography, the use of the Globes, Arithmetic, and Latin Grammar, the answers which the Princess returned were equally satisfactory.
>
> Upon the whole, we feel no hesitation in stating our opinion that the Princess should continue, for some time to come, to pursue her studies upon the same plan which has been hitherto followed, and under the same superintendence. Nor do we apprehend that any other alterations in the plan will be required than those which will be gradually made by the judicious director of Her Highness's studies, as the mind expands, and her faculties are strengthened.

Gratified by this endorsement, the Duchess sent the report to the Archbishop of Canterbury, Dr William Howley, asking him also to examine in person the educational attainments of the Princess.

Howley endorsed the findings of his bishops: he judged the plan of studies to be 'very judicious, and particularly suitable to Her Highness's exalted station'. Three months later, the King died, to be succeeded by his 64-year-old brother, William. Victoria was now only one step away from the throne. The Duchess's unsuccessful manoeuvres to become Regent do not concern us here, except that in order to emphasise the Englishness of Victoria's upbringing, Charlotte, Duchess of Northumberland, replaced Lehzen as governess.

Victoria's education was not simply confined to the classroom. With a further increase in the Duchess's grant by Parliament, the Princess now undertook 'progresses' in order to familiarise herself with the social life of the nation. Together with her mother, she paid visits to historic houses and major cities, receiving loyal addresses. She often made visits to the opera and the ballet in London and, as the journal which she began when she was 14 indicates, she was knowledgeable on musical matters. Holidays were of a simple kind, being spent at such places as Broadstairs, Ramsgate and Tunbridge Wells. Her happiest times, however, were at Claremont, her Uncle Leopold's home, though even here she was closely supervised. There exists an illuminating letter from Feodore, Victoria's half-sister, written in 1843, many years later:

> When I look back upon those years, which ought to have been the happiest of my life, from fourteen to twenty, I cannot help pitying myself. Not to have enjoyed the pleasures of youth is nothing, but to have been deprived of all intercourse, and not one cheerful thought in that dismal existence of ours, was very hard. My only happy time was going or driving out with you and Lehzen; then I could speak and look as I liked. I escaped some years of imprisonment, which you, my poor darling sister, had to endure after I was married ... Thank God they are over![11]

Although we have evidence, based on the ecclesiastical interrogations, of Victoria's educational attainments, it is doubtful if she was by any means a high flier. Admittedly, the journals which she kept before she became queen were expressly written for her mother's satisfaction, but they simply record facts about people and places visited. There is little about herself or her own feelings, and no analysis of the many different events and people whom she encountered over the years. Her education was by no means remarkable; for instance, in an age of science this subject was completely ignored in her curriculum. Added to this was the fact that the Duchess's views of a sound education were largely based on her own, gained in a small German Court. Nevertheless, the circumscribed nature of Victoria's education arguably did have some advantages. As one writer who remembered her speculated, 'A foreign observer and critic once suggested a doubt whether the Queen could have maintained throughout her life her admirable mental equilibrium if education had developed in her high intellectual curiosity or fantastic imagination.'[12] On the other hand, unlike any of her Hanoverian predecessors, she had been brought up in an environment lacking in ostentatiousness or luxury because of her parents' straitened circumstances and was able to take a more sympathetic viewpoint and understanding to some of the problems of her subjects. Taught to value common sense and public virtue, Victoria brought these qualities to bear when dealing with affairs of state or in consulting with her ministers.

For his part, when William IV came to the throne, he expressed a wish to become better acquainted with his niece, but, to his annoyance, the Duchess continued to ignore him. The 'royal progresses' which the Duchess masterminded for her daughter were also the cause of considerable annoyance to the King, and he suspected that the young Princess was being deliberately kept away from the Court. The matter came to a head in August 1836 on the occasion of William's birthday celebrations at Windsor. In a long speech, he strongly criticised the Duchess, referring to her as 'that person', for denying Victoria access to his Court and drawing rooms. Turning to the Duchess he added, 'I am determined to make my authority respected, and for the future I shall insist and command that the Princess do upon all occasions appear at my Court, as it is her duty to do so.' The audience was stunned, and the Duchess, deeply insulted, threatened to leave, while Victoria burst into tears.

Matters were not improved in May 1837 when the ailing King offered the Princess an independent income of £10,000 a year, to be administered by her own Privy Purse. It is a measure of her admiration for her tutor, Dr Davys, that she suggested him as the temporary holder of the post.[13] Later that month, there were public festivities to mark Victoria's coming of age on her eighteenth birthday. Within four weeks, she recorded in her journal on 20 June a description of an historic event:

> I was awoke at 6 o'clock by Mamma, who told me that the Archbishop of Canterbury and Lord Conyngham were here, and wished to see me. I got out of bed and went into my sitting-room (only in my dressing-gown), and *alone*, and saw them. Lord Conyngham [the Lord Chamberlain] then acquainted me that my poor Uncle, the King, was no more, and had expired at 12 minutes past 2 this morning, and consequently that I am *Queen*.

The year before, in May 1836, Leopold had engineered a visit to England of two of Victoria's cousins of the Saxe-Coburg family, Ernest and his younger brother, Albert. Both were intellectually gifted, but she was attracted by Albert's large blue eyes and light brown hair of a colour similar to her own. Victoria felt the separation deeply when the cousins departed the following month. It was not until 15 October 1839, when she had been queen for two years, that she sent for Albert in her closet:

> I said to him, that I thought he must be aware *why* I wished him to come here, – and that it would make me *too happy* if he would consent to what I wished (to marry me).

Within four months, on 10 February 1840, they were married.


Albert's own background and education were, in many ways, as remarkable as those of his wife. His father, Ernest, Duke of Coburg, was a noted profligate and, like the Duke of Kent, burdened with debts. He had married the intelligent and beautiful 16-year-old Princess Louise of Saxe-Gotha-Altenburg in 1817; Ernest was born the following year and Albert on 26 August 1819. Louise left her husband five years later and remarried; she never again saw her sons. The Duke also remarried his niece and Albert was put in the care of a tutor, Christoph Florschütz, who became the dominant influence in his life for the following 15 years.

Victoria had been surrounded by women in her childhood: Albert was largely in the company of men. A shy boy in his youth, Albert was a model pupil who enjoyed his lessons and displayed great self-discipline. At the age of 11 he wrote in his journal, 'I intend to train myself to be a good and useful man.' Although he never had a strong constitution, Albert was a great believer in outdoor activities and physical recreation. His love of the natural sciences was apparent at an early age.[14] Florschütz tutored him in history, geography and Latin, but from the age of 10 he had separate masters for German and Latin. He became even more serious as he reached adolescence, determining to be virtuous, amiable and eager to do good. When he was 14, Albert drew up a programme of study which he decided to follow. How far this regime, which occupied six days a week spread over 14 hours a day, was followed is not known, but its comprehensiveness is impressive:

PROGRAMME OF STUDIES DRAWN UP FOR HIMSELF BY THE PRINCE CONSORT
WHEN IN HIS FOURTEENTH YEAR

| Hours | Monday | Tuesday | Wednesday | Thursday | Friday | Saturday |
|---|---|---|---|---|---|---|
| 6–7 | Translations from the French | Exercises in Music | Reading | Exercises in Memory | Exercises in Music | Correspondence |
| 7–8 | Repetition and Preparation in History | Preparation in Religion | Riding | Repetition and Preparation in History | Exercises in Memory | Riding |
| 8–9 | Modern History | Religious Instruction | Exercises in German Composition | Religious Instruction | Ancient History | Exercises in German Composition |
| 10–11 | Ovid | Ovid | Music | Modern History | Exercises in Latin Composition | Music |
| 11–12 | English | Logic | English | English | Natural History | English |
| 12–1 | Mathematics | Geography | French | Cicero | Logic | French |
| 1–2 | | | Drawing | | | Drawing |
| 6–7 | French | English Exercises | French | English Exercises | French | Geography |
| 7–8 | Exercises in Latin Composition | Written Translation of Sallust | Mathematics | Mathematics | Latin Exercises Sallust | Correspondence |

146

From his first meeting with Victoria in 1836, Leopold and his adviser, Stockmar, planned Albert's education to meet the needs of a future likely prince consort. He became an undergraduate at Bonn University the following year, at that time something of an innovation for a royal prince. As his brother Ernest stated at the time, 'The head of no reigning house would be too willing to see his sons allowed to follow a public course of study at a university.'[15] At Bonn he was able to develop his views on rational education and intellectual freedom, which would, he believed, lead to the making of a perfect world. Education was seen as a boon for the masses in order to improve their intelligence.

It is interesting to compare Albert's educational philosophy, stemming from the Age of Enlightenment, with that of Victoria's at the time. Immediately after her accession, she came under the influence of Lord Melbourne, the Whig Prime Minister. He was exactly 40 years her senior, and Victoria found in him a father figure in whom she could and did confide. Starting with a successful plan, in which Victoria participated, to thwart the future ambitions of Sir John Conroy and the Duchess of Kent, Melbourne spent a considerable amount of his time at Windsor and St James's Palace in the Queen's company. When they did not meet, they often exchanged two or three letters a day.[16]

Victoria not only received sound advice on dealing with matters of state from Melbourne but she was also the recipient of his educational views, which she carefully noted in her journal. Melbourne, a product of Eton and Trinity College, Cambridge, had been Prime Minister since 1835. Two years before Melbourne had taken up that post, a previous Whig government had granted £20,000 to the British and Foreign School Society and the National Society towards building schools for the poor, thus introducing the first elements of state intervention in the provision of education. Controversy continued during the 1830s on such issues as the nature of schooling, whether it should be secular or denominational, the need for the training of teachers at 'normal' schools, school inspection and the imposition of education rates. Melbourne's ministry had inherited many of these problems and, though unenthusiastic about the prospect of further state involvement, he assigned the task of preparing a plan for the government for future action to a keen supporter of the notion, Lord John Russell. Accordingly, in February 1839 Russell proposed the establishment of a Committee of the Privy Council on Education, with the Lord President as its head, to distribute and supervise parliamentary grants for schools and organise a normal school for training teachers. The Committee was set up two months later in April 1839, and appointed Dr James Phillips Kay (later, Kay-Shuttleworth) as its first and dynamic Secretary.[17]

Melbourne's trenchant comments on education at this time impressed the young queen, though she was not always aware of the deliberate irony with which they were tinged:[18]

> Lord M. made us laugh [she noted on 10 February 1839] with his opinion about Schools and Public Education; the latter he don't like, and when I asked him if he did, he said, 'I daren't say in these times that I'm against it, – but I *am* against it.' He says it may do pretty well in Germany, but that the English would not submit to that thraldom: he thinks it much better be left to Voluntary Education, and that people of any great genius were educated by circumstances, and that 'the education of circumstances' was the best; what is taught in Schools might be improved, he thinks.

On the wisdom of training teachers, a practice then unknown in schools, he stated:

> You'll see, they'll breed the most conceited set of blockheads ever known, and that'll be no use whatever; now mind me if they don't.

Melbourne was unsympathetic to the idea of providing education for the lower orders. After dining with the Queen a few days later he once again discussed the subject:

> Walter Scott said, 'Why do you bother the poor? Leave them alone'; don't you think there's a great deal of truth in that?

At almost the same time as the Committee of the Privy Council on Education was being formed, he elaborated on the reasons for his position on the issue:

> 'All that intermeddling *produces* crime', he said. But we said if people didn't know *what* was wrong, they couldn't help committing crime. 'I don't believe there's anybody who doesn't

148

know what is wrong and right', he said. He doubts education will ever do any good; says all Government has to do 'is to prevent and punish crime, and to preserve contracts.' He is FOR labour and does not think the factory children are too much worked; and thinks it very wrong that parents should not be allowed to send their children who are under a certain age to work.[19]

Within a few weeks of the Committee of the Privy Council on Education's being formed, Dr Kay informed Melbourne that it was extraordinary how the appearance of poor children changed when their education was more attended to. Incensed by this statement, Melbourne sent for Kay, the instigator of the successful system of mutual instruction, and told him, 'If you will only let them alone and not be always intermeddling with them. Walter Scott said to a clergyman whom he was writing to, "How would you like it if a nobleman was to come into your house and teach you how to make your beef-steak into a ragout?"'[20]

Middle-class education was equally condemned by Melbourne. He believed that pupils should not learn more than one foreign language. 'You can't *speak* one purely if you know a great many – you mix them.' Greek, he believed, was too difficult. Victoria, drawing on her own experience, agreed, observing that 'learning as much as I did at once prevented one from learning anything very well, and bewildered one'. '"That's very true what you say," Lord M. said, "that's the fault now, they teach too much at once."'[21]

Despite Melbourne's cynical remarks, Victoria developed a more compassionate approach to education. When the Lord President, Lord Lansdowne, sent her a copy of a book entitled *Popular Education, as regards Juvenile Delinquency* in March 1849, she replied:

> It is an extraordinary production for people of the working classes, and there are a great many sound and good observations in it on education; the observations on the deficiency in the religious instruction and in the *preaching* the Queen thinks are particularly true. It likewise shows a lofty and enlarged *view* of education, which is often overlooked.

She was equally sympathetic to the aspirations of the Scottish people. Shortly after paying her first visit to Balmoral, she informed Lansdowne in 1849:

149

The Queen takes this occasion of repeating her hope that *Gaelic* will be taught in future in the Highland schools, as well as English, as it is really a great mistake that the people should be constantly *talking* a language which they often cannot read and generally not write. Being very partial to her loyal and good Highlanders, the Queen takes much interest in what she thinks will tend more than any thing to keep up their simplicity of character, which she considers a great merit in these days.[22]

Unlike Melbourne, Victoria was concerned about the plight of the working classes. She wrote to her daughter in 1872:

You know that I have a very strong feeling on that subject. I think the conduct of the higher classes of the present day very alarming – for it is amusement and frivolity from morning till night – which engenders selfishness, and there is a toleration of every sort of vice with impunity in them. Whereas the poorer and working classes who have far less education and are much more exposed – are abused for the tenth part less evil than their betters commit without the slightest blame. The so-called immorality of the lower classes is not to be named on the same day with that of the higher and highest. This is a thing which makes my blood boil, and they will pay for it.[23]

She also took a close interest in the new schools which were being established throughout the country. In November 1845, one of her maids of honour, Eleanor Stanley, wrote to her mother:

I had a charming drive this morning with Mrs Anson to the Queen's schools near Cumberland Lodge, which are new this year, and very well managed as far as I can judge. The boys' school is quite remarkable, and the master seems a quick, intelligent man, likely to teach well and get them on. I heard an examination on part of Exodus, and I am sure I could not have answered half the questions that they all had at their fingers' ends. The Queen and court are very much afraid of its becoming a show school, and therefore stop all visitors, except those from the Castle, as much as possible, in which they are right, for everybody is rather inclined, naturally, to come and see the Queen's school, especially as she occasionally goes there herself.[24]

It had been Stockmar's manoeuvring, in order to lessen the

150

influence of Lehzen on Victoria, that had been responsible for Melbourne becoming Victoria's guide. Much of this changed with the arrival of Albert and it was accelerated by Melbourne's fall from office in August 1841. Stockmar, who had regularly commuted between Coburg and Windsor, was urgently recalled to England by Albert in the autumn of 1839 when Victoria was confined. As Albert's long-standing mentor, he assumed the role of confidant rather than medical adviser. A month before the birth to the couple of their first child, Victoria, Stockmar wrote to the Prince of the great importance of choosing a suitable nurse, 'for a man's education begins the first day of his life, and a lucky choice I regard as the greatest gift we can bestow on the expected stranger'. This task, however, proved to be a difficult one and shortly after the birth of the Princess Royal, Stockmar admitted, 'the nursery gives me more trouble than the Government of a kingdom would do'.[25] This *cri de coeur* arose from the growing antagonism between Albert and Lehzen over household matters, including the organisation of the nursery. Much to Victoria's sorrow, Lehzen was persuaded to resign in September 1842.

Greville, the diarist, records that when the doctor in attendance informed the Queen that it was a princess, she replied, 'Never mind, the next will be a Prince.'[26] Sure enough, within a year, on 9 November 1841, Prince Albert Edward, the future Edward VII, was born at Buckingham Palace.

## EDWARD VII (1841–1910)

Both Albert and Victoria turned to Stockmar for help on the upbringing of the royal children and in March 1842 he presented a memorandum which contained a suggested framework for their future education. 'Good education', he declares at the start, 'cannot begin too soon. "To neglect beginnings", says Locke, "is the fundamental error into which parents fall."' Stockmar followed Locke's view that education should be concerned with the organisation of experience. '"Nine parts of ten are what they are by their Education", wrote Locke, arguing that educative experiences should be physical as well as mental and spiritual – "a sound Mind in a sound Body" are the opening words of his *Thoughts on Education.*' Stockmar continues that the main task of the tutor is to regulate the child's natural instincts and to keep the

151

mind pure. Teaching should be by living example, for children imitate whatever they see or hear. Stockmar further pointed out:

> The first truth by which the Queen and the Prince ought to be thoroughly penetrated is, that their position is a more difficult one than that of any parents in the kingdom: because the Royal children ought not only to be brought up to be moral characters, but also fitted to discharge successfully the arduous duties which may eventually devolve upon them as future Sovereigns.

The errors committed by previous Hanoverian monarchs as parents were listed. George III did not understand his duties towards his children and neglected them. Only three of his seven sons were educated in England, the rest on the Continent. Stockmar believed that the errors committed by George IV and William IV contributed more than any other circumstance to weakening the respect for and influence of royalty. 'These errors', he continued, 'we can only explain them by supposing, either that the persons charged with their education were incapable of inculcating principles of truth and morality in their youth, or, that they culpably neglected to do so.' He noted that those princes educated abroad were unpopular with the majority of the nation, whilst those educated here were tolerated as possessing at least English faults. The lesson to be drawn from this, Stockmar stated, was 'that the education of the Royal children, from the very earliest beginning, should be thoroughly *moral* and thoroughly *English*'.[27]

Victoria wrote to Melbourne after reading the memorandum, 'Stockmar says, and very justly, that our occupations prevent us from managing these affairs as much ourselves as other parents can, and therefore that we must have some one in whom to place implicit confidence.'[28] In April 1842, Sarah, Lady Lyttelton, sister of the second Earl Spencer and a former Lady-in-Waiting, was appointed as governess. She was a spirited woman who was the mother of five children. About this time, in response to her own daughter-in-law's request for advice on bringing up an 18-month-old daughter, she wrote:

> There is no occasion, believe me, to suppose they [crying fits] mean *bad temper* at her age. As to checking them, I fancy taking very little notice of them is not a bad thing. I own I am against

9. *The Royal Family in 1846*, Franz Xavier Winterhalter, 1846. From left to right: Prince Alfred, Prince of Wales (Edward VII), Princess Helena and Princess Victoria.

punishments; they wear out so soon, and one is never *sure* they are fully understood by the child as belonging to the naughtiness.[29]

An anonymous pamphlet entitled *Who Should Educate the Prince of Wales?*, which was dedicated to the Queen, appeared in 1843 and was eagerly and widely read, not least by Albert and Victoria. The writer dismisses as possible tutors both statesmen (naturally ambitious of ministerial honours) and churchmen (who have 'a propensity for mitres and lawn sleeves'), declaring that 'confiding the education of youth to the clergy is a relic of barbarianism'. Ideally, the tutor should belong to no party, be devoted to the truth, and 'a man of letters ... who had passed through the alembic of adversity, and had come out in pure gold'. The King should regard religion as the first and principal consideration of existence, but not narrowly conceived, so that he may understand the different views of his subjects. In the pamphlet, enlightened writers, particularly Fénélon, Montaigne and Rousseau, are constantly invoked.

The journal *Punch* naturally poked fun at the volume of solemn advice which was being offered. In a piece entitled 'Education of the Royal Infants' it was remarked:

> The public will observe with much satisfaction the appearance above the walls of the garden of Buckingham Palace, two green wooden uprights, with a rope's end attached to each of them. On making inquiry, we have discovered that the objects in question belong to a swing which has been erected in the garden for the use of the Royal Infants. By this admirable arrangement it will be inculcated into their minds at an early age, that even princes are subjected in this life to ups and downs, and that we must all go backward as well as forward; a truth that cannot be too soon impressed on the understanding of infancy.[30]

Even more down-to-earth advice was tendered at the time, such as that of Lord Melbourne to the Queen:

> Be not over solicitious about education. It may be able to do much, but it does not do so much as is expected from it. It may mould and direct the character, but it rarely alters it.[31]

Stockmar's memorandum had been no more than a

background paper for the benefit of the young monarch and Albert. Now, in July 1846, four years later and after the birth of their fifth child, Helena, it was time for Stockmar to expound his views more fully on the education of the Prince of Wales, who was now nearly 6 years of age. Unlike many other contemporary writers on the topic, Stockmar took into account the economic, political and social changes both in England and in mainland Europe which had to be considered. The result was a remarkably perceptive and modern statement on the role of a future monarch.

He warned of the danger of basing a princely education on the existing status quo in a rapidly changing world:

> The extraordinary wealth and luxury of a comparative small proportion of the inhabitants of the British Isles, and the appalling poverty and wretchedness of many among the labouring classes, is another 'anomaly' which is at variance with our natural sentiments of humanity and justice, and finds its chief precedents in the history of ancient Rome, when she was tottering to her fall. Can this condition of things permanently endure in Great Britain?
>
> If coming events cast their shadows before, we may without presumption say that the shadows of great and important changes in the social conditions of Great Britain are already so conspicuously written on the land, that the changes themselves cannot be far distant. The great and leading question therefore is, – whether the education of the Prince should be one which will prepare him for approaching events, or one which will stamp, perhaps indelibly, an impression of the sacred character of all existing institutions on his youthful mind, and teach him that to resist change is to serve at once the cause of God and his country.
>
> Wisdom appears to dictate the superior advantages of the former course.
>
> The education of the Prince should, however, nowise tend to make him a demagogue or a moral enthusiast, but a man of calm, profound, comprehensive understanding, imbued with a deep conviction of the indispensable necessity of practical morality to the welfare of both Sovereign and people.
>
> The proper duty of the Sovereigns in this country is not to take the lead in change, but to act as a balance-wheel on the movements of the social body. When the whole nation, or a large

majority of it, advances, the King should not stand still; but when the movement is too partial, irregular, or over-rapid, the royal power may with advantage be interposed to restore the equilibrium. Above all attainments, the Prince should be trained to freedom of thought, and a firm reliance on the inherent power of sound principles, political, moral, and religious, to sustain themselves and produce practical good, when left in possession of a fair field of development.

It has been claimed that Stockmar's two memoranda represent the Magna Carta of the age of Victoria and are indeed a synthesis of what might be termed Victorianism. The Queen and the Prince were determined to make a break with the past, substituting austere morality for licentiousness and a human concern which transcended insularity. Albert's adoption of Stockmar's principles promoted a new code of ethics which Victoria eagerly embraced. They were to be applied not only in the nursery but were extended to the court, where some semblance of conforming to their views was henceforward expected of officials.[32]

One major problem facing the couple was how to translate Stockmar's fine words into practice. Albert and the Queen themselves prepared a joint memorandum in January 1847 which set out the educational requirements for the four stages of childhood. They agreed that for the first six years, 'the chief objects here are their physical development, the actual rearing up, the training to obedience. They are too little for *real* instruction, but they are taught their language and the two principal foreign languages, French and German, as well as to speak and to read ... Children at this age have the greatest facility in acquiring languages.'[33] Thus, the five royal children were divided into classes according to their age, Alice, Alfred and Helena in the nursery, and Vicky and Edward in an 'elementary education' class. There was no intention of sending Edward to a public school, for Albert regarded them as dens of iniquity. When it was decided to found a public school in honour of the Duke of Wellington, Albert's main concern was that 'it should in *no way* become an Eton or Harrow'.[34]

Much has been written on the wilfulness of Victoria and Albert's eldest son, Albert Edward, Prince of Wales. Educated with his brother, Alfred, from the age of 9, Edward was quickly recognised by his first tutor and a former Eton master and captain of the school, Henry Birch, as extremely disobedient and impertinent to his tutors and unwilling to submit to discipline, as well as being subject to fits of bad temper. At the same time, Edward could be affectionate and early cultivated the art of making friends. Birch initially seemed an ideal choice for Edward, but a clash of wills led to his father approving the use of corporal punishment for the recalcitrant pupil. Stockmar's suggested regime made matters worse, with lessons being given every weekday, including Saturdays. These lessons consisted of calculating, geography and English, all taught by Birch, and German, French, handwriting, drawing and music, taught by a team of experts in their respective fields. Isolated from other boys, their hours of study were increased in 1852, starting at 8 a.m. and finishing at 7 p.m., six days a week; the boys were to be tired out physically by daily bouts of riding, drill and gymnastics. The daily reports on his progress were sent to the Queen and made uncomfortable reading: 'March 8. A very bad day. The Prince behaved as if he were mad, made faces and spat. Poor Dr Becker complained of having heard a naughty word.' Becker, Albert's librarian and Edward's German tutor, warned Albert that the boy's periodic outbursts of destructive rage were a natural reaction to a system of education which placed too great a strain all round, and which could lead to total prostration and collapse. Such an approach was counterproductive: 'Neither kindness nor severity can succeed in such a case.'[35] Nor did Birch's attitude towards his charge ease the situation. After two years, when he was dismissed, he told Prince Albert that, though Edward could not endure chaff or interference of any kind, 'I thought it better, not withstanding his sensitiveness, to laugh at him … and to treat him as I know that boys would have treated him at an English public school, and as I was treated myself.'[36]

With the science of child psychology only in its infancy, other diagnoses were sought to account for Edward's behaviour. Phrenology was at this time very fashionable, and one of its chief exponents, Dr George Combe, was called in over a period of years to report on Edward. At one stage, Combe, after an examination of the royal head, was encouraged by the enlargement of a number of 'moral and intellectual bumps', though he diagnosed danger in the presence of some other protuberances.

It was an unfortunate set of circumstances which would more accurately help to account for Edward's problems. Although in their private lives the Queen and Albert were indulgent parents, quite different standards were applied in carrying out the Princes' and Princesses' educational programme. The children were expected to behave as young adults, with little allowance being made for their youth. For example, Vicky as a child once claimed that Lady Lyttelton had given her permission to wear a pink bonnet after supper. For this untruth, she had had her hands tied together and was very seriously admonished.[37] There were also great differences in personality and temperament between Victoria and Albert. The latter, a deeply serious man, refused to believe that human failure could not be overcome by the use of reason, and, if necessary, coercion. Education was the vehicle for making this possible. Indeed, Albert once said that education was the finest legacy which he could bequeath to his children. Victoria, perhaps because of her upbringing, suffered throughout her life from depression, mood swings and violent outbursts of rage, which could and did lead to friction with Albert. She also found it difficult to give praise. 'How sadly deficient I am', she noted in her journal in 1881, 'and how over-sensitive and irritable, and how uncontrollable my temper is when annoyed and hurt.' Indeed, Stockmar feared that Victoria had inherited some of the madness of her uncle, George III, and he told one of Edward's tutors in 1851, 'He [Edward] is an exaggerated copy of his Mother.'[38] Albert, anxious to safeguard her mental health, attempted to calm her by refusing to join in arguments: in return, Victoria accused him of coolness. On one occasion, Albert, to avoid confrontation, fled to his study and locked himself in. A little time later, there was a loud knock on his door. Anxiously, he asked, 'Who is there?' to receive the imperious reply, 'The Queen of England.'[39] This story illustrates, incidentally, another point: Albert was never popular with the British public and he was conscious of the fact that he was regarded as only the Queen's husband with no other recognised status. It was not until 1857, almost 20 years after their marriage, that Parliament granted him the title of Prince Consort.

Victoria was a person capable of intense physical passion who bore nine children over 17 years between 1840 and 1857. She did not match Albert's genuine affection for and delight in their children, though it must be remembered that she was the first major figure to combine the public role of head of state with the private role of wife and mother.[40] 'It is indeed a pity', Albert wrote to her in 1856, 'that you find no consolation in the company of your children.' Her attitude is best seen in her letters to their eldest daughter, Victoria (Vicky), who in 1858 at the age of 17 had married Frederick, Crown Prince of Prussia and later, briefly, Emperor Frederick III. Towards the end of the same year, when the Princess was pregnant, Victoria wrote to her:

> I know that the little being will be a great reward for all your trouble and suffering – but I know you will not forget, dear, your promise not to indulge in 'baby worship', or to neglect your other great duties in becoming a nurse. You know how manifold your duties are, and as my dear child is a little disorderly in regulating her time, I fear you might lose a great deal of it, if you overdid the passion for the nursery. No lady, and still less a Princess, is fit for her husband or her position, if she does that. I know, dear, that you will feel and guard against this, but I only just wish to remind you and warn you, as with your great passion for little children (which are mere plants for the first six months) it would very natural for you to be carried away by your pleasure at having a child.[41]

A few months later, she admitted that, 'abstractedly, I have no *tendre* for them till they have become human; an ugly baby is a very nasty object – and the prettiest is frightful when undressed – till about four months.' Her advice on children's schooling was equally sobering. She told Vicky in a letter, 'You need not be afraid of their being overtaxed – my children take good care not to overtax their brains or over-exert their fingers; if anyone is overworked it is the teachers and not the pupils, who are really very lazy, and make no effort of their own unless they are forced to do so.' And finally, she warned her daughter, 'You will find as the children grow up that as a rule children are a bitter disappointment – their greatest object being to do precisely what their parents do not wish and have consciously tried to prevent.'[42]

A change of tutor brought no improvement to Edward, who was now 10. Frederick Gibbs, like his predecessor a Fellow of Trinity College, Cambridge, was a successful barrister. His middle-class rather than aristocratic background appealed to Albert. It was under his regime that the hours of schooling were extended and onerous physical activities were increased; it was little wonder that Edward swiftly came to hate his oppressor and this set the scene for the next seven years. However, one innovation for which Gibbs can take credit was his attempt to reduce the two Princes' isolation by forging links with nearby Eton. Edward attended the annual meeting of 'Pop', the social and debating club, and speech days at the college, but this did little to bring him into contact with students of his own age. Reciprocal visits to Windsor Castle by a select group of Etonians led to complaints by Dr Edward Hawtrey, the Provost, about the Princes' behaviour, especially mentioning Edward, who 'had a pleasure in giving pain to others'. 'I feel very sad about him', Victoria wrote to Vicky in March 1858, 'He is so idle and weak.'

To Edward's relief, Gibbs retired in November 1858 when the Prince reached the age of 18. Gibbs's final report to the Queen was not totally without hope:

> Upon the whole it must be remembered that his character is childish for his years, and must for some time be backward ... In his best moments he has a real desire to learn ... These efforts are not long sustained, but they show enough latent power to justify the hope that when he arrives at an age to reflect upon the responsibilities of his position he will rouse himself to greater application from a sense of Duty, and if in the meantime it is possible to furnish him with that elementary knowledge, which is acquired only in childhood, his natural shrewdness and good sense will enable him to understand and efficiently discharge the duties he will be called upon to perform.[43]

Gibbs was succeeded as governor by a soldier, Colonel (later Major-General) Robert Bruce, a mild-mannered and understanding man, who accompanied and reported on Edward during the next four years. The Prince was eager to join the Army, but his parents ruled that this was appropriate only for his younger brother. After a six-month visit to the Continent he once again renewed his plea to train at Aldershot, but his father had much grander plans for the future king.

Although many books have been devoted to the life of Edward VII, comparatively little attention has been drawn to the fact that he was the first English monarch to receive a university education. Even more unlikely, Edward was a student at three different universities – Edinburgh, Oxford and Cambridge. Albert had accepted the chancellorship of the University of Cambridge in 1847 and became involved in attempts to reform university education.[44] In the light of his own enthusiasm for the study of science – it was said of Albert that, except for Lord Brougham, it was not easy to recall any public man who could have talked science with him[45] – he was anxious that Edward should take up the subject. Lyon Playfair, Professor of Chemistry at Edinburgh, had assisted Albert in organising the Great Exhibition of 1851. A future Vice-President of the Committee of the Privy Council on Education, Playfair advised the Prince Consort to send Edward to Edinburgh for four months, July to October 1859, to study applied science under him. The enterprise was a success, though the Press protested at the unnecessary prolongation of the Prince's education.[46] *Punch*, for instance, published at this time some verses entitled 'A Prince at High Pressure', which began:

> Thou dear little Wales, sure the saddest of tales
> Is the tale of the studies with which they are
> cramming thee.

Oxford was next on Albert's list, and he allowed his son to be admitted to Christ Church, but to reside in a separate establishment, Frewin Hall, under the supervision of Colonel Bruce. The cream of the Oxford professoriate directed his studies. These included Arthur Penrhyn Stanley (ecclesiastical history), Friedrich Max Müller (European languages) and Goldwin Smith (modern history), and the young H. A. L. Fisher gave the Prince tuition in law. His teachers reported favourably on his progress, though privately he was soon attracted to fellow students who encouraged him to indulge in riotous living. Albert, meanwhile, had planned the next step in his education.

In January 1861, Edward journeyed to Cambridge for admission to Trinity College. Exactly the same pattern was adopted as at Oxford. The Prince was made to live at Madingley Hall, some five miles from Cambridge, supervised by his staff but otherwise isolated from his fellow students. The Prince Consort paid several visits to Madingley to ensure that his son's studies

10. Revd Henry Birch, tutor to the Prince of Wales (Edward VII), *c.* 1857–58.

11. Frederick Gibbs (centre), tutor to the Prince of Wales (Edward VII) (left), and Prince Alfred (right), Roger Fenton, 1854.

were progressing well and that the staff continued to maintain strict vigilance. Edward's most enjoyable contact was with Charles Kingsley, the novelist and social reformer, who was Professor of Modern History at Cambridge. They met three times a week at Kingsley's house, where the Prince became absorbed by Kingsley's eloquent disquisitions on late eighteenth- and nineteenth-century European history.

In June that year, Edward was granted his long-held wish to experience army life, at Curragh Camp in Ireland. It was there that a few fellow officers smuggled an actress, Nellie Clifden, into the Prince's quarters. By November, rumours of the liaison were circulating round the London clubs. A painful confrontation between Edward and his father followed, when the former admitted to the affair. The Prince Consort travelled to Madingley on 25 November, staying the night after forgiving his son's indiscretion. Shortly after this, Albert developed symptoms of typhoid fever and died aged 42 on 14 December at 11 p.m. Edward, who had been sitting his Cambridge examinations, arrived at Windsor at 3 o'clock in the morning of that day. Victoria blamed her husband's death, wrongly, on Edward's dissolute behaviour and she refused to contact him when Albert was dying. It was only the action of his sister, Alice, which enabled Edward to reach Windsor early in the morning of 14 December. Unable to bear his presence, Victoria dispatched Edward abroad early in February 1862 to propose marriage to Princess Alexandra of Denmark, in the hope of bringing greater stability into his life.

Although relations between the Queen and the Prince of Wales slowly improved, there was now a coldness on Victoria's part which extended to refusing to allow her son any substantial role in royal affairs. As Sir Edward Clark, the former physician to the Duchess of Kent, remarked, 'None who knows the character of the Queen and of the Heir Apparent can look forward to the future without seeing trouble in that quarter.'[47]

It can be argued that Victoria's relationship with her eldest son was a reflection of her own upbringing and education. No previous monarch had been so systematically educated on British lines as Victoria or had been subject to such close and continuous scrutiny. It had been, however, somewhat restricted in scope and in an isolated setting, and was conspicuously aimed by her mother, the Duchess of Kent, at preparing her daughter for the throne. This was probably responsible for her enthusiasm, shared by Albert, for continuing a closely supervised programme of study for the heirs to the throne. In spite of Albert's own enlightened views of education as a means of producing a better society, this was not translated into a liberal regime for his own children.

This chapter includes an account of the most systematic attempt ever made to educate a prince: the Albert–Victoria curriculum based on Stockmar's advice. It is interesting, and perhaps disheartening, that this well-meant programme was so unsuccessful. Edward rebelled against the regime, was never properly educated, but became a successful example of a constitutional monarch, having learned enough to know the limits of his powers.

## NOTES

1. G. Kitson Clark, *The Making of Victorian England* (Methuen, 1965), p. 207.
2. Albert, Prince Consort, *The Principal Speeches and Addresses of HRH the Prince Consort* (John Murray, 1862), p. 190.
3. E. Kaye, *A History of Queen's College, London* (Chatto & Windus, 1972), p. 16.
4. T. C. Hansard, *Parliamentary Debates*, 3 (1825), 27 May, col. 913.
5. G. St Aubyn, *Queen Victoria: A Portrait* (Atheneum, 1992), p. 12.
6. G. Barnett Smith, *The Life of Queen Victoria* (Routledge, 1901), p. 9.
7. C. B. Woodham-Smith, *Queen Victoria: Her Life and Times* (Hamish Hamilton, 1972), pp. 68–9.
8. G. Davys, *A Plain and Short History of England* (Rivington, 1850), p. 257.
9. D. Marshall, *The Life and Times of Victoria* (Weidenfeld & Nicolson, 1972), p. 31.
10. A. Baillie and H. Bolitho (eds.), *Letters of Lady Augusta Stanley: A Young Lady at Court* (Gerald Howe, 1927), p. 76.
11. Viscount Esher (ed.), *The Girlhood of Queen Victoria*, vol. I (John Murray, 1912), p. 18.
12. Ibid., p. 19.
13. A. Plowden, *The Young Victoria* (Weidenfeld & Nicolson, 1981), p. 138.
14. T. Martin, *The Life of His Royal Highness The Prince Consort*, vol. I (Smith, Elder, 1875), p. 8.
15. S. Weintraub, *Albert: Uncrowned King* (John Murray, 1997), p. 55.
16. L. G. Mitchell, *Lord Melbourne 1779–1848* (Oxford University Press, 1997), p. 235.
17. R. J. W. Selleck, *James Kay-Shuttleworth: Journey of an Outsider* (Woburn Press, 1994), pp. 145–6.
18. D. Cecil, *Lord M.* (Constable, 1954), p. 284.
19. Esher, *Girlhood*, pp. 117, 122, 148.
20. Ibid., p. 209.
21. Ibid., p. 303.
22. A. C. Benson and Viscount Esher (eds), *The Letters of Queen Victoria, 1837–1861*, vol. I (John Murray, 1907), pp. 254–5.

23. R. Fulford (ed.), *Darling Child: The Private Correspondence of Queen Victoria and the Crown Princess of Prussia, 1871–1878* (Evans, 1976), p. 51.
24. E. Erskine (ed.), *Twenty Years at Court: From the Correspondence of the Hon. Eleanor Stanley* (Nisbet, 1916), pp. 110–11.
25. P. Crabitès, *Victoria's Guardian Angel: A Study of Baron Stockmar* (Routledge, 1937), p. 125.
26. P. W. Wilson (ed.), *The Greville Diary*, vol. II (Heinemann, 1927), p. 214.
27. E. von Stockmar, *Memoirs of Baron Stockmar*, vol. II (Longman, Green, 1872), pp. 97–100.
28. T. Martin, *The Life of His Royal Highness The Prince Consort*, vol. II (Smith, Elder, 1876), pp. 179–80.
29. H. Wyndham (ed.), *Correspondence of Sarah Spencer, Lady Lyttelton, 1787–1870* (John Murray, 1912), p. 327.
30. 'Education of the Royal Infants', *Punch*, vol. IV (1843), p. 232.
31. Benson and Esher, *Letters*, p. 458.
32. Crabitès, *Victoria's Guardian Angel*, pp. 149–52.
33. R. Rhodes James, *Albert, Prince Consort: A Biography* (Hamish Hamilton, 1983), p. 235.
34. G. St Aubyn, *Edward VII: Prince and King* (Collins, 1979), p. 24.
35. P. Magnus, *King Edward the Seventh: The Most Edwardian of Them All* (John Murray, 1964), p. 26.
36. Ibid., p. 7.
37. H. Pakula, *An Unknown Woman: The Empress Frederick* (Phoenix, 1997), pp. 38–9.
38. F. W. Gibbs, 'The Education of a Prince', *Cornhill Magazine,* Spring (1951), p. 110.
39. St Aubyn, *Queen Victoria*, p. 170.
40. D. Thompson, 'Queen Victoria', *The Historian*, Spring (1997), p. 6.
41. Fulford, *Darling Child*, pp. 143–4.
42. Ibid., p. 202.
43. Gibbs, 'Education of a Prince', p. 119.
44. Martin, *Life of the Prince Consort*, vol. I, pp. 116–20.
45. G. M. Young, *Early Victorian England, 1830–1865*, vol. II (Oxford University Press, 1934), p. 493.
46. S. Lee, *King Edward VII: A Biography*, vol. I (Macmillan, 1925), p. 74.
47. E. Longford, *Victoria R.I.* (Pan, 1966), p. 457.

# 6  *Three Twentieth-century Kings:*

## Social Change and the Survival of the Monarchy

THIS CHAPTER COVERS the period from the education of the future George V to the death of George VI in 1953. It was a period of tremendous social, economic and technical change, during which time Britain passed from the peak of imperial power to the decline of Empire after the Second World War. At the beginning of the period, monarchy was the most common form of government in Europe; by the end, nearly all royal families had fallen, including such great names as the Habsburgs and the Romanovs. The British royal family encountered several crises, perhaps the most damaging being the events leading to the abdication of Edward VIII, but the institution continued to flourish. One of the most important aspects of the social change was reform in education: the period covers a number of major Education Acts, the most important being the Balfour Act (1902), which opened up the possibility of secondary education for a minority – the ladder of opportunity – and the Butler Act (1944) which extended the work of the 1902 legislation by making secondary education universal, compulsory and free.

To some extent the early twentieth-century history of education can be seen as carrying forward the many social and educational reforms of the Victorian age, particularly the expansion of the maintained school system and widening educational opportunities to more and more sections of the community. But the first half of the twentieth century was also a period of dramatic social and political change: the First World War, the extension of democracy, the social unrest leading to the General Strike of 1926, and other events and developments which called into question traditional privileges. It is difficult for

164

those who have grown up in the second half of the twentieth century to appreciate the openness of the social divisions of the late nineteenth and early twentieth centuries. Many parents took great care to keep their children away from their 'inferiors'. This applied to an even greater extent to the royal family. The Duke of Windsor, reflecting on his own childhood, said that he was grateful to his father because he had always taught him not to think of himself as different from or better than other people; but the Duke added: 'To be sure, by other people he meant the children of the well-born.'

Times were, however, changing and the trend was in the direction of overcoming class differences. Much of educational research was concerned with 'political arithmetic', early statistical studies showing the lack of correlation between measured ability and educational opportunity. The Second World War stimulated the demand for more social justice. Increasingly, it was felt necessary for any inequalities to be justified.

Towards the end of the period the 1944 Education Act became a massive landmark of progress towards greater educational opportunity, including free secondary education for all and the possibility of access to higher education. These years also saw much more criticism of educational methods. Many felt that private and maintained schools were rigid organisations, too much concerned with rote learning, mechanical drills and unquestioning obedience. There was much talk of the child as an individual who needed freedom to grow and develop in his or her own way. We shall need to examine the extent to which these trends were reflected in the education of the royal family.

## GEORGE V (1865–1936)

From the time of the birth of George, the second child of the Prince and Princess of Wales, the future King Edward VII and Queen Alexandra, on 3 June 1865 at Marlborough House, there were signs that his upbringing would not remain solely in the hands of his parents. Queen Victoria, the baby's grandmother, was unhappy with the names chosen, George Frederick, on two grounds: that 'George only came in with the Hanoverian family' and that her late husband's Christian name had not been added. It was therefore agreed as a compromise when the child was baptised on 7 July that he should be called George Frederick Ernest Albert.

Some 17 months earlier, Princess Alexandra had given birth to another boy, Albert Victor, known as Eddy, who, it was assumed, would one day become king. The family was completed by three younger sisters, Louise, Victoria and Maud. Both parents were united in their efforts to make their children's lives as happy as possible. 'If children are too strictly or perhaps, too severely treated', the Prince wrote to his mother, remembering his own childhood, 'they get shy and only fear those whom they ought to love.'[1] Princess Alexandra, for her part, a beautiful and cultivated woman, agreed with her husband in believing that children flourish under their mother's eye and she hated being separated from them. The establishing of good relations was as important as formal education and quarrelling between the siblings was frowned upon. In the relaxed home atmosphere, the boys were addressed as 'Prince Eddy' and 'Prince George', never as 'Royal Highness'. At Sandringham, their winter residence, Charles Kingsley, a frequent guest, was a great favourite and often entertained the Princes with his stories. Visits were made each year to their mother's parents in Denmark and to Osborne to see their other grandmother, Victoria. Autumn was spent at Abergeldie Castle in Scotland and during the London season they enjoyed their stay at Marlborough House where an elaborate children's ball was given.[2] Outings to such places as the zoo and the Tower of London were also organised. Sailor suits were worn and occasionally highland costume.[3]

When Eddy was 7 and George nearly 6, it was time for them to begin their formal education. Whilst the girls were to be given their own governess, the boys were placed in the hand of a tutor, John Neale Dalton, a young curate at Whippingham, on the Isle of Wight, who had come to the favourable attention of the Queen. Dalton, a graduate from Clare College, Cambridge with a first in the theological tripos and a third in classics, was a forceful person with firm views on most topics which he expressed in a booming voice; he had a strong temper and made known his belief in equality, which his son, Hugh, a future Labour Chancellor of the Exchequer, was to inherit.[4] For the next 14 years, he was closely involved in the boys' education, gaining George's respect, admiration and affection. Dalton, who was later appointed a canon at Windsor, remained in close touch with George until his death in 1931, an association spanning 60 years.

The daily timetable for Eddy and George at Sandringham was not an arduous one. Homework in English and geography would be prepared before breakfast, then at 8 a.m. there would be either a Bible or a history lesson and an hour later, algebra or Euclid. This was followed by an hour's break for games, then French and Latin and after a main meal at 2 o'clock there was either riding or cricket. The last lessons of the day – writing or music – took place after tea.[5] Dalton was assisted in his work by M. Mariette, who taught French, and Mr Weigall, a drawing master. When they were in London they were taught gymnastics, fencing and dancing with their sisters, as well as being coached in tennis, croquet and football. George became adept also at shooting.

Dalton was soon concerned at the differences in character between the two boys. Whilst George was hardly an intellectual, he was bright and cheerful and applied himself to his lessons. In contrast, Eddy, who was likely to be heir to the throne, was reported by Dalton to be backward, mentioning 'the abnormally dormant condition of his mind', lacking in all 'physical and mental tone' and in 'any habits of promptitude and method, of manliness and self-reliance'. Dalton failed to catch his interest and Eddy's obstinacy and unwillingness to work caused his parents and tutor great anxiety.

The Prince of Wales had long had in mind that the two Princes would benefit from mixing freely with other boys of their own age. This was in sharp contrast to the views of his mother, Queen Victoria, who considered that such an action would lead to mischief, following Albert's belief that boys, if left unsupervised, would 'talk lewdly'. The Prince's intention, however, was to send Eddy to Wellington College, a public school which was originally conceived of by the Prince Consort, its first president, as a military academy with boys in uniform,[6] whilst George, like his great-great-uncle, William IV, would start on a career in the Royal Navy.

A major obstacle to this plan, noted by Dalton, was that it was only with the encouragement of George that Eddy made any effort in his studies. If, therefore, there were to be any improvement in what Dalton darkly called Eddy's 'moral, mental and physical development', it was essential that the two boys should continue to be educated together. For this reason, when

George joined the training ship *Britannia* on the River Dart in Devon in September 1877 as a cadet, Eddy went with him. (It is interesting to note, as one contemporary author claimed, that the heads of some of the leading public schools had been canvassed for their opinion of the possibility of sending the Princes to one of the schools, 'but naturally enough expressed but one opinion, which was that the results would not be beneficial either to the public school which might be chosen or to the princes; and the headmasters were undoubtedly right'.)[7]

Cramming was necessary for George to pass the naval entrance examinations in June 1877 in order to become one of the *Britannia*'s cadets, with Eddy being allowed to accompany his brother without any testing. They were accompanied by Dalton who was able to supervise them throughout the two-year course. 'It is impossible that two lads could be in more robust health or happier than the two Princes are', reported Dalton to the Queen in November 1877, adding possibly with tongue in cheek, 'Their studies are progressing favourably and Mr Dalton thinks there is no fear of the elder Prince working too hard, or overstraining his powers, as your Majesty seems to fear.'[8]

The course itself, with its emphasis on vocational education, was backward-looking in many respects. Concentrating mainly on navigation and seamanship, the course's narrowness of focus was aimed primarily at character building and sea sense rather than giving any sort of liberal education to the young students. Even on its own terms, the course was old-fashioned. The cadets learned to make, reef and furl sails rather than understand the engineering of modern ships; masts and yards featured in the instruction long after the conversion to steam and they were not shown the engine room, as it was considered that they were training to be officers, not engineers.[9] At their father's request they were treated exactly the same as the other 200 cadets, apart from having their own cabin and tutor. George, who was small in stature, was involved in fights with other boys, and though homesick for much of the time, successfully passed the final examinations in 1879.

George had made good progress during the course and the Prince of Wales decided that it would be beneficial to enlarge his naval training by sending him on an extended world tour. As an enthusiastic traveller himself, the Prince believed that one of the

12. Prince Albert Victor and Prince George (George V) as naval cadets, 1877.

essential qualifications of a monarch lay in first-hand experience of the world.[10] Dalton again advised that, in order to stimulate Eddy's mental powers, he should accompany his brother, rather than be sent to a public school which would be unable to cater for his special needs. Dalton's plan was to send the boys on separate ships and thus spread the risk should any tragedy at sea occur; this course of action was approved by Lord Beaconsfield's Cabinet. However, the Prince of Wales, who had already decreed that the Princes, who enjoyed each other's company, should travel together, was furious at this uninvited interference and insisted that his original plan should be followed. Beaconsfield apologised but Dalton at first impetuously handed in his resignation, withdrawing it, however, shortly before the voyage. Accordingly, on 17 September 1879, accompanied by Dalton, the Princes boarded the 4,000-ton HMS *Bacchante* at Cowes. It was to be their home for the next three years.

During this time, Dalton was in complete and overall charge of the boys' education as well as the ship's acting chaplain. Whilst two hours of each day was devoted to school subjects, the rest of the time was occupied with specialised instruction given by some of the warship's officers. The first lieutenant, the Hon. A. G. Curzon-Howe, taught the Princes seamanship, the gunnery lieutenant, C. H. Adair, instructed them in that skill, and the navigating instructor, J. W. Lawless was responsible for providing more general but essential naval information. Dalton was assisted by the assistant paymaster, G. A. F. Sceales, who tried to teach the boys French.[11]

Dalton had always taken a keen interest in naval matters, reinforced by the fact that his brother-in-law was a distinguished officer in the Navy, and he collected sailing prints and models of sailing ships. In later life, his nautical affectations were the butt of much gentle humour:

> A former pupil at St George's Choir School, Windsor, recalled telling a master who had put a lit pipe in his coat, 'You're on fire, Sir.' 'Now Canon Dalton would have put it differently,' came the reply. 'Canon Dalton would have roared out: "I say, Fox-Strangeways, there appears to be a slight conflagration manifesting itself from your portside pocket."'[12]

169

The first voyage took the Princes to the Mediterranean and the West Indies and the last and most substantial journey was the third one, which included visits to South America, South Africa, Australia, Japan and China. George and Eddy were obliged, as part of their education, to keep detailed diaries, which were published in 1886 as *The Cruise of Her Majesty's Ship Bacchante*. The two volumes, consisting of some 1,500 pages, purport to be the boys' own work, except where otherwise stated. However, the long Latin quotations, the detailed accounts of Roman and Greek history which accompany the accounts of their visits and the free and extensive use of poetic allusions make it obvious that the account was heavily edited by Dalton. Nevertheless, as he correctly remarked in the preface:

> It would be absurd to imagine that two young men of their respective ages should take in fully all the information given respecting the various places and people they saw, as older persons might have done. But as these pages will testify, several clear impressions were produced on their minds at each port, which will remain till their dying day.[13]

Dalton also pointed out that the Princes were treated exactly like the other midshipmen and performed all the duties of that rank. 'There was no difference', he wrote, 'not even the slightest, of any sort or kind made between them and their gunroom messmates.'[14]

Whereas Dalton reported to the Prince of Wales towards the end of the first year in May 1880 that Eddy 'sits listless and vacant, and … wastes as much time in doing nothing as he ever wasted', at the same time he praised George's progress in his studies and his enjoyment of naval life. In January of that year while at sea, George had successfully sat the examinations for a midshipman. It was from this time that he began to keep a daily diary in his large, round handwriting and with shaky spelling; he was to continue with it until three days before his death 56 years later.

Although it was largely due to Dalton that George's education had been reasonably successful, it was his mother, Princess Alexandra, who significantly shaped the Prince's character. She instructed Dalton on how he should deal with different aspects of life affecting the Princes. For instance, 'Politics of any kind, home or foreign, should be as much as possible kept from them', and they should 'take a *broad* view of everything and they should not be influenced by party spirit either in politics or religion'.[15] The Princess had a particular affection for George, and he returned her love in full, as his letters to her show: even in old age he would address her in his correspondence as 'Darling Motherdear'.

After the *Bacchante* had returned to England in August 1882, one of the first ceremonies which awaited the young Princes was their confirmation. This took place at Whippingham, Dalton's former church, in the presence of the Queen and the Prince and Princess of Wales. The Archbishop of Canterbury, Archibald Campbell Tait, in his speech laid down what was to become the foundation of George's philosophy when he became king:

> Experience has already taught you that the life of a true Englishman cannot be a life of mere pleasure; it must be above all things a life of duty. Duty first, pleasure afterwards; and the truest pleasure coming from the discharge of duty: and so Englishmen are what they are. To teach this practically – not to teach people to say it, but to teach them to feel it and act upon it, is the object of all good education. For a boy or young man it matters comparatively little whether the lesson is learnt by poring over his books at home, in spite of many temptations to idleness; or whether, subjected to a strict discipline, he wanders over the world with the privilege of seeing what others read about, and learns much as to men and places that can scarcely be known without being seen. It is not the details of education that are most important, but the general principles on which it is conducted.[16]

One important deficiency in the Princes' education needed to be remedied: the inability, in spite of many efforts, of either of them to speak either French or German, which were the *lingue franche* of the European educated classes. The Prince of Wales was a surprisingly good linguist and both parents were concerned that, apart from English, the boys were only fluent in their mother's native tongue, Danish. In an attempt to overcome this, the boys were sent to Lausanne for six months, accompanied by Dalton and M. Gabriel Hua, who subsequently taught French at Eton.

Dalton, hoping to capitalise on their interest in adventure stories, gave them several Alexandre Dumas novels to read. The move drew a reprimand from the Princess, who was, like her husband, good at languages. 'Though I have no doubt that Dumas' novels are very interesting still I cannot help think that *Novels* are not useful reading and do the boys no good. In French literature there are so many useful and most entertaining books in the shape of memoirs and historical works which would be far better for them.'[17]

The two brothers were parted for the first time when in 1883 Eddy, after intensive coaching by Dalton at Sandringham, became a student at Trinity College, Cambridge. This exercise proved to be futile, though he was awarded an honorary LlD; his subsequent time as an army officer proved to be equally unsuccessful. In contrast, George's career in the Navy flourished. He was appointed to the West Indian and North American Squadron as a sub-lieutenant and in the following year returned to England for further training at the Royal Naval College, Greenwich. The range of subjects studied was impressive. It included geometry, algebra, trigonometry, physics, mechanics, practical navigation and nautical astronomy, with practical navigation his best subject and mechanics his worst.[18]

His advancement in the Navy owed little to his royal title. In 1885 George was gazetted lieutenant after serving under Captain (later Admiral of the Fleet) J. A. Fisher, gaining first class in gunnery, torpedo work and seamanship, missing a first in pilotage by 20 marks. Fisher explained this latter lapse as follows: 'The yarn is that one of his examiners, an old salt-horse sailor, didn't think it would do to let him fancy he knew all about it.'[19]

George's next posting, to HMS *Thunderer*, brought him into contact with a sailor for whom he had the greatest admiration, Captain (later Admiral Sir Henry) Stephenson, an old friend of his father who also served as his equerry. On hearing the news of his new posting, George wrote to him from Sandringham: 'I would sooner serve under you than with any other Captain. And I am quite sure I shall be very happy all the time I am on the *Thunderer* ... We have just had a capital week, we killed over 5,000 head in four days.'[20] On the same day the Prince of Wales also wrote to Stephenson:

> I feel that in entrusting my son to your care I cannot place him in safer hands only don't *spoil* him *please*! He is sharp and quick and I think likes the Service, but he *must* be kept up to his work, as *all* young men of the present day are inclined to be lazy.[21]

By this time, George had grown a beard, but behind his phlegmatic exterior there were signs of prolonged adolescence. At the age of 21 he wrote to his mother from Corfu:

> You will be going to Sandringham almost at once I suppose for dear Papa's birthday. How I wish I was going to be there too, it almost makes me cry when I think of it. I wonder who will have that sweet little room of mine, you must go and see it sometimes & imagine that your little Georgie dear is living in it.[22]

By 1890 George had risen to the rank of commander, having had charge first of a newly commissioned torpedo boat and then a first-class gunboat.

At the end of the following year, George was recovering at Sandringham from an attack of typhoid fever. His brother Eddy had earlier become engaged to Princess Victoria Mary, known as Princess May of Teck, and the couple spent Christmas 1891 with the family. In January 1892, Prince Eddy became ill, developed pneumonia and died six days later on 14 January at the age of 27. Despite Eddy's many failings, including strong rumours of his links with the London homosexual underworld,[23] George was shocked and heartbroken at his brother's death and the end of a long and close friendship.

George and Mary, who had known each other from child-hood, were drawn together by their mutual grief. Within the royal family, there was also a fear that should George die without heirs, his eldest sister, Princess Louise and her commoner husband, the Duke of Fife, would succeed to the throne. A marriage between George and Mary was therefore to be encouraged as her mother, Princess Mary Adelaide, daughter of the Duke of Cambridge was a first cousin of Queen Victoria. George, as heir presumptive, was created Duke of York in 1892 and he married Mary on 6 July the following year in the Chapel Royal, St James's Palace.

George's naval career came to an end but this did not mark the finish of his formal education. Before his marriage, he was sent to

Heidelberg for two months in one more futile attempt at improving his German. Mary was intellectually his superior and from the beginning was determined to widen his knowledge. He rarely read a book for pleasure and his main interests were shooting, sailing and philately. She was also aware of the fact that her husband was likely one day to be king as his father, the Prince of Wales, was now 53. She helped him to speak French and she read her favourite books to him. Mary used his enthusiasm for stamp collecting to explain the history and geography of the different countries.[24] He had little appreciation of the arts and once said that his favourite opera was *La Bohème*, as it was the shortest one.

To prepare him for his future role as king, George studied with a young Cambridge don, Joseph Robson Tanner, of St John's College. Tanner was an expert on constitutional history and the author of three books on the subject relating to the Tudor and Stuart periods. Probably another reason for the choice of Tanner was that he was an authority on English naval history, especially on the activities of Samuel Pepys at the Admiralty. Tanner set George the formidable task of reading and analysing Walter Bagehot's book *The British Constitution*, and he wrote a summary and comments in a school notebook which survives at Windsor. One interesting sentence of Bagehot's on which George made no comment was, 'Theory and experience both teach us that the education of a Prince can be but a poor education and that a royal family will generally have less ability than other families.'[25] Certainly this experiment was not approved by all the royal family. Lord Riddell, the newspaper proprietor and friend of Lloyd George, reported a conversation between the politician and George V exactly 20 years later:

> The King told him that when he was a youth a course of reading had been provided for him by some educational expert. This included Bagehot. One day Queen Victoria saw him reading Bagehot's economic essays. She was displeased that he should be studying such a radical writer.[26]

Further instruction to repair the gaps in his knowledge of English constitutional history was given when his father became Edward VII, though one royal biographer has stated that the standard achieved was that of 'the average public school boy at the leaving age'.[27]

13. Revd John Neale Dalton, tutor to Prince Albert Victor and Prince George (George V), 1892.

There is little doubt that George's naval training and education had much influence on his actions after he became king in 1910. The qualities which he possessed as a sailor, the ability to carry out orders without questioning, the need to perceive problems without examining the subtleties of the situation and the closed world of the wardroom hardly prepared him for the more hectic world of politicians and constitutional crises. On the other hand, he possessed other qualities which were to his advantage. George's devotion to duty, his belief in tradition, his robust health and the possession of domestic and public virtues combined with a lack of imagination, which made the routine of kingship less onerous, made him popular with the people.

### EDWARD VIII (1894–1972, ABDICATED 10 DECEMBER 1936)

There can be few monarchs whose life has come under such detailed public scrutiny as that of Edward VIII, later Duke of Windsor. Many writers have been attracted to him as a subject for their books, mainly because of his abdication over his wish to marry an American divorcee, Wallis Simpson. More detail was added when the ex-king published three books relating to different aspects of his life and reign. The interplay between his upbringing and his education throws considerable light upon his later actions.

Edward, known as David in the family, the eldest son of the Duke of York, later George V, was born at White Lodge, Richmond, on 23 June 1894. By Queen Victoria's wish, he was named after her own 'darling Eddy': his other Christian names were Albert, after the Prince Consort, Christian, after Queen Alexandra's father, and the four British patron saints, Andrew, David, George and Patrick. David was the first of six children, the other five being Albert, Mary, Henry, George and John. His mother, Princess Mary, disliked the routine of childbearing and had little interest in her children as babies. Soon after the christening, which was attended by 12 godparents, mainly German, and the Prime Minister, Lord Rosebery, the new family moved to York Cottage, a former hunting lodge on the Sandringham estate. This was to be their main family home for many years.

David was handed over to a nurse, Mary Peters, who was

given full responsibility for his care. A woman of unstable temperament and with severe mental problems, 'Nanny' made the first three years of his life a misery. David's parents liked to see their children at teatime each day and Mary Peters made the occasion a nightmare. As David later recalled:

> Before carrying me into the drawing-room, this dreadful 'Nanny' would pinch and twist my arm – why, no one knew, unless it was to demonstrate, according to some perverse reasoning, that her power over me was greater than that of my parents. The sobbing and bawling this treatment invariably evoked understandably puzzled, worried, and finally annoyed them. It would result in my being peremptorily removed from the room before further embarrassment was inflicted upon them and the other witnesses of this pathetic scene. Eventually, my mother realised what wrong, and the nurse was dismissed.[28]

One biographer has surmised at the possible effect of this period of care on David's future relationships with women.[29] Mary Peters's successor, Charlotte Bill, a cheerful cockney woman known as 'Lalla', provided the love and affection which had so far been lacking in the child's life.

The household was augmented by Mlle Hélène Bricka, a former governess to David's mother. A domineering woman of French Alsatian origin and a devoted teacher, she was widely read and had studied modern history and social issues.[30] David and his younger brother, Albert, known as Bertie, were the main recipients of her teaching. The boys were taught reading and writing, history, French and German. Canon Dalton was responsible for religious instruction. It was at this time that David learned to crochet, a skill in which he liked to indulge throughout his life.

Their father ensured that the regime was a fairly strict one, made worse by the fact that they were made to wear schoolroom costume, consisting of starched Eton collars and ties, jackets and long stockings up to their thighs. Nothing was to be out of place. As the Prince remarked, 'We were always on parade, a fact that he would never allow us to forget.'[31] It was a relief for the boys when their parents went on a tour of the colonies and they were moved close to their grandparents. Mlle Bricka was greatly concerned that their school work was being neglected, as indeed it was. As part of the conspiracy, when the new King and Queen took the children to Sandringham for a two-week stay, Mlle Bricka was left in London in order not to spoil their fun.

The death of Queen Victoria marked a new stage in David's education. His parents, now the Prince and Princess of Wales, made changes in the supervision of the two boys. Mlle Bricka was retired and 'Lalla' Bill was transferred to supervise their sisters. 'Lalla' was replaced by Frederick Finch, who in time became David's valet, and a male tutor, Henry Peter Hansell. Hansell, who was born in Norfolk and educated at Malvern, had read history at Magdalen College, Oxford and then taught at Rossall and later Ludgrove, an independent preparatory school. Hansell was an inadequate tutor, more interested in church architecture, the classics, and physical prowess than inspiring his young charges in their studies. He created a small schoolroom on the first floor of York Cottage which accommodated desks, a blackboard and bookshelves. The boys followed the same routine experienced by their father when he was of school age: preparation before breakfast, lessons from 9 a.m. to 1 p.m. and again between tea and supper. Their schoolwork took priority over other pleasures. When the Princess of Wales attended a children's party in the middle of the week, taking with her Princess Mary and Prince Henry, her hostess expressed regret that the she had not brought the two elder Princes as well. 'Saturday is their only half-holiday', replied the Princess. 'We never allow anything to interfere with their lessons.'[32]

Hansell had to call in outside help to teach French and German. M. Hua, the Prince of Wales's own former tutor, was recalled from retirement from Eton to teach French, and Professor Eugen Oswald taught them German. Cecil Sharp, the folk music collector, was engaged to teach singing. He reported to the Prince that David and Bertie were able to sing no fewer than 50 songs, stating that the two boys possessed 'a musical instinct and ability far above the average'.[33] When their father realised one day that they could not calculate the average weight of stags which he had shot at Abergeldie, he engaged a master to teach them mathematics.[34] David took an intelligent interest in history, as Lord Esher, a close friend of the royal family, noted after taking the boys on a visit to Westminster Abbey:

> Prince Edward remarked of the Duke of Buckingham that he was a 'wicked man' – and when I asked him why, he said he gave bad advice to Charles I. He knew that Buckingham had been murdered at Portsmouth by Felton. I think he must have been reading Dumas![35]

The only occasions when David and Bertie mixed with other boys was when J. Walter Jones, the master of West Newton village school near Sandringham, persuaded their father to let them participate in games of football, made up of boys from the school. Whenever Hansell was away, Jones would take the Princes for nature walks and they were fascinated by his knowledge of the countryside.

To Hansell's credit, he was forthright in telling the Prince of Wales that, in his opinion, his sons would benefit from attending a normal preparatory school instead of being educated in isolation.[36] Not only would the lively pair be subject to firmer discipline but their academic progress would be accelerated. Neither of the boys was unintelligent and were willing, if not eager, learners. The Prince, however, was adamant that they should follow his own educational route, telling Hansell, 'My brother and I never went to preparatory school. The Navy will teach David all that he needs to know.'

Princess Mary, a shy person and totally subservient to her husband, was unwilling to challenge this view. Before her marriage, she had been an earnest student at the University Extension lectures given in Richmond, becoming an avid reader of George Eliot and Thomas Carlyle.[37] Later, she became a passionate collector and was a good judge of furniture and china.[38] Nevertheless, she shared her husband's distrust of intellectuals, and was not academically ambitious for her sons. Prince George, who had enjoyed a good relationship with his own father, nevertheless believed that a strict regime was bene--ficial for the children and should, inevitably, involve fear. He is reported to have once told his friend Edward, 15th Earl of Derby, 'My father was frightened of his mother; I was frightened of my father, and I am damned well going to see to it that my children are frightened of me.'[39] A slightly more generous explanation was later give by the Countess of Airlie, who was appointed a Lady-

14. Mlle Hélène Bricka, governess to Prince Edward (Edward VIII) and Prince Albert (George VI), 1893.

in-Waiting at Sandringham in 1902:

> King George V and Queen Mary have often been depicted as stern
> unloving parents, but this they most certainly were not.
> Remembering them in my early days at Sandringham, before their
> family was even complete, I believe that they were more
> conscientious and more truly devoted to their children than the
> majority of parents in that era. The tragedy was that neither had
> any understanding of a child's mind. They themselves had been
> brought up in particularly loving homes ... but they did not
> succeed in making their own children happy.[40]

It is unfortunate that David and Bertie were not given the same
educational opportunities as their younger brother Henry, later
Duke of Gloucester. Born at the beginning of the century, he was
a delicate child who, Hansell believed, required special treatment. The Prince was reluctantly persuaded to let Henry become
a day boy at a preparatory school, St Peter's Court, Broadstairs,
where he flourished. Even so, the Prince of Wales grumbled that
learning Latin verses was a 'pure waste of time', and insisted that
he learnt French and German instead. Henry subsequently
attended Eton, the first member of the royal family in direct line
of succession to the throne to do so.[41]

When David was 12, he was entered for admission to the Naval
College at Osborne, a junior Royal Naval college which replaced
the training ship *Britannia*. David's spelling was bad, he knew no
Latin, and had little mathematics. Despite the fact that he
narrowly failed to pass the written examinations (though he
obtained high marks in the *viva voce*), he was accepted for the
course.[42] One relief was that he was not accompanied by his tutor,
Hansell. The Prince of Wales's instructions were the same as *his*
father had given the college, that his son was to be treated in
exactly the same way as any other cadet. The change from a
sheltered, comfortable and privileged environment to sharing a
dormitory with 30 boisterous, and in some cases bullying, boys
came as a shock to him. Princess Mary did not agree with her
husband on her son's treatment. At the beginning of David's
second year at the college, Lord Esher recorded a conversation he
had had with her:

Princess: George refuses absolutely to make any distinction between the boys at Osborne and David.

E: I think he is right.

Princess: But George goes too far. I am most anxious that David should learn German. Captain Sinclair [one of the joint commanders at Osborne] objects, and says he *must* do what all the other boys do, and nothing different. You see how George has suffered from not knowing French and German. The other day in Paris *I* enjoyed everything. But he was not really amused. He knows nothing about pictures or history. He is told something about Francis I, and it conveys nothing to him.[43]

David's confidence grew during his second and last year at the college when he was joined by Bertie, and he was instructed by his father to supervise his brother in his studies. From being not far from the bottom of his class list at the end of the first term, David had worked his way up to reach an average grade. Esher commented at this time, after meeting the youth, 'He is wonderfully improved. Osborne has made him unshy, and given him good manners. He talked just like an Eton boy.'[44]

In May 1909, David, as was expected, entered Dartmouth, which he found 'much nicer'. His compatriots were now two years older, and he had made a number of friends. Academically, he did not shine; he showed a little promise at English, German and history but remained abysmally poor in all branches of mathematics.

David's life was to change in May 1910 when his grandfather, Edward VII, died and his father became King George V. He was now the Duke of Cornwall and, as heir apparent, the time had come for him to learn something about politics and statecraft. George arranged, through Hansell, that David should substitute for his engineering class the study of civics. One of the masters, George H. F. Cookson, arranged for him to read two daily newspapers, the *Morning Post* and the *Westminster Gazette*, the former a Conservative and the latter a Liberal newspaper. David wrote to his father, 'It is ever so much more interesting for me to follow the political proceedings now that I have been taught something of the country's constitution.' However, the King was not happy with this balance of views and considered *The Times* to be a safer option. David fell in with his father's wishes. 'I have changed the papers as you wished', he told the King, 'and Mr Cookson quite agreed, and said that he thought *The Times* put everything clearer and more to the point. So I now take *The Times*.'[45]

A few weeks after his sixteenth birthday, David was created Prince of Wales at an elaborate investiture at Caernarfon Castle. George V had already begun to consider the future career of his eldest son. David's entry into public life was postponed because of his apparent immaturity. In Esher's estimation, 'The boy is a mere child now, much of which is due to the limitations of his tutor [Hansell], a man, however, in whom the King reposes great confidence.'[46] Because of his involvement in the Coronation ceremony of his father, which took place in June 1911, David was obliged to forgo his last term at Dartmouth. This was a bitter blow, for he had set his heart on undertaking a final cruise which would qualify him as midshipman. But to his delight, a few weeks after his investiture, David was sent for by the King and informed that it had been decided by his ministers and the royal family that he should continue his career in the Royal Navy.[47] George V personally ordered that his son should serve during the summer on the battleship HMS *Hindustan*, carrying out his duties like any other junior officer. One irritating feature of the voyage for Edward was that Hansell was to accompany him, to coach him in school subjects in between his naval duties. After three months at sea, David was called to Sandringham to be told by his father that, in view of his position as Prince of Wales, he would have to leave the Navy as it was 'too specialised'. Instead, he would be making educational visits to France and Germany, as George had done after he had left the Navy. This was to be followed by a spell at Oxford. When it became clear that Hansell was behind the change of plan, David responded in unambiguous terms. As he wrote in his autobiography, 'What I had to say to the poor man after I left the Library was – to use a highly satisfactory American phrase – nobody's business.'[48]

Only three Oxford colleges were considered, Christ Church, New and Magdalen. Lord Derby advised the King that New College was unsatisfactory because the Archbishop of York, Cosmo Lang, had mentioned that there was much unspecified 'trouble' there; Christ Church, Derby believed, was also out of the question as, according to him, it was a college 'apparently where all the *nouveaux riches* go and where the sole object seems to be to spend money and prove themselves men instead of being what they are – boys'.[49] Magdalen suffered none of the disadvantages of the other two colleges. Hansell had also urged the selection of his own former college, and it was decided that the Prince would start at Oxford in October 1912. Before that, he spent five months in France, accompanied by a French tutor, M. Maurice Escoffier, who was on the staff of the Ecole des Sciences Politiques, and, inevitably, Hansell. Escoffier could speak little English, but by the end of the tour he had gained a far greater mastery of English than David had of French.

The King had asked the president of Magdalen, Sir Herbert Warren, to ensure that his son was treated in the same way as other undergraduates, whilst at the same time creating a situation which was aimed at isolating him from his contemporaries. Nothing had been left to chance. Warren had been summoned to Buckingham Palace to meet the Prince and was interviewed on more than one occasion by the King and Queen on the necessary arrangements for the Oxford sojourn.[50] One interesting new feature of David's student days at Oxford was that, unlike his father and grandfather, he was resident in the college itself rather than in a separate establishment. From the beginning, he was carefully supervised; he was given an equerry, Major the Hon. William Cadogan, his own valet, Finch, and Hansell, who occupied a room directly below his. It was even planned that Lord Derby's son, Edward Stanley, should be sent to Magdalen so that he should have a companion. David wrote to Bertie shortly afterwards, 'It is an awful situation and I only wish I was back quietly in the only service – the navy.'

The Prince had been excused the entrance examinations to the university as he was not taking a degree, and it was not certain at first if his course of study, which was aimed at broadening his educational horizon, would extend to a second year. He was at a disadvantage with the other undergraduates as he brought with him many of the practical skills which were a product of his naval training, whereas most of the other students had received a traditional public-school education, which fitted them well for their studies.

David's two years at Oxford did little to stimulate a love for learning. He attended a number of lectures at first but found many of them boring; individual tutorials were more to his liking. He studied French with M. Berthon, German with Professor Hermann Fiedler, history with Charles Grant Robinson, and political economy with the Revd Lancelot Ridley Phelps. Once a week the Prince, together with six other undergraduates, met Warren to study the humanities, with some emphasis on poetry. Warren was an uninspiring and unhelpful tutor, and the essays which David had to write for him did not encourage him to explore English literature on his own. Warren wrote of his pupil two years later, 'Bookish he will never be.'[51]

The most enjoyable sessions were with Sir William Anson, the Warden of All Souls, who taught him constitutional law. Anson, a splendid teacher with a good sense of humour and a kindly disposition, was also a practising politician, representing Oxford University as its MP for 15 years. He had been the first Parliamentary Secretary to the newly formed Board of Education and had assisted in the passage of the 1902 Education Bill through the House of Commons. Anson usually gave the Prince an hour's instruction on Monday mornings before going up to London to attend to parliamentary business. David made progress in the subject and over the two years they became personal friends. Anson reported to a colleague:

> The Prince wants to have a thorough knowledge of all the Constitutions. We have long done the English Constitution, and several of those of the chief countries: last week I got up the Swiss Constitution for his benefit, and I am now engaged in acquainting myself with that of Japan for the same purpose.[52]

During the Easter and summer vacations of 1913, the Prince made visits to Germany, accompanied by Professor Fiedler. He stayed with King Wilhelm and Queen Charlottte of Würrtemberg, the Grand Duke of Mecklenburg-Strelitz, saw the latest aircraft of Count Ferdinand von Zeppelin, and spent one night at the palace of Kaiser Wilhelm II. David wrote home stating that he had enjoyed seeing so many of his relatives.

By the time David left Oxford, he had blossomed socially, if not academically. He had become a good horseman under Cadogan's tuition, rode with the south Oxfordshire hounds and ran with the university beagles. Possessing great stamina, he indulged in many sports, including football, golf, tennis, shooting and polo and enjoyed motoring. His friend Chips Channon once remarked, 'He takes up things with violence … His amazing energy makes him indulge frantically in exercise, or stay up all night.'[53] He joined the Officers' Training Corps, rising to the rank of corporal and trained conscientiously as a soldier. It was at Oxford that he first developed his love of clothes, becoming well known for his dandyism. Whenever he was able to slip away from his guardians, he joined in the social activities, drinking, sometimes to excess, smoking and dancing. At the end of his second year at Oxford, as David remarked almost four decades later, 'The inhibitions from which I had suffered began to disappear, and I gained confidence in myself. In short, I was growing up.'[54] By this time he was also gaining a reputation for party-going and leading a hectic social life.

The Prince left Oxford, with the agreement of his parents, in June 1914 to start a career in the Army. With the outbreak of the First World War in August, he was given a commission in the Grenadier Guards, even though, standing at 5 feet 7 inches, he was 5 inches short of the regulation height. He was bitterly disappointed not to be allowed to see active service, and was instead attached to the staff of the headquarters of Sir John French, Commander-in-Chief of the British Expeditionary Force in France. He was highly embarrassed to be awarded the Military Cross although he had seen no fighting. One benefit which arose from his many visits to Allied troops in the different theatres of war, was that he met for the first time a range of people from every walk of life and from many different countries. The Prince acknowledged this when he wrote, 'My education was widened in the war, not through book or theory, but through the experience of being under all kinds of conditions with all manner of men.'[55]

After the war, the Prince's preparation for kingship, when he was given many more official duties to perform, was handicapped by poor father–son relations, aggravated by the Prince's tendency to disregard instructions from the King and advice from his own staff. His advisers were later to complain that the Prince insisted on his traditional rights but wanted to modify traditional practices which were not to his personal taste. He developed a dangerous inclination to make public utterances which were clearly of a political nature, such as the pro-German speech to the British Legion in 1935. David, who only read newspapers, failed to have a good grasp of the duties and responsibilities of a modern constitutional monarch. The events leading to his eventual abdication from the throne after the death of his father in 1936 showed his lack of understanding of his constitutional position and of the limits of his powers as a king. To some degree, this was clearly a failure of education and training. Exactly how much blame can be attached to those failures, as compared with his selfishness and the weakness of his own personality, it is impossible to say. But better education should certainly have been attempted. It is also difficult to assess how much of the problem was more fundamental and structural, that is, of the constitution itself. Should the constitution be formulated in such a way as to cater for monarchs who are neither very intelligent nor very hardworking?

On the other hand, Hector Bolitho, one of the more perceptive contemporaries of Edward VIII at the time of his Abdication, laid much of the blame for the monarch's failure on the events of his formative years. Writing in 1937 he stated:

> Most people have the opportunity of living in a chosen community, and those who join the Services or go to universities carry some of their friends with them from one sphere to the next. The Prince never enjoyed this privilege. Nothing seemed permanent to him except the responsibilities of his inheritance. He made friends at Osborne, but they went to sea while he stayed ashore. He sailed in the *Hindustan*, but he left the ship's company to go to Oxford. He was unable to enjoy the influence which growing friendships would have been for him. The lessons in personal loyalty which he would have learned through friendship seemed to pass him by. In considering the years of his education it is important and just that one should remember the many changes of which he was the victim, and understand, therefore, why it was not easy for him to remain loyal to a central purpose in the development of his mind and character.[56]

## GEORGE VI (1895–1952)

George VI was, like his brother Edward VIII, an example of a royal who did not view the prospect of becoming king with any enthusiasm. (Edward VII, by contrast, is reported at one stage to have remarked, 'I don't mind praying to the eternal Father, but I must be the only man in the country afflicted with an eternal mother.') Albert Frederick Arthur George, Prince Albert, known in the family as Bertie, was the second son of George Duke of York, later George V, and Princess Mary. He was born on 14 December 1895, the anniversary of the death of the Prince Consort, at York Cottage, Sandringham. His elder brother, David, was only 18 months older than him, though they were very different in temperament and character.

From an early age, Bertie suffered from poor health. He was placed in the care of the same cruel nurse who had caused David such anguish. As Bertie's official biographer has written:

> So completely did she disregard his wants and comforts that he was frequently given his afternoon bottle while driving in a C-sprung victoria, a process not dissimilar from a rough channel crossing – and with corresponding results. It is not surprising that the baby developed chronic stomach trouble, which may well have laid the foundation for the gastric complaint from which he was later to suffer so acutely.[57]

He was highly strung, excitable and nervous as a child, took rebuffs to heart and was prone to outbursts of anger. Bertie was subject to the same discipline as Edward had suffered at the hands of his father. 'Now that you are five years old', the Duke of York told his small son, 'I hope you will always try and be obedient and do at once what you are told, as you will find it will come much easier to you the sooner you begin.'[58] When David and Bertie visited their parents at teatime, the Princess would read them stories taken from royal history.

By the age of 7, Bertie had joined his brother to begin his formal education under Henry Hansell's tuition. He was from the start overshadowed by David's more outgoing and confident nature, though there were other reasons for his poor performance as a pupil. By nature, he was left-handed, but his parents, regarding it simply as unorthodox, insisted that he

15. Children of the Prince of Wales (George V) drilling, with the piper, Cameron and Forsyth. Left to right: Prince Henry, Princess Mary, Prince Albert (George VI) and Prince Edward (Edward VIII), 1905.

should be forced to write with his right hand. One result of this was that he developed a nervous stammer which remained with him for the rest of his life.[59] This handicap was to prove serious in the oral practice of foreign languages with his French and German tutors, where he would sometimes know the answer but had difficulty in uttering it.[60] As a result, he was wrongly described by his German teacher, Dr Oswald, as 'inattentive and playful'. When asked by Bertie's father to explain exactly what this meant, Oswald reluctantly explained, 'Your Royal Highness, it isn't only that Prince Albert is inattentive; but when I scold him, he just pulls my beard.'[61]

A further disability was that, like his father and all his brothers except David, Bertie suffered from knock knees. In an attempt to correct this defect, a system of splints had been devised which Bertie wore during the day and, for a while, also at night. The experiment proved to be a painful one for the wearer, though the Prince bore it stoically. 'I am sitting in an arm chair with my legs in the new splints and on a chair,' he wrote to his mother. ' I have got an invalid table, which is splendid for reading but rather awkward for writing at present. I expect I shall get used to it.'[62] Nevertheless, Hansell was soon reporting that the splints were affecting his pupil's progress. The situation improved slightly when he was allowed to dispense with them during the day.

The Prince's weakest subject was mathematics, despite the efforts of his tutor, Martin Davis. The combination of an unequal temperament and physical disabilities led to angry explosions. 'Division by 2 seems to be quite beyond him', reported Hansell to Bertie's father. 'Prince Albert has caused two painful scenes in the bedroom this week.'[63]

However, there was much compensation for these setbacks. He was on very good terms with his two closest siblings, David and Mary, who was 18 months younger than him. Bertie followed the high-spirited duo into many kinds of mischief. He admired David's easy charm and lack of inhibition, and was fond of his sister, though it has been claimed that, being sandwiched between two such attractive and outgoing children, Bertie caught little of the limelight.[64] David was the natural leader of the threesome. Reginald Esher described a scene he had witnessed at Windsor when David was 9 and Bertie was 8:

It was queer looking through a weekly paper, and coming to a picture of the eldest with the label 'our future King'. Prince Albert at once drew attention to it – but the elder hastily brushed his brother's finger away and turned the page. Evidently he thought it bad taste.[65]

When David departed from the schoolroom for Osborne in the spring of 1907, Bertie was joined by his brother Prince Henry, who was some five years younger. Hansell made Bertie 'head boy' of the small establishment, hoping that it would give him a greater sense of responsibility, but Bertie did not respond to this minor challenge.

Unlike his elder brother, Bertie was on reasonably good terms with his parents. Harold Nicolson, in writing his official biography of George V, was warned by Sir Owen Morshead, the librarian at Windsor Castle, that the trickiest part of his book would be in dealing with the King's relations with his children. 'The House of Hanover', he declared, 'like ducks, produce bad parents. They trample on their young.'[66] This was less true in Bertie's case. The future George V recognised the similarities they shared in character, ranging from their sobriety, industry and religious convictions, to their tastes in countryside sports, especially shooting. In 1923, the King wrote to Bertie, now Duke of York:

> You have always been so sensible and easy to work with and you have always been ready to listen to any advice and to agree with my opinions about people and things, that I feel that we have always got on very well together (very different to dear David).[67]

Much later, after the Abdication crisis, Walter Monckton, a close confidant of the Duke of Windsor, recorded a conversation which he had had with Bertie, now King George VI:

> I was sitting with him in his room at Balmoral Castle when he told me that this was the only room in which he had real discussions with his father. He said that his father had always treated his brothers as if they were all the same whereas in fact they were totally different in character. He then said: 'It was very difficult for David. My father was so inclined to go for him. I always thought it a pity that he found fault over unimportant things – like what he wore.'[68]

Bertie saw comparatively little of his mother because of official ceremonial duties or social activities at home or overseas with her husband. Princess Mary had become more repressed since her marriage to Prince George and rarely showed any emotion in his presence. The children did not feel close to her either. Bertie confided to his brother David in 1928 when King George was seriously ill:

> Through all this anxiety she never once revealed her feelings to any of us. She really is far too reserved; she keeps too much locked up inside herself.[69]

In 1909, when Bertie was 13, he joined his brother David at Osborne; the entrance examination in December had involved much cramming for the mathematics paper, but he did very well at English, French and history. The interview itself had been a great worry because of his shyness and stutter. In his first term at Osborne, he was withdrawn and suffered from homesickness, having been thrust into an environment quite strange to him. However, he soon gained in confidence and found it easy to make long-term friends. With the death of his grandfather, Edward VII, in 1910, he believed that he was safe in the knowledge that, unlike David, he would not be haunted by the shade of the monarchy.[70] He was fortunate in coming under the influence of two exceptional officers, Lieutenant William Phipps and Surgeon-Lieutenant Lewis Greig. The former, who was a good athlete, encouraged the young prince to display his talents for games which won the admiration of his fellow cadets. Greig was then an assistant medical officer who first looked after the Prince when he had a bout of whooping cough, and who proved to be a role model for Bertie: he was to remain a close friend, holding various official household posts until the Prince's marriage to Elizabeth Bowes-Lyon in 1923.

Despite his efforts, the Prince struggled to make any academic progress, remaining near the bottom of the list in the termly examinations. But his tutor wrote of him hopefully, 'With Prince Albert's mercurial temperament all things are possible.'[71]

Albert joined his comrades at the Royal Naval College, Dartmouth in January 1911. To improve his confidence, he was assigned two officers, Engineer-Lieutenant Sydney Start, who gave him coaching in mathematics and engineering, and Lieutenant Henry Spencer, who furthered his skills in horse riding, tennis and other sports.

When his father was crowned King George V in June, Albert's participation in the Coronation ceremony involved his absence from Dartmouth. His poor showing in the summer term examinations – 67th out of 68 – was followed by tuition for two hours a day in physics and mathematics at Balmoral by James Watt, the science master from Osborne. Some slight improvement was noticeable as a result and by Christmas he was placed 63rd in the list.

Life at Dartmouth was not all serious. He was punished, together with 16 other cadets, for setting off fireworks in the lavatory on Guy Fawkes night. The Prince, together with the other malefactors, received six strokes of the cane, though Albert subsequently maintained that as the cane had broken at the fourth stroke, he should not have received the remaining two.

His confirmation earlier in the year had been a moving and spiritual experience which remained with him for the rest of his life. Bertie had matured and made more progress during his last six months at Dartmouth and he ended his final term 61st out of the 68 cadets.

His initial naval education ended when he made a training voyage on the cruiser HMS *Cumberland* in January 1913: the tour included visits to the West Indies and Canada. Although he was supposedly treated like any other cadet, Bertie had to perform some ceremonial duties during the course of the voyage. His stammer made this aspect of the tour a painful one and he subsequently entered into a pact of secrecy with another cadet, whose features were remarkably like his own, to carry out such duties for him. Bertie had a puckish sense of humour, and later in the voyage persuaded another cadet to talk to the press as if he were the Prince himself. His stand-in assured the assembled reporters that he received no special privileges except that he wore a bowler hat on Sundays. Shortly after the end of the six months' voyage, Bertie attained the rank of midshipman.

In the autumn of that year, he received his first appointment, to the battleship HMS *Collingwood*, which was ordered to join the manoeuvres in the Mediterranean. In theory, he was a mere midshipman, but as the King's son he was singled out for special treatment. When the Commander-in-Chief, Mediterranean, and the admiral commanding the battleship went to stay with King George's friend, Lord Kitchener, in Cairo, Bertie was taken with them to be presented to the Khedive.[72]

He was still serving aboard the *Collingwood* when Britain declared war on Germany in August 1914. Later in the same month he was diagnosed as having appendicitis and was operated upon. Bertie subsequently suffered from a series of illnesses, particularly gastric attacks, which limited his opportunities for active service. He was on board the *Collingwood*, but in the sick bay, in May 1916 when the First Squadron engaged the German High Seas Fleet at Jutland. When the battle began, Bertie leapt out of bed and watched the proceedings from the top of a gun turret until a salvo of German shells passed over his head, causing him to take rapid cover. This was to be the high point for the Prince during the war, for illness once more intervened, and his naval career came to an end in December 1917.


Air power had proved to be a new and powerful dimension of warfare on the Western Front and plans were laid for the establishment of the Royal Air Force in April 1918. King George was anxious for one of his sons to be identified with the new organisation, and Bertie was appointed in January 1918 to HMS *Daedalus*, a training station at Cranwell, Lincolnshire, for officers and boys of the Royal Naval Air Service and the Royal Flying Corps. He was given responsibility for supervising the 2,500 boys on the camp and proved to be a strict disciplinarian. 'I never trouble my head about myself now', he wrote to his mother, 'as I feel a different person.' Even so, he was not allowed to lead a normal officer's life, living with Louis Greig and his wife in a nearby village. This pattern was repeated when he was posted to St Leonards in Sussex.

With the war about to end, the King decided that Bertie should not make a quick return to civilian life, as there had been some malicious gossip about his prolonged absence from active service.[73] Instead, he was sent to Belgium to join the staff of the Commander-in-Chief of the Royal Air Force on the Western Front. When he returned to England, Bertie learnt to fly, though without much enthusiasm, and became the first member of the royal family to receive his wings as a pilot.

He was now 23 years of age and would have liked to have remained in the services. His father had, however, decided differently. Bertie wrote to one of his former tutors at Dartmouth in July 1919, 'I am giving up a service career now, and go to Cambridge in October for a year, to learn everything that will be useful for the time to come.'[74] He was sent to Trinity College, Cambridge, accompanied by his less gifted brother, Prince Henry. With the recent experience of David's sojourn at Oxford still vividly in mind, the King insisted that his sons should not live in college. A house in Trumpington Road, about a mile from Trinity, was leased and they were joined once more by Greig, now Bertie's equerry, and his wife, as watchdogs.

The year's course of study embraced history, civics and economics. Like his mother, Bertie was fascinated by history and he was inspired by one of his tutors, J. R. M. Butler, who had served in Gallipoli and Egypt during the war.[75] Butler was the author of *The Passing of the Great Reform Bill*, published in 1914, and Bertie enjoyed his tutorials with him. The Prince also read Dicey's *Law of the Constitution* and Bagehot with great interest. According to a recent biographer, he became an expert on the subject, later showing a greater understanding of constitutional issues than either his official legal adviser or even Winston Churchill.[76] Another young tutor, Dennis Robertson, who had also been a distinguished soldier, introduced the Prince to economics. Robertson was an expert on industrial fluctuation and money; his lively teaching was to be of practical use to Bertie in the coming years.

After the First World War, there was social unrest in Britain, caused by high unemployment and poor living conditions. At a meeting at the Albert Hall on the third anniversary of the Russian Revolution, the King's name was hissed and there was some nervousness in Court circles.[77] In 1919, Bertie had met the Revd Robert Hyde, who, as a temporary civil servant, had made a study of the working conditions of men and boys in factories. In the previous year, Hyde had set up the Boys' Welfare Association to improve their working conditions and to 'provide proper facilities for the maximum enjoyment of the workers' free time'.

At the end of the Easter term 1920, Bertie left Cambridge and was created Duke of York by his father. Now with more time on his hands, he agreed to become the Association's president. He took his position seriously, visiting factories, coal mines, building sites and various other workplaces, talking to workers and management about their problems. His brother David nicknamed him 'The Foreman', a soubriquet which was used within the family for many years.[78] The Association, which changed its name to the Industrial Welfare Society, continued to be one of the Duke's major interests until he became king. As late as 1930, Bertie told the Prime Minister, Ramsay MacDonald, that 'he would be very glad if he could be used as a figurehead for any movement or organisation for encouraging industrial progress'.[79]

An interesting development from the work of the Industrial Welfare Society was the Duke's idea that it would be beneficial if ways could be explored in which boys from public schools and industry could be brought together in a common purpose. He put forward a plan whereby 100 public schools and 100 industrial firms would each nominate two boys to attend a camp at New Romney, on the Kent coast, where the participants from different walks of life could live and play for a week as a community in order to gain a better understanding of each other. The Duke of York's Camps, in which the Duke himself participated – the image of Bertie joining in the singing and actions of 'Underneath the Spreading Chestnut Tree' is an enduring one – was an idealistic experiment which received widespread publicity and ended only with the outbreak of the Second World War in 1939. When Clement Attlee became Prime Minister six years later, he remarked that Bertie, now George VI, had a 'real knowledge of industry and understood the mind of working people very well'.[80]

Bertie's education, both formal and informal, had lasted much longer than that of many of his predecessors. He had more physical obstacles to overcome than his elder brother, which left their mark on his character, and he had to endure the same strict upbringing as his five brothers and sisters. It was little wonder that he regarded the abdication of his brother in 1936 as a personal tragedy. As he told his cousin, Lord Louis Mountbatten:

> Dickie, this is absolutely terrible. I never wanted this to happen;
> I'm quite unprepared for it. David has been trained for this all his

life. I've never even seen a State Paper. I'm only a Naval Officer, it's the only thing I know about.'[81]

Nevertheless, his reign was a successful one. As one writer has observed, 'George VI had grown steadily into the practice of kingship and became, in a little over ten years, the standard by which the monarchy itself was to be measured.'[82] A religious man who hid his deeper feelings, conscious of his constitutional responsibilities and conducting a model family life, he helped to restore the monarchy to a popularity which had not been witnessed for many reigns. His unusual lengthy and practical education probably played an important part in bringing this about.

The period covered by this chapter encompassed several major educational reforms: not simply the establishment of free primary and secondary education as a right for all children, but also the making of higher education more accessible. Educational ideas and theories continued to develop, and it began to be accepted that high-quality education was a prerequisite for a developed democratic society.

These changes tended to progress at the same time as further advances were made towards limited monarchy. In many other countries, the contradiction between democracy and hereditary monarchy proved too great, and many of the famous royal dynasties disappeared. In Britain a form of constitutional monarchy survived. Two of our three kings, George V and George VI, adapted very well to their constitutional role, but Edward VIII failed dramatically. His reign served as a reminder that unsuitable kings could be removed, and as a demonstration that constitutional monarchy was so firmly entrenched as part of the British way of life that it could survive one unsuitable monarch, provided that he did not stay too long.

The education of both Edward VIII and George VI was very similar, almost identical, but the outcome was completely different. The lesson to be learned from that is not clear: it might mean that personality counts for more than training, or, alternatively, that the education and training programmes which were provided were inadequate. Had they been better, Edward

16. Henry Hansell, (left), tutor to Prince Albert (George VI) and Prince Edward (Edward VIII) with the children of the Prince of Wales (George V) and others: Prince Edward (Edward VIII), white jumper, Prince Albert (George VI), dark clothes, Prince Henry, lying on sledge, Princess Mary, and Prince John, with lady on sledge, Sandringham, 5 January 1908.

VIII might have become a perfect constitutional monarch. As educationists, we reluctantly come to the conclusion that the former hypothesis is the more likely.

NOTES

1. G. Battiscombe, *Queen Alexandra* (Constable, 1969), p. 121.
2. E. E. P. Tisdall, *Unpredictable Queen: The Intimate Life of Queen Alexandra* (Stanley Paul, 1953), p. 107.
3. A. A. Smith, *Our Sailor King* (John F. Shaw, 1910), p. 13.
4. H. Dalton, *Call Back Yesterday: Memoirs 1887–1931* (Muller, 1953), p. 24.
5. H. Nicolson, *King George the Fifth: His Life and Reign* (Constable, 1952), p. 7.
6. G. F.-H. Berkeley, *Wellington College: The Founders of the Tradition* (Newport, Mon., R. H. Johns, 1948), p. 21.
7. J. E. Vincent, *His Royal Highness the Duke of Clarence and Avondale* (Murray, 1893), p. 62.
8. G. E. Buckle (ed.), *The Letters of Queen Victoria*, 2nd series, vol. II, 1870–78 (John Murray, 1926), p. 575.
9. E. A. Hughes, *The Royal Naval College, Dartmouth* (Winchester Publications, 1950), pp. 21–2.
10. P. Gibbs, *George the Faithful: The Life and Times of George V* (Hutchinson, 1936), p. 19.
11. M. Harrison, *Clarence: The Life of HRH the Duke of Clarence and Avondale* (W. H. Allen, 1972), p. 46.
12. B. Pimlott, *Hugh Dalton* (Cape, 1985), p. 10.
13. Prince Albert Victor and Prince George of Wales, *The Cruise of Her Majesty's Ship Bacchante, 1879–1882*, vol. I (Macmillan, 1886), p. viii.
14. Ibid., pp. x–xi.
15. Battiscombe, *Queen Alexandra*, p. 141.
16. Prince Albert Victor and Prince George of Wales, *The Cruise of HMS Bacchante*, vol. II, p. 800.
17. Harrison, *Clarence*, p. 16.
18. K. Rose, *King George V* (Weidenfeld & Nicolson, 1983), p. 17.
19. J. Gore, 'George V', in L. G. Wickham Legg (ed.), *Dictionary of National Biography, 1931–1940* (Oxford University Press, 1949), pp. 315–16.
20. J. Stephenson (ed.), *A Royal Correspondence: Letters of King Edward VII and King George V to Admiral Sir Henry F. Stephenson* (Macmillan, 1938), pp. 62–3.
21. Ibid., p. 64.
22. Nicolson, *King George V*, p. 38.
23. T. Aronson, *Prince Eddy and the Homosexual Underworld* (Murray, 1994), p. 117.
24. A. Edwards, *Matriarch: Queen Mary and the House of Windsor* (Hodder & Stoughton, 1984), p. 57.
25. Nicolson, *King George V*, p. 63.
26. Lord Riddell, *More Pages from My Diary* (Country Life, 1934), p. 218.
27. J. Gore, *King George V: A Personal Memoir* (Murray, 1941), pp. 247–8.
28. Duke of Windsor, *A King's Story* (Cassell, 1951), p. 7.
29. Edwards, *Matriarch*, p. 39.
30. J. Pope-Hennessy, *Queen Mary* (Allen & Unwin, 1959), p. 172.
31. Duke of Windsor, *A Family Album* (Cassell, 1960), p. 24.
32. Gibbs, *George the Faithful*, p. 95.
33. A. H. Fox-Strangways, *Cecil Sharp* (Oxford University Press, 1933), p. 52.
34. F. C. Donaldson, *Edward VIII* (Weidenfeld & Nicolson, 1974), p. 18.
35. M. V. Brett (ed.), *Journals and Letters of Reginald, Viscount Esher*, vol. I (Ivor Nicholson & Watson, 1934), pp. 330–1.
36. Hansell had earlier successfully coached the Duke of Connaught's son, Prince Arthur, for entry to Eton.
37. Smith, *Our Sailor King*, p. 69.

38. C. Hibbert, *Edward: The Uncrowned King* (Macdonald, 1972), p. 4.
39. R. S. Churchill, *Lord Derby 'King of Lancashire'* (Heinemann, 1959), p. 159.
40. J. Ellis (ed.), *Thatched with Gold: The Memoirs of Mabell, Countess of Airlie* (Hutchinson, 1962), p. 112.
41. N. Frankland, *Prince Henry, Duke of Gloucester* (Weidenfeld & Nicolson, 1980), p. 30.
42. P. Ziegler, *King Edward VIII* (Collins, 1990), p. 20.
43. J. Lees-Milne, *The Enigmatic Edwardian: The Life of Reginald, 2nd Viscount Esher* (Sidgwick & Jackson, 1986), p. 188.
44. Brett, *Viscount Esher*, vol. II, p.305.
45. Duke of Windsor, *A King's Story*, p. 74.
46. Donaldson, *Edward VIII*, p. 35.
47. W. and L. Townsend, *The Biography of HRH The Prince of Wales* (Albert E. Marriott, 1929), p. 70.
48. Duke of Windsor, *A King's Story*, p. 81.
49. Churchill, *Lord Derby*, p. 157.
50. L. Magnus, *Herbert Warren of Magdalen* (John Murray, 1932), pp. 180-1.
51. *The Times*, 18 Nov. 1914, p. 11.
52. H. H. Henson (ed.), *A Memoir of the Right Honourable Sir William Anson* (Oxford, Clarendon Press, 1920), p. 132.
53. R. Rhodes James (ed.), *Chips: The Diaries of Sir Henry Channon* (Penguin, 1970), p. 67.
54. Duke of Windsor, *A King's Story*, p. 104.
55. Ibid., p. 126.
56. H. Bolitho, *King Edward VIII: His Life and Reign* (Eyre & Spottiswoode, 1937), p. 16.
57. J. W. Wheeler-Bennett, *King George VI: His Life and Reign* (Macmillan, 1958), p. 17.
58. Rose, *King George V*, p. 55.
59. A. A. Michie, *The Crown and the People* (Secker & Warburg, 1952), p. 126.
60. P. Howarth, *George VI* (Hutchinson, 1987), p. 14.
61. Duke of Windsor, *A King's Story*, p. 39.
62. Wheeler-Bennett, *King George VI*, p. 28.
63. D. Duff, *George and Elizabeth: A Royal Marriage* (Collins, 1983), p. 38.
64. C. Warwick, *King George VI and Queen Elizabeth* (Sidgwick & Jackson, 1985), p. 27.
65. Brett, *Viscount Esher*, vol. II, p. 53.
66. J. Lees-Milne, *Harold Nicolson: A Biography* (Chatto & Windus, 1981), p. 230.
67. Rose, *King George V*, p. 309.
68. Lord Birkenhead, *Walter Monckton: The Life of Viscount Monckton of Brenchley* (Weidenfeld & Nicolson, 1969), p. 124.
69. Pope-Hennessy, *Queen Mary*, p. 514.
70. H. Bolitho, *George VI* (Eyre & Spottiswoode, 1937), p. 31.
71. Wheeler-Bennett, *King George VI*, p. 45.
72. S. Bradford, *King George VI* (Weidenfeld & Nicolson, 1989), p. 57.
73. D. Judd, *King George VI: 1895–1952* (Michael Joseph, 1982), p. 43.
74. Wheeler-Bennett, *King George VI*, p. 126.
75. S. W. Roskill, 'Sir James Ramsay Montagu Butler', in Lord Blake and C. S. Nicholls (eds), *Dictionary of National Biography, 1971–1980* (Oxford University Press, 1986), p. 113.
76. Bradford, *King George VI*, p. 86.
77. Michie, *The Crown and the People*, p. 131.
78. During the First World War, rumours that the King and Queen were only lukewarm in their support of the Allied war effort led in 1917 to King George changing the title of the dynasty to the House of Windsor. On hearing this, the Kaiser expressed his wish to see a performance of Nicolai's well-known opera, 'The Merry Wives of Saxe-Coburg-Gotha'.
79. T. Jones,*Whitehall Diary*, ed. K. Middlemas, vol. II: 1926–1930 (Oxford University Press, 1969), p. 247.
80. T. Burridge, *Clement Attlee: A Political Biography* (Cape, 1985), p. 216.
81. Wheeler-Bennett, *King George VI*, p. 294.
82. K. Middlemas, *The Life and Times of George VI* (Weidenfeld & Nicolson, 1974), p. 202.

# 7 The Two Elizabeths and the Heirs to the Throne:
## Continuity and Tradition

ONE OF THE more spectacular features of British society over the last four decades of the twentieth century has been the growth of public concern over the provision of and equal access to education. An incidental result of this movement has been a growing curiosity about the schooling of royals which has not been witnessed since the early years of Victoria and Albert's marriage.

At the time when Elizabeth ascended the throne in 1952, planners and politicians were preoccupied with coping with the effects of the postwar population explosion. Towards the end of the 1950s, however, a series of committees began to investigate the need for reforms in the system in order to enable wider access to secondary and higher education. The Crowther Committee's Report *15 to 18*, commissioned 'in the light of the changing social and industrial needs of society' and published in 1959, recommended the raising of the school leaving age to 16; this was achieved in the years 1972–73. In 1960, the Beloe Committee on secondary school examinations turned public attention to a large number of secondary school pupils who were effectively barred from taking recognised public examinations. A new structure was recommended which ultimately led to a large increase in those taking school examinations. But perhaps the most far-reaching reforms followed the Robbins Report (1963), which called for a large expansion in the provision of university places and the creation of more universities. As a result the number of students has doubled over the past four decades.

Not only were educational opportunities rising but the structure of the education system itself was changing. There had

197

been growing disenchantment among parents of all classes with the '11-plus' examination which segregated children into different types of school at this age. In 1965 the Labour government set out the different ways in which local education authorities were to establish comprehensive schools. The momentum continued under both Conservative and Labour governments until the 1980s. This led to the ending of selection procedures in the majority of local education authorities.

The public schools also came under scrutiny. A Public School Commission, established in 1965 'to advise on the best way of integrating public schools within the State system', opened one of the chapters in its report, 'Some people have objected to the assumption in our terms of reference that the public schools are a divisive influence. One answer to this objection is that public schools themselves think they are.'[1]

Critics of these schools were not confined to one party. Sir Robin Williams wrote in a (Conservative) Bow Group pamphlet *Whose Public Schools?* in 1957:

> The public schools – as at present organized – therefore attract a degree of envy and resentment which is unhealthy in a stable democracy. Even if only to divert this potentially destructive emotion, Conservatives ought to consider the desirability of broadening the basis of recruitment to the public schools.[2]

Though outright reform has not taken place, the public-school image has been changing. The term 'independent' has replaced 'public' and co-educational schools are now not uncommon. It is still true, however, in the words of evidence submitted to the Public Schools Commission by governors and heads of such schools, that 'only the better-off can afford to send their sons to us, and our parents, therefore, all come from the upper income brackets'. Despite the acceptance of the principle of equality of educational opportunity, especially since the 1944 Education Act, the independent schools have not only survived but have flourished. This may be regarded as a contradiction, a paradox or an interesting example of English hypocrisy. In any case, the result has been that education in England has remained more class based than in any other modern society. As we shall see in Chapter 8, this presents the royal family with a problem; should they follow the example of the upper classes (and others) who buy a privileged education; or should they attempt to identify with the other 93 per cent of the population and make use of free maintained schools? The second alternative has not been seriously considered.

The public's fascination with royalty in all its manifestations has been greatly enhanced by the coming of television and the greater coverage, both in words and picture, in the press. An example of this, unthinkable in an earlier age, occurred during Prince Charles's schooldays at Hill House, Cheam and Gordonstoun. Finally, it should be remembered that all the main political parties now place quality of education at the top of their agendas. It is not surprising, therefore, that decisions regarding the most appropriate form of education for potential heirs to the throne, now made in the full glare of publicity, need to be approached with great care and caution.

### ELIZABETH THE QUEEN MOTHER (1900–)

We have already described in a previous chapter the boyhood and training of Elizabeth's father, Albert, Duke of York, later King George VI. In great contrast, Elizabeth's mother, Elizabeth Bowes-Lyon, now popularly known as the Queen Mother, was brought up in a very different environment. She was the ninth of ten children of one of the outstanding women of her time, Nina Cavendish-Bentinck, and her husband, Claude Bowes-Lyon, who succeeded as the 14th Earl of Strathmore and Kinghorne. Born eight months after the turn of the new century, on 4 August 1900, Elizabeth was already at the age of 13 months being called 'the Princess' because of her charm and bearing. The Strathmores, one of the oldest Scottish families, carried on the tradition of service and loyalty to causes which Elizabeth absorbed from her father. Elizabeth's mother, a warm and vivacious person, had written a children's book on British plants and took a personal interest in her family's education. Elizabeth had her first lessons in drawing, painting and dancing from her and soon learned to value each person on his or her merits and how to put people at their ease.[3] Lady Strathmore was widely read, had a talent for music and art and was an admirer of the teaching of Froebel which emphasised the value of play.[4] She encouraged her family to become self-confident, and life at

Glamis Castle was a relaxed one. Busier times were spent at their southern homes at St Paul's, Walden Bury, Hertfordshire, and 20 St James's Square, London.[5]

Elizabeth and her brother David were taught to read and write and were introduced to Bible stories by their mother. When she was 6 a governess was employed, Clara Knight, known as Allah, who was also in charge of the nursery. She developed in the children a love of history and literature, and there were also French and German governesses. Accomplishments for young ladies in the form of dancing, singing and piano playing were included in the curriculum. It is interesting to note that at one stage a boarding school education was considered for Elizabeth, but this was ultimately rejected.[6] Instead, when the family were at their London home in St James's Square, she was sent to the Misses Birtwistle's Academy at 30 Sloane Square. It was a broad curriculum and Elizabeth excelled at history, French, scripture and literature, winning a prize for one of her essays.

For some unknown reason, Elizabeth's parents decided to withdraw her after two terms, probably considering that a private governess was more appropriate. Now that girls were being entered for public examinations it was desirable that she should direct her efforts towards this end. In July 1914, Elizabeth passed the Oxford Preliminary Examination in seven subjects – English, arithmetic, history, geography, French, German and drawing. A few weeks later, with outbreak of the First World War, her formal education came to an end.

Her engagement in January 1923 to Albert, Duke of York, who was second in line of succession to the throne, came as a surprise to the general public. The novelty lay in the fact that the royal family had for the previous 140 years always married royal, and usually foreign, wives. Elizabeth, a commoner, was the first British wife of royalty since James II, then also Duke of York, had married Lady Anne Hyde. After their marriage, the Yorks had no settled home. They were first at the White Lodge in Richmond Park but it proved to be too expensive to run. While negotiations for a London house were in progress, their first child, Elizabeth, was born on 21 April 1926 at the Strathmores' London home at 17 Bruton Street.

ELIZABETH II (1926–)

In 1688 James II's second wife, Mary of Modena, a Catholic, had given birth prematurely to a boy, and there was a suspicion by the Whigs that the baby had died and a substitute smuggled into the palace in a warming pan. Since then it had been the custom for a Minister of the Crown to witness royal births. Accordingly, William Joynson-Hicks, the Labour Home Secretary, was called to Bruton Street on the birth of Elizabeth. It was not until 1948, when Prince Charles was born, that this archaic custom was finally abolished.[7]

When Elizabeth was 5 months old the Yorks moved into 145 Piccadilly, within easy reach of Buckingham Palace. The family was completed in August 1930 with the birth of a second daughter, Margaret Rose, though this time the Duchess chose her parents' Scottish home, Glamis Castle, for the occasion.

In bringing up their children, the Yorks chose for their staff women who would provide stability by staying in their posts for a considerable time. Continuity was assured with the appointment of the Duchess's own former nanny, Clara Knight (Allah) and of Margaret MacDonald (Bobo) as under-nurse; the latter who later became the Princess's royal dresser, gave 67 years' service in all. In March 1932, when Elizabeth was 6 and Margaret 2 years old, a Scottish teacher, Marion Crawford, was appointed as governess for a trial period of a month but remained in the post for 17 years. The appointment was an unusual one. 'Crawfie', as she was called, was only 22 and had taken a two-year teacher-training course at Moray House, Edinburgh. She was filling in time teaching the children of one of the Duchess of York's sisters when she was invited to become governess to the Princesses.

In 1950, after her retirement, Miss Crawford published an account of her time with the York household entitled *The Little Princesses*. It provides some valuable insights into royal thinking as well as Miss Crawford's on what was considered an appropriate education for the Princesses. Written in a bland manner, the book's publication was nevertheless widely condemned in Court circles as breaking confidences.

Crawfie was surprised at the extent to which she was left in charge of the children. She wrote later:

> No one ever had employers who interfered so little. I had often the feeling that the Duke and Duchess, most happy in their own married life, were not over concerned with the higher education of their daughters. They wanted most for them a really happy childhood, with lots of pleasant memories stored up against the days that might come and, later, happy marriages.[8]

She found that Princess Elizabeth could already read. The Duchess, following the example set by her own mother, had begun to read aloud Bible stories and had introduced the Princesses to a wide range of children's books.[9] George V, on meeting Miss Crawford for the first time, made clear his priorities for the governess: 'For goodness sake', he boomed, 'teach Margaret and Lilibet to write a decent hand, that's all I ask of you. Not one of my children can write properly. They all do it exactly the same way. I like a hand with some character in it.'[10] His wife, Queen Mary, on seeing the first draft of the proposed curriculum, suggested that history, geography and Bible reading should figure more prominently and that the study of genealogical trees should be included. Arithmetic she considered to be of less importance.

There were two striking features of the finally agreed curriculum. One was that it was did not attempt to be highly academic in character, possibly reflecting Crawfie's own background. The second was its remarkable similarity to that endured by Elizabeth's nineteenth-century forebears. The weekly timetable, occupying six days, followed a regular pattern. Lessons of 30 minutes' duration, began at 9.30 a.m. on Mondays with religious knowledge, though for the rest of the week that period was occupied with arithmetic. In all there were four sessions of history, two on grammar and single lessons on geography, poetry, literature and composition. From 11 a.m. to midday was devoted to recreation, followed by an hour's reading, both silent and aloud. After lunch, there were more recreational activies such as painting, music (mainly singing) and dancing. Saturday mornings were occupied with the revision of the week's work. One of Miss Crawford's more original ideas was to cultivate the Princess's interest in the fine arts. To this end each week she had one of the great masterpieces from the Royal Collection brought from the store and placed on an easel in the classroom. Visits to art galleries to view the great masterpieces were made with their governess and, on occasions, with Queen Mary. But, as one royal biographer, has written, 'All it can confidently be stated that the future Elizabeth II acquired from these exercises was the ability to keep walking with every expression of great interest on her face when her feet were hurting her and it was getting towards teatime.'[11]

At a very early age she was encouraged to take a keen interest in animals, especially horses. Her large collection of miniature horses, which she saddled each morning and were kept on the landing outside her bedroom, is reminiscent of Victoria, who was equally isolated, with her collection of dolls. The Princess was only 5 when, riding a Shetland pony, she accompanied her father in Northamptonshire at a meet of the Pytchley hounds. Riding instruction became a regular feature of the curriculum. Dogs, in the absence of fellow playmates, also provided much-needed companionship.

The official school day ended at 4.45 p.m., when tea might be taken with a select group of children such as their Harewood cousins. Whenever possible, the Princesses' parents tried to spend the hour before supper playing games of various sorts with them. Conscious of the sternness of his own upbringing, the Duke of York was anxious to ensure that his own children enjoyed their parents' company. The family became a close and devoted unit which the different forms of media were quick to portray. This concern for the welfare of their children extended to the Princesses' education as well as their social life. After becoming king in 1936, George VI inspected the schoolroom in Buckingham Palace where he had been taught as a boy – a dark attic room with equally dark portraits on the walls. Miss Crawford, who was with him at the time reported:

> The King stood in the doorway for a few minutes looking round in silence – no doubt remembering his own childhood spent up here, doing lessons on gloomy afternoons. I remember he turned away slowly, shutting the door behind him. 'No', he said, 'that won't do.'[12]

Certainly a premium was placed on happiness and for this reason formal education, especially for girls at that time, was not taken too seriously. It may seem strange that the Duchess of York, who was successful at public examinations as a girl, did not wish her daughters to follow her example. However, it could be argued that the Duchess was not, at the time, unlike her daughter Princess Elizabeth, being prepared as a future monarch.[13] It was considered sufficient to inculcate good manners and deportment with an emphasis on accomplishments and sport rather than on intellectual achievements. There is evidence to show that this attitude was not confined to Court circles. It was reported by *The Times* on Elizabeth's tenth birthday that her studies had been planned 'in consultation with the leading educationalists in the country' and had then received Cabinet approval.

However, it is not certain that the Duchess was in favour of a restricted type of education. A book entitled *Queen Elizabeth the Queen Mother*, published in 1966 and written by Dorothy Laird, states on the title page that the Queen Mother gave assistance to the author in preparing the first authorised biography of her. While the Queen Mother admitted that 'given the choice *between* [her italics] higher education and good character training, she would make her choice without a second's hesitation. If both could be achieved, so much the better'. The passage continued:

> When Princess Elizabeth was seven, plans for her education were reviewed. Both the Duke and Duchess of York wished to send Princess Elizabeth to school, believing that it would be good for her to have the normal experience and discipline of a schoolgirl. But the King was adamant: Princess Elizabeth was third in the line of succession, it had always been traditional that the heir to the throne should be privately educated, and he wished his granddaughter to be privately educated too ... The Princesses were the grand-daughters of the Sovereign and their upbringing was more than normally important.[14]

In 1936 events moved rapidly and unexpectedly. Within the space of that one year there were three Kings of England. George V died, Edward VIII abdicated and the Duke of York, with the greatest reluctance, became George VI. The family's move to Buckingham Palace involved a number of changes for Princess Elizabeth. She was now heir presumptive and, like Victoria in her time, she had to be groomed for possible succession. Shortly after the King's accession, *The Times*, in an obviously carefully mounted public relations exercise, outlined the extent of

Elizabeth's course of study:

> It covers not only the normal school subjects, but many others, such as economics, upon which, as possible future Queen, she must be more than usually well informed. It is, indeed, a little frightening to contemplate the curriculum that confronts the heir to a modern Throne, languages, history, economics, deportment – these subjects and many others have to be studied more deeply than by ordinary school children. Princess Elizabeth is already making progress with French and German. Latin, of course, is essential for anyone who wishes to understand fully the working of British law and constitution, for many of the vital documents are in this 'dead language'.
>
> The King and Queen have helped her in her languages by speaking to her, and 'French lunch' was quite an institution at '145'.
>
> Queen Mary helps with deportment and bearing instruction and the Princess already shows signs of being exceptionally graceful in her bearing. Riding lessons and music lessons have all helped to prevent Princess Elizabeth's education from becoming too 'stodgy'. She has regular hours of study like any school child and only the most exceptional event is allowed to interfere with them.

A further consequence of her new status was that it was considered important for her to become better acquainted with constitutional history. The Princess received twice-weekly lessons from the Vice-Provost of Eton College, Henry Marten. There were also sessions dealing with knowledge of the British Dominions, including the consequences for the British constitution of the 1931 Statute of Westminster. During the Second World War, these lessons continued in the form of a correspondence course with assignments being returned by post.[15] The amount of time devoted to history was also increased. Marten was responsible for the tutoring and the Vicomtesse de Bellaigue assisted in teaching French and European history.

The routine continued after the outbreak of the Second World War when the family were at Windsor. By 1943, when the Princess reached the age of 18, the press made great claims for her educational achievements. A magazine editor wrote to the palace to check a list of books and authors, supplied by 'a friend near the

Court', which the Princess is supposed to have read. Amongst them were works by Coleridge, Keats, Browning, Tennyson, Scott, Dickens, Trollope, Robert Louis Stevenson, G. M. Trevelyan, Conan Doyle, John Buchan and Peter Cheyney; she also expressed a liking for the Brontës, for historical novels and stories about the highlands. A recent biographer of the Queen has commented:

> Was it true? If such accounts were even half accurate, the Princess would have been a strong candidate for a place at university, where she might have extended her intellectual range. Neither university nor even finishing school, however, was considered as a possibility. Instead, like a butcher or a joiner, she apprenticed for the job she would be undertaking for the rest of her life by doing it.[16]

Another close parallel between Elizabeth and Victoria is to be found in the arrangements made to ensure that close personal supervision was constantly maintained. When the family moved into Buckingham Palace in February 1937 after the Abdication, Margaret MacDonald, the assistant nanny, was asked to sleep in the Princess's bedroom to provide both continuity and companionship.[17]

Her grandfather, George V, was especially fond of Elizabeth and with Queen Mary played a full part in supervising the daily life of the two Princesses when their parents were making official visits abroad. However, both grandparents lacked warmth in their relationships with others, and the Princesses never forgot the 'hollow feeling' which their grandmother inspired, or conquered their dread at receiving a summons from Queen Mary.[18] The latter strongly upheld the convention, for instance, that no member of the royal family should be seen to smile in public,[19] a formality which the new Queen ignored. Similarly, on the return of the Yorks from a visit to Australia in 1927, George V welcomed his son home with the words, 'We will not embrace at the Station before so many people', and added, 'When you kiss Mama, take your hat off.'[20]

In contrast, the Yorks made a point of ensuring a happy childhood for the Princesses, who were treated as if they were the same age,[21] with an emphasis on fun. Games, charades and mild horseplay were part of family routine and built up for the

17. Princess Elizabeth (Queen Elizabeth II) and Princess Margaret with their governess, Marion Crawford (right), having their first ride on the London Underground, May 1939.

Princesses a lasting devotion to their parents. Miss Crawford tells the story of how the children were warned, on the day of their uncle's Abdication, that 'when Papa came home to lunch at one o'clock he would be King of England, and they would have to curtsy to him as they had always curtsied to their grandparents'. 'And now you mean we must do it to Papa and Mummie?' Lilibet asked, 'Margaret too?' 'Margaret also', Crawfie instructed, 'and try not to topple over'. However, the notion of curtsying to their parents was quickly dismissed and Queen Mary remained the only member of the family regarding whom this custom continued.[22]

If the Princesses' lives had been up to now a rather goldfish bowl existence, Crawfie had attempted to alleviate the situation by making links for the Princesses with the outside world. She was instrumental in overcoming the King and Queen's resistance to forming the 1st Buckingham Palace Company of Girl Guides, of which Princess Elizabeth, along with other children, became a member. There were also bus and Underground rides and visits to shops such as Woolworths, though they were accompanied by two detectives and a Lady-in-Waiting. Queen Mary was also responsible for taking them to art galleries, museums and exhibitions and acquainting them with other members of the royal family. The removal to Windsor during the Second World War also widened the Princesses' experience of the outside world.

The Royal School in Windsor Park, formerly for children of employees at the castle, was now augmented by evacuees from London's East End, and the headmaster wrote a yearly panto-mime which included parts for the two Princesses; they were staged at Christmas at the castle before a large audience. There were also Girl Guide meetings, including camping, and a regular dancing class was held at Windsor.

Wartime provided a further opportunity for the Princess at least partly to break through the barrier of isolation. In April 1942, on her sixteenth birthday, Elizabeth registered at the Windsor labour exchange as the law required in preparation for some form of war work. She was eager to join one of the women's services, but the King was concerned on security grounds to postpone the decision. In February 1945, with the war in Europe nearing its end, she was allowed to join the Auxiliary Territorial Service as No. 230873 Second Subaltern Elizabeth Alexandra Mary Windsor.

She successfully completed a six-week course in driving and vehicle maintenance, and the striking images in the press of the Princess in uniform, engaged in routine tasks, were warmly received by the public as contributing to the war effort; but the impact of the apparent democratisation of the royal family was weakened by the fact that the rank was an honorary one and that the Princess returned to Windsor each night to sleep.

Looking back over her education, it might be claimed that it had been unduly limited by being placed initially in the hands of one person, Marion Crawford, who had no experience of university-level study. The curriculum was, as with the Princess's predecessors, mainly geared to preparing her for the monarchy and the performance of ceremonial duties. A recent sympathetic biographer has said that 'her curriculum was far from exacting … According to a tactfully understated assessment in the 1950s (by Miss Crawford), it was "wide rather than deep", without any forcing, or subjection to a classical discipline. It was perhaps a misfortune that there were no peers to offer competition, or examinations to provide an incentive.'[23] It could be argued, though, that much valuable informal education took place through her parents and grandparents; the warm, personal relationship which existed with her own parents, so unusual with previous monarchs, helped to form the stable and sensitive character of Elizabeth which were valuable assets when she became queen.

## PRINCE PHILIP (1921–)

There could be no greater contrast between the education of Princess Elizabeth and that of her husband-to-be, Prince Philip of Greece. Some five years older than her, he was born on 10 June 1921 on the island of Corfu whilst his father, Prince Andrew, the brother of the King of the Hellenes, was involved as a soldier in an unsuccessful campaign against the Turks. In the following year, Prince Andrew was obliged to resign as a lieutenant-general by the new Greek military government and took his family into exile in France.

Philip was the youngest of five children, with four elder sisters. Though the family was not without means, his mother, Princess Alice of Battenburg, found it necessary to open a boutique selling traditional Greek products in Paris while his father busied himself in writing his autobiography. Philip had strong connections with England. His mother was the sister of Lord Louis Mountbatten, the last Viceroy of India, and his grandmother, Victoria, the Marchioness of Milford Haven, resided at Kensington Palace. Philip became acquainted with England at an early age and as his parents drifted apart (his father finally left his mother, who became a nun, in 1929), his English relatives pondered over his future education.

Philip's first school was a progressive pre-preparatory establishment, the MacJannet Country Day and Boarding School, known as The Elms, at St Cloud, a suburb of Paris where the family now lived. It was not altogether a happy experience and at the age of 8, in 1929, he was sent to England to attend Cheam, the exclusive preparatory school at Headley on the Berkshire Downs. Founded in Surrey in the early seventeenth century, it prepared boys for the common entrance examination to public schools. The curriculum, which was largely geared to meet this need, was dominated by Latin and Greek, with English Literature, French and arithmetic. Teaching methods were old-fashioned and corporal punishment was employed to keep discipline. Philip, an advocate of corporal punishment, claimed in a speech given when he later returned to the school that its administration had made a man of him.[24]

He excelled at sports, winning the all-school diving championship when he was not yet 12 and he tied for the first place in the high jump. In academic subjects, his knowledge of French was, not surprisingly, excellent and he shone at history. His reports characterised him as a high-spirited and independent-minded youth.

The next phase of Philip's education came about through a fortuitous series of circumstances. In the eight months between December 1930 and August 1931, while Philip was in England, all of his four sisters married German aristocrats. Philip's second sister, Theodora, had married Berthold, Margrave of Baden. His father, Prince Max, had been the last Imperial Chancellor of Germany and he took a keen interest in social welfare. His friend and former secretary was Dr Kurt Hahn and they together decided to establish a public school based on the English model but also drawing on other traditions. Prince Max once said of the school, 'I am proud of the fact that there is nothing original here.

We have cribbed from everywhere, from the public schools, from Goethe, from Plato, from the Boy Scouts.'[25] The school was set up at first in a wing of the family home, Schloss Salem, on the German shore of Lake Constance in 1920; Hahn was the headmaster and the school at first consisted of 28 boys.

The philosophy of the school was formulated by Hahn. It had, according to one of the earliest teachers at Gordonstoun, been conceived of during a period of prolonged illness as a young man following sunstroke, when he was forced to spend long periods in the semi-dark.[26] Hahn had studied at Oxford and four German universities and had built up a reputation for eccentricity and absent-mindednesss and wore a long black cape and a wide-brimmed hat. His system was based upon seven principles: to give children the opportunity for self-discovery; to train the imagination; to provide periods of silence for reflection; to give opportunities for self-effacement in a common cause; to make games prominent in the curriculum but not at the expense of other activities; to free the sons of wealthy and powerful people from a sense of privilege; and character-building, which was the most important.[27] The regime was a rigorous one, with high praise being given for physical fitness and self-reliance. Hahn himself wrote that before breakfast, 'all boys ran slowly for 400 yards, preferably on their toes. All boys skipped in the morning and did physical drill at night. Many climbed a rope each day. Four times a week, all the year round, academic studies in the morning had a 45-minute break for the practice of running, jumping and javelin throwing.' In addition, all boys were given tasks of physical labour involving building and construction works.[28]

Philip left Cheam earlier than usual in order to enrol at Salem in September 1933 when he was 12 years old. Hitler was now in power in Germany and there was a clash between the explicitly pacifist philosophy of the school and that of the National Socialist Party. Further, Hahn was Jewish and he was subsequently arrested for openly criticising the regime in speeches and in the press. It was only the intervention of several European educationists and the British Prime Minister, Ramsay MacDonald, that enabled Hahn to be freed and allowed to leave the country. After only two terms at Salem, Philip left for England.

Hahn, recovering in Scotland from his ordeal, made plans to

reopen his school in Britain. With the help of friends, he was able to take out a lease on Gordonstoun House, an eighteenth-century mansion set in 300 acres of land, at Elgin in Scotland, to continue his Salem experiment. Hahn introduced two new elements into his British school. The first arose from the inspiration Hahn had found in the Cistercian monks who had once inhabited Salem: altruism was therefore stressed. The second stemmed from what he considered was the immoral climate which existed in most public schools. Hahn hoped to combat this menace with his aim 'to kindle on the threshold of puberty non-poisonous passions which act as guardians during the dangerous years'.[29] The school motto, *Plus Est En Vous*, translatable as 'There is more in you', set out the challenge facing the boys. To test their resourcefulness, expeditions in a variety of conditions at home and overseas were mounted. Links with the community, another of Hahn's ideals, were forged, with boys participating in a range of local activities. The school had its own auxiliary fire-fighting unit linked with the Elgin fire brigade; it helped man a coastguard station and it had an ocean life-saving team as well as a mountain rescue team. Exchange visits with pupils from other countries were also arranged in order to spread the gospel of internationalism.

In 1934 Philip rejoined the school in its new home; there were 30 pupils in all, mainly refugees from Germany. He quickly adapted to the regime and was prepared for the icy showers and the predominantly vegetarian diet. Philip set himself daily targets in running and the high jump and became team captain of both cricket and hockey.[30] He was a reasonably good but not outstanding sailor and had many opportunities to display his skills. His maternal grandfather, Prince Louis of Battenberg, had had a distinguished naval career, becoming First Sea Lord. One of the school's ships in which Philip sailed was the *Prince Louis*, named after his grandfather. Some 20 years later, he recalled the experience:

> It is not so long ago that I cannot remember what it was like to go sailing in those ships. In fact, I remember only too well the times when I was wet, cold, miserable, probably sick, and often scared stiff, but I would not have missed that experience for anything. In any case the discomfort was far outweighed by the moments of intense happiness and excitement. Poets and authors down the centuries have tried to describe those moments but their

descriptions, however brilliant, will never compare with one's own experience.[31]

In later years, the Prince defended the Gordonstoun philosophy, with its emphasis on character building, perhaps at the expense of more traditional school subjects:

> It's somehow got the reputation of being a spartan, rigorous, generally body-bending sort of organisation. In fact it isn't at all, and never has been. It's a misunderstanding of what it's all about. I think it rationalises the whole of the physical activities. Instead of this obsession with games, which is the standard public school thing – the idea that you've got to be good at football or cricket or whatever it is to get anywhere – we in fact had a great many more activities. That is why it got that reputation. Because if you say that there's sailing, and rugby, and mountain climbing and all these things, it's bound to sound as if ... But these are alternatives, they're not necessarily absolutes, not everyone does everything.[32]

By the time Philip left Gordonstoun in the spring of 1939 to enter the Royal Naval College, Dartmouth, the school had grown to 150 pupils. His last report stated that 'he has the greatest sense of service of all the boys in the school'. However, there remained an ambivalence in his attitude towards Gordonstoun. While he could write in an appeal brochure, 'I must confess that I enjoyed my days at Gordonstoun', he told one of his biographers, Basil Boothroyd, about the 'irksome regimentation' and the 'ghastly foot-slogging'. Nevertheless, it is a fact that all three of his sons – Charles, Andrew and Edward – received part of their education at the school.

Philip's later educational philosophy was formed by Hahn's example. As His Royal Highness the Duke of Edinburgh, Philip was given a platform in his public addresses to air his views on a wide range of topics. On his installation as Chancellor of Edinburgh University in November 1953, Philip chose to discuss education, confessing that one reason was 'because I wanted to find out something about the subject myself'. In his speech he addressed the question of formulating a *raison d'être* for schooling in the twentieth century:

> The process of education that I wish to discuss starts in the schools, but, unfortunately, the very term 'education' means different things to different people. To some it means mere book

learning and the ability to pass examinations, some again concentrate on the powers of reasoning and observation, to others it means a preparation for life and citizenship, but to most of us it means a bit of all these things.

The difficulty is that while the purely book learning side can be measured by standards and examinations, the development of character is highly individual and cannot be measured by classes or at stated intervals. Neither can the training of intellect and the development of character be done separately, because character will be formed whether it is guided into the right paths or whether it is neglected, and no amount of intellectual training will make up for that neglect.

In addition, life in school should be so ordered that it is in a real sense a preparation for life in a larger community; it is out of classroom hours and away from home that many of the practical lessons of life are taught and learned. The schools therefore have this further duty, to teach the young to live as members of a community with all that that implies in learning to give and take and play their part in a common life.

Whatever the meaning of education, then, there can be no doubt that all schools have the threefold responsibility of training the intellect, actively developing character, and providing a practical preparation for life.[33]

He also observed that National Service, which then existed, was 'a very important character building experience', quite apart from its importance from a military point of view.

Philip discussed with Hahn possible ways to sponsor young people in the concept of challenge. Hahn himself had been co-founder in 1941 of the Outward Bound Sea School at Aberdovy, Wales. Subsequent Outward Bound residential schools for boys and girls, which later included Mountain schools, introduced healthy activities for many thousands of youths. The time was now ripe, with National Service coming to end, for a more ambitious scheme to be devised.

In 1956 the Duke of Edinburgh's Award scheme was launched from Buckingham Palace. The statement mentioned that 'it is designed as an introduction to leisure-time activities, a challenge to the individual to personal achievement and as a guide to those people and organisations who are concerned about the development of our future citizens ... I am quite sure that all who enter and all those who help to run it will gain that special sense of satisfaction which comes from the discovery of hidden abilities and from helping others to overcome a challenge.'

The scheme, available to organisations and individuals between the ages of 14 and 25, has been a great success; between 1956 and 1991 more than 2 million young people have taken part in it. Awards are given in four different sections – service, expeditions, skills and physical education.

The range of interests, which include life-saving, youth leadership, drama, sailing and expeditions on land or sea, have been criticised as being somewhat elitist in nature. However, Philip's interests also extended, on a different level, to fund-raising on behalf of existing organisations, such as the Federation of Boys' Clubs and the Central Council for Physical Recreation. His view of the need to make each new generation aware of the possibilities for 'healthy recreations and useful service' closely echoes that of his schooldays mentor, Kurt Hahn.


PRINCE CHARLES (1948–)

The marriage of Philip to Princess Elizabeth in November 1947 brought together two people who had undergone very different educational experiences, one a cloistered and lonely learning process and the other a mixture of the traditional and experimental public school curriculum. A study of the education considered appropriate for their eldest child, Charles, not only reflects these differences but also demonstrates the changing public perception of what a royal education might be in the modern world.

Charles was born on 14 November 1948 at Buckingham Palace whilst Clarence House was being made ready for the family. Only five days before his birth, Letters Patent were issued under the Great Seal which allowed Philip and Elizabeth's offspring to bear the rank of prince and princess. Within a week of the birth, at least one of the Sunday papers was already speculating about the schools to which the new prince might eventually be sent. The public debate on the most appropriate type of education for the sons and daughters of royalty was to continue during the following years.

After Philip and Elizabeth moved to Clarence House in July

1949 when Charles was 8 months old, the baby was installed in the nursery under the care of two nurses, Helen Lightbody and Mabel Anderson. Though both were unmarried, the former was officially called 'Mrs' because of her seniority. Even before his mother became queen, there were long periods of separation from his parents. Philip was still a sea-going naval officer and Elizabeth joined him at Malta for Christmas 1949 while Charles was looked after by his grandparents. A similar situation occurred in 1951, when Elizabeth and Philip made an official visit to Canada and the United States. Easier means of transport, especially air travel, with a consequent increase in official visits abroad, resulted in Charles seeing less of his parents as a child than some previous royal children. His fourth birthday party was the first his father had attended.[34]

The death of his grandfather George VI on 5 February 1952, when Charles was 3, had a number of important consequences. With his mother now queen, he had become heir apparent with the title of Duke of Cornwall. Serious consideration had to be given to preparing him for kingship. It was decided to appoint a governess when he reached the age of 5. Miss Catherine Peebles, known as Mipsy, like Miss Crawford a Scot, was put in charge of his lessons at Buckingham Palace. For parents who were praised for the enlightened way in which their children were brought up, it seems strange that Charles was taught on his own rather than with others, whereas his younger sister and brothers were not similarly isolated.[35] The main reason given was that Charles was a shy boy and would therefore flourish in a one-to-one situation.

For the next three years, Charles began the day at 9.30 a.m. with prayers and Bible stories, then lessons followed in history geography, writing and arithmetic; he showed little aptitude for the latter. At the age of 6, at the request of his mother, French was added to the curriculum. The afternoons were devoted to either painting or drawing or tours of London's beauty spots and museums. Dancing lessons were introduced when he was 7. The only time when he joined the company of other boys was a twice-weekly session at a Chelsea gymnasium, where he could experience rope-climbing, exercises and ball games. Surrounded in his everyday life by women only and with comparatively little contact with his parents – half an hour in the morning and when possible after teatime – Charles was prone to embarrassment and self-consciousness. One writer described the situation at this time as follows:

> A good deal of what was important in his life was lived internally, within the bounds of his own imagination. Miss Peebles discovered that she had to deal with a vague child, or, perhaps more accurately, a child who still had only a vague relationship to the outside world. He was resistant to concentrating, not thirsty for knowledge, but on the other hand very conscientious.[36]

The Queen and Prince Philip had encouraged Miss Peebles to adopt a policy of 'no forcing' with Charles and up to a point it had succeeded. He was now of an age when his contemporaries would have been attending a primary school, and public speculation was rife on the next step which would be taken. Philip issued a statement through the unlikely medium of the British Information Service in Washington which included the momentous sentence, 'The Queen and I want Charles to go to school with other boys of his generation and to learn to live with other children and to absorb from childhood the discipline imposed by education with others.' Charles, therefore, was to be the first heir to the throne to be educated during his schooldays outside the walls of a royal palace.

The breaking down of his isolation was not before time. In any case his friend and companion Helen Lightbody had retired and Mabel Anderson was now looking after his younger sister, Princess Anne. In the Christmas vacation before starting school, when Prince Philip was on a four-month overseas visit, the Queen arranged for a tutor-companion for the young Prince, the head of a Sussex preparatory school, Michael Farebrother.[37]

The school chosen was an exclusive preparatory boys' day school, Hill House in Hans Place, Kensington. Its headmaster and founder, Colonel Henry Townend, an Oxford Blue at football and a champion swimmer, had been invited for tea at Buckingham Palace in October 1956. Accordingly, in the following January in the glare of press publicity, Charles, wearing the school uniform, began his half-day attendance at Hill House (it later became full-time). Townend ran the school on Swiss lines, emphasising that little hands, if kept busy, would not get into mischief. Latin, French and geography were taught by the head, and his wife, a former nurse, taught anatomy, first aid and general knowledge.

18. Prince Charles with other pupils from Hill House School, Knightsbridge, 1957.

Although games were not dominant, there was an emphasis on physical fitness, with Townend joining in games of football with the boys. Corporal punishment was avoided and serious misdemeanours led to the confiscation of the school tie. The school catered for 5- to 10-year-olds, and Townend aimed at cultivating a family atmosphere with himself as a father figure. Teaching groups consisted of eight or nine pupils.

One of the first tasks which his teachers found necessary was to acquaint him with the value of different coins, many bearing his mother's head; Charles was unaware of money at that stage, never having the need to handle it. Examinations were set at the end of every term and the results were posted on the school notice board. Parents were encouraged to come to the school and scrutinise the lists if they so wished, but the Queen and Philip never made the journey. Apart from arithmetic the first term's report was quite satisfactory.

After two terms, Charles's parents decided that it was time for him to move on. There had been an uproar during the year (1957) when Lord Altrincham, later John Grigg, published an article in the August issue of the *National and English Review* pointing out how far the Court was behind the times and how out of touch with the sentiments of the people.[38] Altrincham also challenged the decision to send Charles to a private preparatory school in the first instance, asking 'But will she have the wisdom to give her children an education very different from her own?', and questioning whether the Queen would ensure that 'he mixes during his formative years with children who will one day be bus-drivers, dockers, engineers etc., not merely with landowners or stockbrokers?'[39]

A book published a decade later, *To Be a King*, by Dermot Morrah, then Arundel Herald Extraordinary and an influential figure in palace circles, attempted to answer Altrincham and others who had favoured Charles's attending a state school. He put forward the view that the Prince 'should be educated from the very beginning so as to fit him for his unique position [as future monarch]. It can only be arranged in what is called the "private sector".' It was clearly better, in his view, that Charles should enter the private sector 'on the ground floor'. Another objection to a state school education for the Prince was put forward:

Compared with Hill House, in its secluded corner of Hans Place, the council school had far less effective defences to keep at bay those who would inevitably come crowding for a glimpse of the Prince. Its teachers would be more likely to be overawed by their responsibility; the other children, drawn from much humbler strata of society, would be more inclined to treat him as a fabulous animal coming from an unknown world. Not only would the emphasis on his peculiar position, which the Queen wished to play down, be reasserted: his presence would be a disturbing influence in the school itself and react adversely on the education of his fellow-pupils.[40]

This argument ignored the great public interest in royal watching. When Charles was sent to the exclusive Cheam School in September 1957, the event attracted headlines in the national newspapers for 68 of the first 88 days. The decision to choose Cheam was not taken lightly. The Queen had previously visited several schools in order to inspect the facilities and to talk to the teaching staffs; schoolmasters were also invited to the informal palace luncheon parties which were instituted in May 1956. Various reasons were put forward for finally choosing Cheam, particularly that it was not a crammer and also that Charles's cousin, the Marquis of Milford Haven, was already at the school and could provide company if necessary. The main reason, however, was given later by Prince Philip, who made the actual decision:

> When Charles first went to school one of the problems we were confronted with was 'How do you select a prep school?' In the end he went to Cheam, where I had been. But this is something better understood in this country than almost anything else – that people very frequently do what their fathers have done. People said, 'Oh, he's gone because his father went', and there was no further argument.[41]

Like her mother, the Queen placed great importance on speaking French well and in the holidays at Balmoral before Charles started at Cheam, he had a full-time tutor-companion, Mlle Bibiane de Roujoux.

While Hill House had been the first day school attended by an heir to the throne, Cheam was the first boarding school to be chosen. Without doubt the experience came as a shock to Charles.[42] He had never been away from home on his own before

218

and his natural shyness was an obstacle. This was not helped by the fact that his father before him had been a success at sport when he was at Cheam, being a member of the school's cricket, soccer and rugby teams while Charles was not a natural athlete. Continuing press interest in his activities tended to aggravate the situation. As a result the editors of the national newspapers were invited to Buckingham Palace at the end of Charles's first term at the school to hear from the headmaster how their activities were making normal life at the school impossible. Following this, most of the papers called off their vigil at the school.

It could be argued that 'normal' schooling was in any case almost impossible. For instance, as at Hill House, while his fellow pupils called him 'Charles', his teachers addressed him as 'Prince Charles'. In addition, press interest was inevitably revived when in July 1958, the Queen, without first telling Charles, announced at the Empire and Commonwealth Games in Cardiff that she had created Charles Prince of Wales. Nevertheless, he was rated by his teachers as a good average schoolboy. During his time at Cheam Charles was reasonably successful, with history and art as his best subjects, but mathematics was still a weakness. He also discovered that he enjoyed acting, once taking the inappropriate part of the lead in the play *Richard III*.

The school, even for its time, was run on old-fashioned lines. For example, after washing and dressing in the morning the pupils were presented to the matron for inspection: this was followed by prayers, a formal handshake with one of Cheam's two headmasters and then breakfast. The school's house system was based on four divisions, named after Commonwealth countries, Australia, Canada, New Zealand and South Africa; out-door activities, which were much encouraged, followed the lines of Baden-Powell's teachings. The curriculum was necessarily traditional, as it was geared towards the common entrance examination.

After four years at the school and with Charles now 13 years of age, it was time to consider the final phase of his school education. His name had been put down for Eton at birth, but it was not a foregone conclusion that it would be the ultimate choice. There were different views expressed on the subject. Both the Queen and the Queen Mother favoured Eton, but the others involved in the discussion, Prince Philip and Lord Mountbatten, were not so sure. The Queen, Prince Philip and Charles had visited Gordonstoun, the other main contender, in September 1961 when they were at Balmoral. It was decided subsequently that it was not too forbidding a prospect and in the following January the Queen publicly announced that her son would be starting at his new school at the beginning of May 1962.

Perhaps the most compelling argument in favour of Gordonstoun came from Prince Philip. He had been impressed in retrospect by his own schooldays there and he hoped that its unorthodox approach to education might draw Charles out of his shell. Another advantage over Eton was that Gordonstoun is some 500 miles away from London and therefore not so accessible to the attentions of the press, or so it was believed. In addition, the school did not require potential pupils to sit the common entrance examination, so there would not be the embarrassment of possible failure. However, to avoid the charge of special treatment, Charles took the examination and passed it successfully.

The decision was not universally welcomed. Lord Beaverbrook's *Daily Express* ran a campaign challenging the wisdom of sending Charles to a public school, especially Gordonstoun.[43] From a different perspective, the Queen's great-aunt, Princess Alice Countess Athlone, on hearing the news was reported to have said, 'I am sorry the Prince isn't going to Eton. He would make many more contacts there which would stay with him through life.'[44] Certainly, as one royal commentator has pointed out, it would have been far more 'trad' for Charles to have been an Old Etonian: 'Instead, the heir to the throne was brought up with ideas of toughness and self-testing that might have been familiar to the Black Prince or Prince Hal, but not since.'[45]

The school had changed in a number of respects since Philip's day. Kurt Hahn, the headmaster, had retired, though his philosophy still permeated the school's activities. Charles was fortunate to fall under the influence of some outstanding members of staff, including his housemaster Bob Whitby, the art teacher Bob Waddell, who encouraged his talents in this field, and the English teacher Eric Anderson, later head of Eton, who inspired Charles to take part in the plays which Anderson brilliantly produced. He also learned to play the cello, took part in the school orchestral concerts and sang in the choir.

There was a temporary halt to his studies at Gordonstoun following the Queen's visit to New Zealand in 1963 where she stated that 'before long our children will be able to see for themselves this prosperous and happy country'. This promise was quickly pursued by Sir Robert Menzies, the veteran Australian Prime Minister, during a visit to Balmoral in July 1965 during the Commonwealth Conference. As a result it was arranged that Charles should spend a term at Geelong Anglican Grammar School, a leading public school near Melbourne, not at the school itself but at its annex, Timbertop, some 200 miles away in the bush. The headmaster was a disciple of Hahn and had established Timbertop so that fourth-year boys could embark on various adventure activities which were beneficial for character training. A journalist writing in the *Daily Express* in October 1965 shortly before Charles's departure for Australia praised the Timbertop scheme, whilst criticising the British state education system:

> Let us examine the question of Prince Charles and your rate bill … We must have new universities on almost every hill and down. We must have glorious new schools with whole walls of plate glass and lavatories like the Ritz. Nothing we say (in public) can be too good for the young people. Yet now consider the case of Prince Charles. Quite rightly (and much to the credit of his parents, I think) he is getting the best education in the world. Soon, in Australia, he will live and be taught in a hut like a lumberjack. In fact, he could as easily be an apprentice in a logging camp doing lessons in his spare time. Excellent. Yet it raises this question: Just how necessary is all our massive and swelling system of State education? Are our children really being really enriched by it? If a shack in the woods, with an axe and a saw, is good enough for Prince Charles, do all the rest of our young people truly need those vast new educational palaces?[46]

In fact, the writer was quite inaccurate about the Prince's role at Timbertop, for although still only 17, he was acting as an assistant master at the school, teaching English and constitutional history and taking part in the expeditions. The experience proved to be a confidence booster for Charles, who discovered for the first time his ability to talk unselfconsciously to a wide range of people. His stay with the school was extended by a term in order that he could go with the boys to New Guinea. Despite some criticism in the Australian press directed at Menzies for not placing the prince in a state school, the visit was considered a success on educational and other grounds.

Charles had previously taken his General Certificate of Education 'O'-level examinations (school-leaving examination for 16 year olds) in six subjects and had passed in five of them: English language, English literature, history, Latin and French. He initially failed in mathematics but subsequently passed. No science or social-science subjects were attempted. He returned to Gordonstoun having lost two terms' lessons in Australia during his second year of studying for 'A'-levels (principal examination for 18-year-old school-leavers, normally a requirement for university study). In his last year at school, 1967, he was made head boy or, to use the Gordonstoun terminology, 'Guardian'. His examination results were no more than adequate, a 'B' grade for history and a 'C' grade for French.

Charles's next step in his education had already been the subject of both formal and informal discussions shortly after he reached the age of 18. On 22 December 1965, the Queen assembled a select group of people who could offer their expert advice.[47] Prince Philip acted as chairman; the other members of the group were his uncle Lord Louis Mountbatten, who had recently retired as Chief of the Defence Staff, Sir Charles Wilson, Principal and Vice-Chancellor of Glasgow University and chairman of the Committee of Vice-Chancellors and Principals, Dr Michael Ramsey, the Archbishop of Canterbury, Dr Robin Woods, Dean of Windsor and Harold Wilson, then Prime Minister.

There were different viewpoints expressed by the committee during the session. Two of the members, Sir Charles Wilson and Harold Wilson, were Oxford graduates of Corpus Christi and Jesus Colleges respectively. Ramsey had been an undergraduate at Magdalene College, Cambridge and President of the Union and Regius Professor of Divinity at the university. Woods was not only a graduate of Trinity College, Cambridge, but two of his own sons were undergraduates there at the time. It was agreed in principle that Charles should attend an English rather than a Commonwealth or a Scottish university. Harold Wilson, reflecting public concern on the need for the monarchy to change with the times, recommended a redbrick, that is, a non-Oxbridge, university. Mountbatten, who had briefly studied at Christ's College, Cambridge, held forthright views on the subject. He favoured Trinity College, where Charles's grandfather, George VI, had been a student, to be followed by a spell at Dartmouth and subsequently into active service in the Royal Navy. Trinity College was also favoured by Woods, partly on the grounds that the student population contained a high proportion of students from state grammar schools and partly because the college's Master, R. A. Butler, a former senior statesman, had held many high offices in Conservative governments and was therefore well known to the royal family. After a discussion lasting over two hours,[48] it was generally agreed that Cambridge seemed the most suitable destination and Woods was delegated to visit the university to seek out a suitable college and submit a report to the Queen. He subsequently met the Vice-Chancellor and a number of heads of colleges. In the end, six were chosen for the short list, with their academic proposals, accommodation and security arrangements set out by Woods in a memorandum. Trinity College emerged as the clear favourite.[49] It is interesting to note that Charles was not present at the meeting, though he was happy with the decision.

When the Queen publicly announced the next stage in Charles's education, there was some feeling expressed that only a privileged youth of his rank would be admitted to Cambridge to take an honours degree on the strength of two modest 'A' levels and without outstanding academic ability. But the other side of the case was put by one contemporary writer:

> He was not expected to be a paragon of learning. Those who hope to find academic brilliance in princes rarely steer their arguments to logical conclusions. What if the future King were to turn out to be a scholar, a genius, a seer, a mystic? The last learned monarch was the first Stuart King of England and sixth of Scotland whose theories of hereditary Divine Right plunged his dynasty into darkness and death. James was both talkative and pedantic, ever ready to spell out principles of government when silence would have served him better: he was not unlike some pernickety don. The Prince of Wales of his day [Charles I] inherited from his father notions that delivered him to the executioner in Whitehall.[50]

Two aspects of Charles's university career were unique. No previous heir to the throne had been expected to take a full degree course and in competition with other students. He was also the first to reside in college and not be isolated with his own staff in a separate establishment. But in many ways he was treated very differently from the other 650 Trinity students. From the time he entered the college in September 1967, Charles had direct access to the Master, having a key to a private staircase to the lodge which led to Butler's study. The Master set aside three-quarters of an hour each evening to discuss with the Prince a range of matters and was a formative influence upon him. As Anthony Howard has remarked in his biography of Butler, 'There is no doubt that the notion of playing Melbourne to the Heir to the Throne was something that pleased him enormously'.[51] It was at Butler's insistence that the palace had been weaned away from the notion that the Prince should have a specially designed two-year course and not risk taking a degree.[52]

Charles was also given in New Court his own room, a private bathroom and kitchenette which had been altered and redecor-ated. He was allowed to keep a car on the premises, a privilege not granted to other freshmen, and he carried out several official duties during his undergraduate years. Nevertheless, he partici-pated fully in college life, making music in orchestras and choirs and joining in the theatrical activities which abounded. Charles studied archaeology and anthropology for part one of the tripos examinations under an inspiring supervisor, Dr Glyn Daniel. Daniel took him on a tour of France at Easter to see the Palaeolithic cave art of the Dordogne and the megaliths in the Carnac region.[53] Charles was awarded an upper second at the end of his first year. He changed to history in his second year and found the subject increasingly absorbing; he was particularly fascinated with his forebear, George III, whom he considered had been unfairly treated by posterity. It was at this time that he spent a controversial term at the University of Wales College at Aberystwyth in preparation for the ceremony of his investiture as Prince of Wales that summer. This proved to be a distraction from his studies, though in June 1970, at the end of his third and final year at Cambridge, he emerged with a lower second-class honours Bachelor of Arts degree.

Charles's formal education was now complete: it now

remained to follow the path favoured by his father and Lord Mountbatten, a spell of service in the armed forces. Charles himself stated at the time that the experience would be useful in teaching him about people as well as giving him new skills. He entered the Royal Air Force College, Cranwell, in March 1971 and during the six months he was there gained his wings as a pilot. A more arduous career followed in the Royal Navy. He started at the Royal Naval College, Dartmouth, as an acting sub-lieutenant and then served on ships in many parts of the world in a number of different capacities for the next five years. On leaving the service in December 1976, he was promoted to commander.

Members of the royal family have come under increasing criticism in recent years for failing to adopt a distinctive role for themselves apart from the purely ceremonial. Charles has been largely exempt from such criticism. It is widely held that he found the right solution to finding useful work by his close involvement in the field of public welfare. As early as 1973, while he was still in the Navy, Charles had chaired a meeting at Buckingham Palace with representatives of the social services, the Church and the police, at which he made an impassioned speech about Kurt Hahn and Gordonstoun and its schemes of out-of-school activities, especially its involvement with the local community. Charles told the meeting that he wished to offer his services in helping disadvantaged and delinquent youth in the wider society.[54]

Since then he has been closely involved in several schemes which have at least partly answered this need, and is patron of more than 400 organisations, over a half of which are explicitly philanthropical.[55] Outstanding has been the Prince's Trust, formed in 1976, a multi-million-pound concern which has provided grants to some 47,000 young people in order to set up their own businesses or to help others; out of this has grown the Prince's Trust Volunteers which enables people to learn how to work in teams and participate in community projects. The Youth Business Initiative, which became the Prince's Youth Business Trust in 1986, was set up 'to educate, advise and support young unemployed people with a view to setting up small businesses of their own'. As president of Business in the Community, a partnership between business, government and the community, the Prince was able to persuade many of Britain's major companies to establish a network of enterprise agencies which created several thousand new jobs each year.[56] Another project in which he became closely involved arose from Hahn's establishment of Atlantic College in 1962 at St Donat's in Wales, an international sixth form co-educational independent school. As the movement spread to other countries, it became the United World Colleges with Mountbatten as its first president. Charles succeeded him, warning his uncle that he had his own views as to the duties of the president.[57] He remained in the post until 1993.

Hahn's influence is also seen in Charles's great interest in community architecture and his campaign against modern ugly buildings, in the regeneration of inner cities, and in the promotion of complementary medicine, as well as in giving a lead to organic farming, successfully practising this approach on the Highgrove estate. Some of his speeches on these topics have been attacked for their partisanship which some consider to be out of place coming from the heir to the throne and one who has had enjoyed a privileged upbringing. An example of this occurred over a television broadcast in June 1997 when Charles claimed that state education had failed, that its standards were poor, and that these were due to the fashionable approach to teaching methods and the abandonment of a disciplined structure in schools. He also indicated that there was not enough emphasis on the social and moral development of pupils. The speech was condemned in the press for being out of date and out of touch with the problems facing schools. Those institutions which Charles and his children had attended, one writer pointed out, with their well-paid teachers, small classes, excellent facilities and set in green spaces, ill-prepared him to pronounce on educational matters.[58] This judgement should be modified to take into account Charles's real interest in educational issues and the plight of young people without basic skills; this can be seen in the Highgrove seminars where educational topics are discussed and the visits to inner city schools which he has made.[59] How far his controversial pronouncements on education could be considered to be entering the political arena is a debatable point. Certainly, the choice of schools for his own sons, William and Harry both being at Eton, indicate that the traditional world of nannies, pre-preparatory and public schools seems likely to be continued.

PRINCE WILLIAM (1982–)

Although attempts were made to keep the details of William's early upbringing confidential, a good deal is known as a result of leaks and oblique mentions in various biographies and books about the royal family. It is clear that both Diana and Charles were more directly involved with caring for William than had ever been the case with earlier generations of royalty, even to the extent of occasionally bathing William and putting him to bed when he was a baby. Tradition was also broken by the young Prince's travelling with both parents to Australia and New Zealand before his first birthday. There were, of course, plenty of other carers, nursemaids and nannies, but the parents were directly involved more than ever before.

Another break with royal tradition came at the age of 3, when, instead of being taught at home by a tutor, William was enrolled as a part-time pupil at Mrs Mynor's Nursery School, or kindergarten, in west London, the kind of private establishment catering for the children of the affluent and well connected that Diana herself had worked in before her marriage. William stayed with Mrs Mynor until 1987, when he transferred to Wetherby School in Kensington, a pre-preparatory school, where he remained for three years as a day pupil before becoming a boarder at a conventional preparatory school, Ludgrove School in Wokingham. At all these establishments William was a cooperative and reasonably high-achieving pupil, and he became a prefect in his final year at Ludgrove. His curricula and extracurricular activities were typical of boys destined for an elite independent school and Oxford or Cambrdige University.

In 1995, at the normal age of 13, having passed his Common Entrance examination, William began his five years at Eton, the most famous independent school in England and the most exclusive. He followed the normal Eton curriculum, but in classes much smaller than in state schools (a ratio of about 12 pupils to one teacher, compared with at least 20 to 1 in most state schools). He also wore the distinctive Eton uniform which marks off these boys from the less privileged: black tail coats with striped trousers, white shirts and ties.

William's timetable would have varied from winter to summer, but a typical Eton day has a pattern something like the following:

| | |
|---|---|
| 7.30 a.m. | First School (the first lesson of the day) |
| 8.15 a.m. | Breakfast |
| 9.20 a.m. | Chapel (Church of England service) |
| 9.40 a.m. | Second School |
| 10.30 a.m. | Break |
| 10.55 a.m. | Third School |
| 11.55 a.m. | Fourth School |
| 1.00 p.m. | Mid-day meal (still called 'dinner' at Eton) |
| | Games or other extra-curricular activities |
| 3.30 p.m. | Fifth School |
| 4.15 p.m. | Tea |
| 5.00 p.m. | Sixth School |
| 6.00 p.m. | Private study |
| 7.45 p.m. | Supper |
| 8.20 p.m. | House Prayers |
| 8.30 p.m. | Private study |
| 10.00 p.m. | Lights out |

William seems to have thrived on this regime, passing 12 subjects at the General Certificate of Secondary Education (GCSE) examination, and proceeding to study geography, biology and the history of art for the Advanced-level examination.

Independent boarding schools in England have sometimes been described as 'total institutions'; the above timetable would reinforce the view that the boys are kept occupied for a greater proportion of the day than boys and girls in state schools. Even during their time off, boys are under the care and vigilant supervision of their housemaster, whose responsibility it is to know each member of his house very well as an individual and to help him through any personal difficulty. For example, when Diana died suddenly, William's housemaster, Dr Andrew Gailey and his wife would certainly have been concerned to comfort him when he showed signs of distress. William was also accompanied everywhere by his personal bodyguard/detective, who was even required to sleep in the study/bedroom next to William's.

In some respects, this kind of regime has much to commend it for teenage boys whose contact with the outside world might be problematic. On the debit side, however, there are many disadvantages in sending a royal prince, heir to the throne, to

228

Eton. First, the greatest drawback is that Eton is not only an expensive independent school, it is probably the most exclusive school in England, where Prince William will meet only a very narrow section of the future citizens of the country. (This is one of the points that John Grigg made in his well-known articles.) Second, by attending Eton, William has become involved in such upper-class 'sporting' activitives as beagling (hunting hares with dogs), which many today find offensive and cruel. Third, there may be pressures to reform Eton and similar independent schools by encouraging a less exclusive admissions policy. It would be unfortunate if members of the royal family were drawn into such a dispute, which might become very acrimonious. Fourth, it is questionable whether the conventional GCSE and Advanced-level curriculum will be adequate for a future monarch (this will be discussed in Chapter 8). Fifth, Eton has the reputation for having an 'old-boy' network even more pervasive than that of most independent schools. It is as unfortunate for a future king to be part of such a network as it would be for him to become a freemason. If any activity *is* controversial in a democracy it is is surely unwise for the royal family to take part in it. Finally, throughout this book, we have noted the enduring problem that heirs to the throne have often been brought up in such an atmosphere of privilege that it makes it difficult for them to play the part of a modern, constitutional monarch. Eton may be too special, encouraging the Prince to think of himself as different from those of his subjects who have not shared these privileges.

### PRINCE HARRY (1984–)

Prince Harry has followed almost exactly in the footsteps of his elder brother:

| | |
|---|---|
| 1987–89 | Mrs Mynor's Nursery School |
| 1989–92 | Wetherby School in Kensington as a day boy |
| 1992–97 | Ludgrove Preparatory School as a border |
| 1997 | Eton, joining William at Dr Gailey's house, Manor House |

Apparently, Harry is not as academic as William, and it was

necessary for him to spend an extra year at Ludgrove in order to reach the standard in his examinations that even royal princes are expected to achieve in order to proceed to Eton; but in 1997 he passed all his Common Entrance papers in English, mathematics, science, French, geography, history and religious education.

In addition to their schools, William and Harry have benefited from the companionship of Alexandra (Tiggy) Legge-Bourke. After the Prime Minister announced the separation of Charles and Diana in 1992, Charles appointed Ms Legge-Bourke as a companion/nanny to the two Princes whenever they were staying with him. Her official position was assistant to the Prince of Wales's Private Secretary, but her duties were almost entirely recreational and social, for example, helping to teach the boys to hunt and shoot rabbits. Clearly, she was chosen for her social rather than her intellectual accomplishments, since her academic qualifications consist of four passes at the General Certificate of Education, Ordinary-level examinations and a Montessori teaching certificate, which would not have qualified her for employment in a state school but nevertheless enabled her to open her own kindergarten, 'Mrs Tiggiwinkles', in 1985, which closed in 1988 after some financial dififculties.

At the end of the twentieth century, education has become a high priority for all political parties but is still full of controversial issues. To some extent controversy over Queen Elizabeth II was avoided at the time by keeping her education away from the public gaze. This 'private' solution then appeared reasonable; in retrospect, it has been criticised, partly because it continued the tradition of isolating young members of the royal family, partly because the curriculum was narrow and undemanding.

For Prince Charles a different decision was made: he was to attend schools and universities, following programmes which would be as close to normal as possible. This pattern, too, has been criticised, by some because the schools were independent, and by Charles himself because he found the Gordonstoun regime at times uncongenial, notwithstanding the fact that his father had enjoyed it.

For Prince William, second in line of succession, a more traditional school was chosen; but Eton is, more than any other school in England, associated with a privileged, upper-class lifestyle. It remains to be seen whether Prince William can overcome that disadvantage, and also learn to cope with what we have described earlier in this book as the occupational hazard of monarchy: growing up in the midst of deference, and learning to believe that being royal means being above normal social and moral rules. On that may depend the future of the monarchy itself.

## NOTES

1. Public Schools Commission, *First Report*, vol. I (HMSO, 1968), p. 55.
2. Quoted in D. Childs, *Britain since 1945: A Political History* (3rd edn, Routledge, 1992), p. 150.
3. D. Duff, *Mother of the Queen* (Muller, 1965), p. 334.
4. C. Warwick, *King George VI and Queen Elizabeth* (Sidgwick & Jackson, 1985), p. 20.
5. G. Wakeford, *Thirty Years a Queen* (Robert Hale, 1968), p. 42.
6. G. Forbes, *My Darling Buffy: The Early Life of the Queen Mother* (Richard Cohen, 1997), p. 59.
7. The Duchess of York was anxious that the birth of her second child, Princess Margaret, should take place at Glamis. The Home Secretary, J. R. Clynes, was obliged to stay at a nearby castle on 24-hour alert for 15 days until the baby was eventually born on 21 August 1930. A. Edwards, *Royal Sisters: Elizabeth and Margaret, 1926–1956* (Collins, 1990), pp. 31–3.
8. M. Crawford, *The Little Princesses* (Cassell, 1950), p. 20.
9. Margaret soon joined her sister in the classroom. Miss Crawford remarked, 'It was not always a very easy matter to teach, at the same time, two children of such different ages, character and development', ibid., p. 43.
10. Ibid., p. 16.
11. R. Lacey, *Majesty: Elizabeth II and the House of Windsor* (Hutchinson, 1990), p. 120.
12. Crawford, *Little Princesses*, p. 40.
13. Evidence that Elizabeth had naturally developed a strong sense of duty at an early age is given in M. Crawford, *Queen Elizabeth II* (George Newnes, 1952), p. 47.
14. D. Laird, *Queen Elizabeth the Queen Mother* (Hodder & Stoughton, 1966), p. 132.
15. Edwards, *Royal Sisters*, p. 82.
16. B. Pimlott, *The Queen: A Biography of Elizabeth II* (HarperCollins, 1996), p. 69.
17. Laird, *Queen Mother*, p. 168.
18. Warwick, *King George and Elizabeth*, p. 141.
19. K. Rose, *King George V* (Weidenfeld & Nicolson, 1983), p. 42.
20. Warwick, *George and Elizabeth*, p. 69.
21. S. Bradford, *King George VI* (Weidenfeld & Nicolson, 1989), p. 153.
22. Crawford, *Little Princesses*, p. 39.
23. Pimlott, *The Queen*, pp. 23–4.
24. T. Heald, *The Duke: A Portrait of Prince Philip* (Hodder & Stoughton, 1991), p. 36.
25. Ibid., p. 41.
26. H. L. Brereton, *Gordonstoun* (W. & R. Chambers, 1968), p. 127.
27. Hahn's final report to the parents for boys leaving the school emphasised character above academic achievements. A foolscap page was devoted to the former aspect; this was supplemented by an account of progress made in the traditional subjects. R. Arnold-Brown, *Unfolding Character: The Impact of Gordonstoun* (Routledge & Kegan Paul, 1962), p. 25.
28. Alexandra, Queen of Yugoslavia, *Prince Philip: A Family Portrait* (Weidenfeld & Nicolson, 1966), p. 49.
29. A. Holden, *Charles, Prince of Wales* (Weidenfeld & Nicolson, 1979), p. 112.
30. J. Parker, *Prince Philip: A Critical Biography* (Sidgwick & Jackson, 1990), p. 189.

31. Prince Philip, HRH Duke of Edinburgh, *Selected Speeches, 1948–1955* (Oxford University Press, 1957), p. 136.
32. B. Boothroyd, *Philip: An Informal Biography* (Longman, 1971), p. 125.
33. Prince Philip, *Speeches*, p. 76.
34. S. Bradford, *Elizabeth: A Biography of Her Majesty the Queen* (Heinemann, 1996), p. 277.
35. G. and H. Fisher, *Charles: The Man and the Prince* (Robert Hale, 1977), p. 41.
36. D. Morrah, *To Be a King* (Hutchinson, 1968), pp. 35–6.
37. G. Wakeford, *The Heir Apparent: An Authentic Study of the Life and Training of HRH Charles, Prince of Wales* (Robert Hale, 1967), p. 66.
38. In a television interview, Altrincham claimed that the Queen was surrounded by people of 'the tweedy sort' and he advocated 'a classless and Commonwealth Court'. E. Healey, *The Queen's House: A Social History of Buckingham Palace* (Michael Joseph, 1997), p. 375.
39. Lord Altrincham, 'The Monarchy Today', *National and English Review*, 149, August (1957), p. 63.
40. Morrah, *To Be a King*, p. 48.
41. P. Junor, *Charles* (Sidgwick & Jackson, 1987), p. 32.
42. As Miss Crawford wrote, 'The matron of a small boys' school once told me that on the first nights of school terms, most of her homesick little boys wept, not for mummies, but for their nanny. She was much more than a paid servant; she was their childhood.' Crawford, *Little Princesses*, p. 43. And Lady Diana Cooper once reminisced, 'We were all of us perfectly accustomed to middle-aged men, when they got home, not going to see their old mothers and fathers but bounding upstairs to see their nannies.' J. Gathorne-Hardy, *The Rise and Fall of the British Nanny* (Hodder & Stoughton, 1972), pp. 105–6.
43. For example, on 25 January 1956, the newspaper reported that Gordonstoun was not represented in the list of 87 public schools whose pupils gained open scholarships and exhibitions to universities.
44. Wakeford, *Heir Apparent*, p. 146.
45. E. Longford, *Royal Throne: The Future of the Monarchy* (Hodder & Stoughton, 1993), p. 114.
46. *Daily Express*, 30 October 1965, p. 12.
47. One of the group, Woods, wrote later, 'We were amused to learn that Queen Victoria had given a similar party when she was uncertain as to how to occupy her son, who was to become Edward VII.' R. Woods, *Robin Woods: An Autobiography* (SCM Press, 1986), p. 175.
48. R. Crossman, *The Diaries of a Cabinet Minister*, vol. I, 1964–66 (Hamilton/Cape, 1975), p. 420.
49. Woods, *Autobiography*, p. 175.
50. Wakeford, *Heir Apparent*, p. 213.
51. A. Howard, *RAB: The Life of R. A. Butler* (Cape, 1987), p. 390.
52. Lord Butler, *The Art of the Possible: The Memoirs of Lord Butler* (Hamish Hamilton, 1971), p. 260.
53. G. Daniel, *Some Small Harvest: The Memoirs of Glyn Daniel* (Thames & Hudson, 1986), p. 205. Daniel was also a television personality, acting as chairman of the popular panel game *Animal, Vegetable or Mineral*.
54. Holden, *Charles, Prince of Wales*, p. 234.
55. F. Prochaska, *Royal Bounty: The Making of a Welfare Monarchy* (Yale University Press, 1995), p. 264.
56. A. Holden, *Charles, A Biography* (Weidenfeld & Nicolson, 1988), p. 150.
57. P. Ziegler, *Mountbatten: The Official Biography* (Guild Publishing Company, 1985), p. 694.
58. L. Purves, 'A Period of Silence, Sir', *The Times*, 17 June 1997, p. 22.
59. B. Passmore, 'The Prince and the Inspector', *Times Educational Supplement*, 20 June 1997, p. 9.

# 8 Lessons of the Past and the Future of Royal Education

IN CHAPTER 1 WE attempted to analyse the British view of monarchy and how it has changed. In later chapters we related that view to the education that royals had received, or should have received, from the Tudors to the late twentieth century. We come now to the question of the possible future of the monarchy and the kind of education future kings and queens may need in the twenty-first century. Part of this speculative analysis is an assumption that the monarchy will survive in some form, despite recent criticisms. We have seen, however, that there were several contradictions built into the British view of monarchy which have become increasingly important since the general acceptance of democracy as part of the British way of life. To what extent are the monarchy and equality compatible? Given sufficiently modest definitions of both concepts, it would seem that they are not incompatible although they may not always be completely comfortable together. Part of the problem of compatibility may be the view that the royals themselves have of the monarchy in a democratic age.

In considering the future of the monarchy, including the education of future kings and queens, it may be useful at this stage to review very briefly the earlier chapters of this book. Education of future monarchs has always been the product of a mixture of educational ideas and other kinds of thinking, especially social and religious beliefs and political ideologies. This is not to suggest that these views on education were always consciously formulated theories: it is more likely that they were usually assumptions based on what might have been regarded as commonsense. But commonsense views, including ideas on

233

education, change over time. We always need to look at education in its historical context.

The range of educational provision for past monarchs has been very wide, and some of the difference can be explained in terms of changing political and social conditions. There has been a steady move away from quasi-absolute authority to constitutional monarchy with extremely limited powers or prerogatives; we have observed that there are elements of royal education which have survived. Part of our task has been to identify and comment on those common elements. In the end, it may be that the differences are more interesting than the similarities, but we should start with some common principles.

The following is, we suggest, a minimum list of the knowledge, skills and attitudes required of all the monarchs from the sixteenth century until today. We shall then see how these general headings have been modified over the five centuries. In each case we will evaluate the quality of the educational programme offered and also attempt to relate that quality to the successes and failures of the monarch concerned. We shall, of course, need to bear in mind that it is much easier to judge the quality of an educational programme on paper than it is to assess its relative importance in practice compared with an individual's personality. Another constant feature is what we have identified as an occupational hazard of sovereignty: that the upbringing of kings and queens can be seen to encourage them to believe that they are different from other mortals and that normal laws and rules of moral behaviour do not necessarily apply to them. This last danger can range from very serious 'crimes', which resulted in the execution of Charles I or the expulsion of James II, to trivial examples such as Princes Charles allegedly encouraging his sons to jump a ski-lift queue. (By contrast, Princess Diana was praised for queuing with the two Princes at Marks & Spencer.) We know that power tends to corrupt, but what effect does a lifetime of being flattered and treated with exaggerated reverence or veneration have, even where little or no power is now involved? What kind of education should accompany or replace the flattery?

The education of future kings and queens might also be seen as a special kind of vocational training. In addition to a good general education, now regarded as the right of every child, what else is desirable? The following topics cover five broad areas which were important in the past and are likely to have continued significance in the future:

1. A knowledge of *history* has always been important – especially constitutional history, including 'statecraft' and legal aspects of the constitution. It is essential for monarchs to know about the mistakes made in the past, perhaps in order to avoid repeating them. We have already noted several problems which have arisen partly because kings and queens were ignorant of established rules or conventions. Under this general heading, some aspects of political geography, and the history of other societies should also be included.

2. Some would suggest that even more important than history and statecraft would be having a sound *moral education*: monarchs have always had decisions to make and they should be made fairly, having just regard for rights and duties. In the past, monarchs also had judicial powers over life and limb which were not always exercised in the best possible way. In the twentieth century, moral decisions are more likely to involve questions of personal lifestyle as well as complex issues of setting priorities and providing examples.

3. Closely connected with the ability to make fair decisions is the general process of *decision-making*, including developing judgment in appointing advisors. It is essential for a monarch to be able to make decisions without undue delay, knowing when to ask for and to take advice, but to avoid being taken in by the flattery of manipulators and sycophants. Important decisions include those on marriage – when and to whom. Some have suggested that in the twentieth century this is the most important decision a monarch or future monarch has to make.

4. Some knowledge and understanding of *economics and finance*, both national and personal, including the problems of balancing a budget at both levels. In the past, for example, many monarchs underestimated the crippling cost of war. Now, it is more important to be able to balance a personal budget, but this should be achieved in the context of understanding national finances. The connection between private royal wealth and public financing of the monarchy is a

delicate issue, when the estimated cost to the state of the royal family is about £50 million a year.

5. Finally, a British monarch has needed to be well versed in the understanding of religious controversies, in particular *theological* issues within the Church of England. This may no longer be as important as it was in the sixteenth and seventeenth centuries, but there are still important issues to be addressed, as long as the Queen is still the titular supreme governor of the Church of England and Defender of *the* Faith. Even without that challenge, the position of the Crown in a multicultural, multifaith Commonwealth is complex.

Readers will have made their own judgements, from the evidence presented in Chapters 2 to 7, about the changes over time of the role of sovereign and how well individual kings and queens were prepared for their roles. We will do no more than briefly recapitulate the evidence, taking into consideration both the move towards constitutional monarchy and the kind of education received.

Henry VII, the first of the Tudor monarchs, managed to acquire a good education and was concerned that his children should also be well educated. It has generally been argued that Henry VIII was given excellent tuition according to the ideas of Renaissance education prevailing at the end of the fifteenth century. He was well versed in languages and literature, exceptionally talented in music, and scholarly about the religious controversies of the Reformation. His failures were, first, financial: he indulged in unnecessary and costly foreign campaigns. Second, few of his biographers have found it possible to leave his private life without some criticism. One of the weaknesses of the Renaissance view of education was that it emphasised form and etiquette at the expense of ethics. Henry was selfish and disregarded the rights and feelings of others. It is particularly difficult in his case to decide how much of his failure was a question of education or his personality or the occupational hazard of kingship.

By the time that Henry's son, the future Edward VI, was educated, the theory was changing: the Renaissance ideal was giving way to the ideological concerns of the Reformation. The curriculum for Edward was still based on some Renaissance ideas and practices, but they were subordinated to the need for Edward to become a Protestant Prince. By contrast, his sister Mary was an early illustration of Counter-Reformation zeal in an education programme explicitly designed to produce a Catholic queen who would return the country to the old religion.

Henry's second daughter, Elizabeth I, received what was by sixteenth-century standards, an excellent general education: she achieved high standards in Latin, French, Italian, Greek and history. But what about her vocational training? She was incapable of making up her mind about almost anything. And when she did, eventually, come to a difficult decision, she frequently blamed others for her own inadequacies. In the notorious case of the execution of Mary Queen of Scots, Elizabeth, having signed the death warrant, on hearing that Mary had been executed, blamed one of her secretaries, William Davison, for acting with undue haste. Davison was arrested, tried and sentenced to a heavy fine and to remain in the Tower of London during the Queen's pleasure. And at this point in the story Elizabeth apparently wanted to punish not only Davison but also to hang some other members of her Privy Council. Her inadequate understanding of her constitutional powers caused her to believe that a monarch's rights included the arbitrary privilege of executing any of her subjects at will. It was only with difficulty that Burghley and other senior advisers added to her education by persuading her that her powers did not stretch that far. In other areas Elizabeth's performance was mixed. She understood the theological disputes well enough to steer a middle course for the duration of her reign; she also managed to live within her personal means as well as avoiding any national economic crises. But she was not always good at recognising flattery.

During the Stuart period, significant changes took place both in terms of the role that monarchs played, and also in the education that they received. The difference between the first and the last of the Stuarts is very great. James I was thoroughly educated in the Renaissance tradition, modified by his Puritan tutors, and prepared for the English crown as well as that of Scotland. He, like Henry VIII, was particularly well-versed in the relation between the Crown and the Established Church. He was also well advised to avoid pressing his own views of absolute monarchy too far when faced with any opposition from the English Parliament. His main failings were economic and moral. James's son, Charles I, was not only well educated but was a man of great taste and aesthetic judgement, a distinguished collector and patron of the arts. He also thought of himself as a highly moral character, and in some respects he was, but he was frequently guilty of failing to keep his word, and of deserting his friends and followers when they most needed his support. His most obvious educational failing was, however, that he did not appreciate the limits of his own powers in relation to Parliament and national laws. He paid a high price for inadequate training.

The Commonwealth period saw the development of many social, political and educational ideas, but they were not much in evidence in the education of any of the later Stuart kings and queens. On the other hand, the interregnum made permanent differences to the role of the sovereign. Charles II was the first of the monarchs under consideration whose general education was neglected, not least because the Civil War interrupted his studies very seriously. This does not seem to have made him a failure as a king, except that his personal and public extravagance further weakened his constitutional position. His understanding of moral behaviour also left something to be desired. But he was always careful enough politically to avoid 'going on his travels' again. James II had also suffered from a disorganised formal education, but it would be dangerous to link that too closely to his lack of success as king. However, it is clear that his limited sense of history distorted his view of kingship so that he failed to appreciate the limits of what a monarch could do within the post-Commonwealth concept of sovereignty. Monarchy had moved further away from absolutism than James was prepared to acknowledge. The fact that he was a Roman Catholic might have been overcome if he had possessed greater understanding of his position. His problems were also made more difficult by his poor understanding of economics.

With the Abdication of James II the move away from strong royal authority to a monarchy with reduced powers continued. Some of what had been regarded as royal prerogatives were now restricted by Act of Parliament. This may have been just as well because the education of both of James II's daughters, Mary II and Anne, would have been inadequate for exercising real power. The Renaissance view of education had almost disappeared, together with the notion that women should be educated as well as their male relatives. In Mary's case, William was the effective sovereign; Queen Anne's husband did not become king, but her own monarchical role was extremely limited: she took advice on most occasions, apart from a few incidents which did not seriously threaten the monarchy. Financing long periods of war meant that parliaments were needed every year, and ministers began to decide on the date of dissolution, although in theory this was still a royal prerogative. With the development of the Whig and Tory political parties, the selection of ministers was becoming a party matter rather than the choice of the sovereign.

The education of the Hanoverian kings represented a break with English tradition: the German ethos of the court of the first two Georges has frequently been commented on. This distanced them from English politics as well as giving them a different view of education. George I and George II were reasonably well educated by the standards of their day, although they were not much affected by the dominant theories of the eighteenth century – the Enlightenment. Science and rational thinking were less important factors in their education than traditional expressions of culture such as literature, art and music. By contrast, George III considered himself to be completely English, but it is difficult to evaluate the suitability of his education as his reign was dominated by his sporadic insanity. Parliament demonstrated its right to declare a king unfit to rule and to appoint a regent in his place. George IV had what appeared to be a conventional education, but he still blamed his upbringing for his adult failures; and he never understood English politics. William IV was the first of the sailor kings; joining the Navy at 13, his training was more rigorous than his education. He was king in 1832 when the great Reform Act was passed, but that was in spite of William rather than because of anything he did in the cause of democracy. He was anti-Whig to an extent that stretched the flexibility of the constitution. The Hanoverian contribution to our heritage was mainly aesthetic, notably in architecture.

Queen Victoria had a strange, isolated educational experience. Despite the strong opinions of Baron Stockmar, it would seem that there was no clear theory or educational policy such as had operated in Tudor or Stuart times. Few monarchs or advisors at this time acknowledged the importance of that aspect of social education which involves sharing educational experiences. There were other gaps in her educational knowledge and experience, and she was seriously lacking in imagination. Fortunately, her better-educated husband provided a good influence in some respects: somewhat belatedly, the Enlightenment reached the English court, despite the reactionary views of the Prime Minister, Lord Melbourne. Unhappily, the views of the Queen and Albert on education – a kind of encyclopaedism – were applied too rigidly in the case of the future Edward VII. The Albert and Victoria curriculum paid too much attention to content and not enough to human nature. They also continued the policy of keeping the future king away from the supposedly undesirable company of his social inferiors. The Prince for a long time rebelled against so much inculcation of knowledge and moral values. His post-school education was less disastrous, but much damage had been done by then, though Edward gained more from his university tutors than might have been expected. The loss of real political powers had its advantages: monarchs began to be seen as apolitical, standing above disputes in Parliament.

In the twentieth century, royal education became even less theory based and more haphazard, depending on the ideas, or lack of ideas, of the tutors and governesses. Sovereigns also generally accepted their much more limited role as constitutional monarchs. Edward VII, much to the surprise of some of his subjects, played the role graciously. His son, George V, continued in this new tradition, although his education was generally thought to be inadequate: it was a naval officer's training rather than preparation for kingship. Despite this he became almost a model of constitutional monarchy; this may well have been because he was aware of his own deficiencies and was advised by Arthur Bigge, later Lord Stamfordham. Stamfordham's advice was, however, not infallible and he was regarded by some Liberal politicians as being biased towards the Conservative Party.[1] George's lack of knowledge was less important because he was prepared to take advice, but is it an acceptable situation for a king to be so dependent on the availability of good advice? Is this a problem for education or is it a constitutional issue?

The short reign of Edward VIII brought to a head many of the problems and contradictions of the British style of monarchy in the twentieth century as well as the education and training needed for it. Edward, unlike his father, had been expected to inherit the crown and had been prepared for it. In retrospect it would seem clear that the choice of tutor was ill considered, and that the Osborne–Dartmouth schooling was far from ideal. The damage having been done, Oxford University could not have been expected to educate a prince who lacked the will to study. He also had a closed mind on too many issues. The fact that his brother George had much the same education may well indicate that Edward's failures had as much to do with his personality as with formal education, but his education and training certainly failed to modify his personality sufficiently. For example, Edward understood the unwritten constitution well enough to want to change it, and he would have liked to have become Edward the Innovator. He failed to realise that the kind of innovation that he wanted was incompatible with constitutional monarchy. George, on the other hand, was content to revert to his father's example of taking advice, even when he was personally opposed to the political counsel he received.

What kind of educational programme would encourage kings to take proper advice? Or should the role be changed to remove the remaining royal prerogatives and make advice less crucial? The major lesson of Edward's reign was not immediately accepted: the reality was that there was a serious tension between parliamentary democracy and a monarchy that was constitutional but still retained some of the trappings of power. Had Edward been more astute he might have put that contradiction to the test by exercising his prerogative. In the event he was no match for the adroit politician, Baldwin, and the fundamental issue was temporarily avoided. Perhaps part of the curriculum for future monarchs should be concerned not only with the unwritten constitution, but also include constant reminders that a lifetime of deference may lead to delusions of being superhuman. Edward's problem was that he seemed to believe that he was a superior being who deserved obedience, despite his incompetence and unsuitability as king. Another lesson to be learned from 1936 might be that a future king should be prepared for the correct or constitutional use of what remains of royal prerogatives. Ironically, had Edward VIII received better training of this kind he might have defied Baldwin, got his own way about Mrs Simpson without abdicating and remained as a very unsatisfactory king.

George VI was exposed to the same kind of inadequate education as his elder brother: an unimaginative tutor, a narrow naval training curriculum and a too brief period at university with an imperfectly planned curriculum. The main difference, apart from George having a wife who encouraged him to act effectively within his constitutional limits, was that he did not wish to innovate but simply to do what he saw as his duty. He took as a role model his father, who had reigned with little controversy for 26 years. Personality rather than educational training seemed to be the key factor. He took advice, but the advice was, as we shall see later in this chapter, limited and biased.

Elizabeth II, unlike her father, was trained for the monarchy from an early age although her general education was narrow and undemanding. She grew up at a time when the prestige of the royal family was high. For the whole of her father's reign and about the first 30 years of her own, the contradictions of the British monarchy were not an open problem, although from time to time academics and others concerned with the constitution raised questions about the future, including the need for a written constitution. Elizabeth's education was far from ideal, yet she managed to cope with the problems of her role – at least until the next generation of royals began to give offence to her subjects in a variety of ways. It is doubtful whether her understanding of the constitution and of economics is sufficient to overcome the present tensions and contradictions unaided. It seems that the Labour government which took office in 1997 has undertaken the task of helping her to enable the monarchy to survive as an institution into the twenty-first century. But have either of the future kings – Charles or William – been adequately prepared for that changed role? Probably not: David Cannadine was not impressed by Charles's education, stating: 'Despite having read history at Cambridge, the Prince's sense of the past is, like that of most royals, romantic, escapist and superficial.'[2]

Since Tudor monarchs had real power it was very important for them to be properly educated for the exercise of power. In earlier chapters we were able to point out the deficiencies in royal preparation which caused problems. As the power of kings and queens diminished over the years, education has become less crucial in that respect, but more important in others. Without a written constitution, a future monarch has to be educated to understand the many complex precedents associated with, for example, the royal prerogative on the dissolution of Parliament or the appointment of a Prime Minister. If there were a written constitution the educational task would be considerably simpler. It might also be argued that with the development of constitutional monarchy, the role of Private Secretary to the monarch has increasingly included an element of providing education and training.

PRIVATE SECRETARIES AS ROYAL EDUCATORS

A fascinating insight into the role of Private Secretary was provided by Arthur Ponsonby's biography of his father, Henry,[3] who was Queen Victoria's Private Secretary for 25 years (1870–95). As background to that account, Arthur Ponsonby outlined a brief history of the post. Before the reign of George III, the Home Secretary as the King's constitutional adviser acted as his Private Secretary, partly because it was thought undesirable for anyone other than a Privy Councillor to have access to Cabinet secrets. But when in 1805 George III became almost blind, a temporary exception was made with the appointment of Lieutenant-General Sir Herbert Taylor. As Regent, George IV had no official Private Secretary but he used the Keeper of the Privy Purse, Sir William Knighton, whose main task was to avoid even greater debts accumulating. In 1830, William IV recalled Taylor from retirement; he was very useful for the advice he gave at the time of the Reform Bill, although William's behaviour bordered on the unconstitutional.

Queen Victoria did not have an official Private Secretary until 1861, when General Charles Grey was transferred from Prince Albert's service: he served the Queen until his death in 1870, when he was criticised for not standing up to her more often. Colonel (later Major-General Sir Henry) Ponsonby then was appointed, but he did not become a Privy Councillor until 1880. The appointment met with some opposition because he was regarded as possessing radical tendencies on military matters. Arthur Ponsonby proceeded to give an account of his father's extremely difficult task of advising the Queen until his retirement in 1895, when he was replaced by Arthur Bigge. Since then there has always been an official Private Secretary.

Part of Henry Ponsonby's difficult role was to advise and to educate the Queen whilst not giving her the impression that he was more knowledgeable than she was. He often disagreed with her views but said nothing unless there was some danger of the Queen's reactionary opinions becoming entangled with government policy. His role was complicated by the fact that he owed loyalty not only to the Queen personally but to the sovereign as an institution and to the country (and therefore sometimes to the government). Much of what went on between the Queen and her Private Secretary now seems trivial in the extreme. We might even be tempted to ask why someone accustomed to military command could have subjected himself to what Ponsonby described as 'impetuosity and inconsiderateness'. Ponsonby was clearly helped by his sense of humour. Victoria appears to have accepted his advice on matters that might have been considered beyond his role: 'The Duchess of Roxburgh recommended the novels of Marie Corelli. She began one of them. But on Ponsonby courteously informing her it was "bosh" she seems not to have proceeded any further.' She also used her Private Secretary as a means of delivering 'despotic' instructions to her children, especially the haemophiliac, Leopold. Ponsonby's tact often avoided difficulties between the Queen and the Prince of Wales. The general impression gained from the biography is that the post was, even with such a diplomatic figure as Ponsonby, virtually impossible to perform, whilst the monarch possessed, or thought she possessed, powers as head of state. In his review of the biography Harold Laski took the opportunity to make some relevant points about Private Secretaries in general. He spoke of 'dignified slavery', for example. He began his review by saying 'Little by little our knowledge accumulates of the complicated metaphysics of limited monarchy.' He also suggested that the problem of royal education was 'insoluble'. His proposal by which the metaphysics of constitutional monarchy could continue was 'to keep the Crown a dignified emollient, to confine its acts to ceremonial, to maintain the ultimate faith of parties in its neutrality'.

Sir Francis Knollys[5] served as Private Secretary to Edward VII for the whole of his reign. He seems to have interpreted his role largely in terms of preserving royal prerogatives: his educational role was limited by the fact that Edward was very set in his ways by the time that he became king, having waited a long time for Victoria to die. Knollys continued as Private Secretary to George V, but jointly with Arthur Bigge. The importance of Sir Arthur Bigge to George has already been mentioned. When still Prince of Wales in 1907, George wrote to Bigge: 'What would have happened to me if you had not been there to prepare and help me with my speeches? I can hardly write a letter of any importance without your assistance.'[6] When George became king, he continued to be very dependent on Bigge, and later on Clive Wigram who took over as Private Secretary from 1931 to 1936.[7] But Stamfordham's advice was occasionally disturbingly reactionary: he feared that 'each successive erosion of the royal prerogative heralded the destruction of both the monarchy and a stable society'.[8] Wigram too had a tendency to reinforce rather than to moderate some royal opinions: for example, he shared the King's dislike of foreigners. He also lacked judgement about priorities: while he was Assistant Private Secretary, on the day before the battle of Passchendaele in the First World War, he was worried about whether women munition workers inspected by the Queen should be told to remove their gloves.

Alan Lascelles[9] as Assistant Private Secretary might have advised and educated George V's son Edward when he was Prince of Wales and later as Edward VIII, but the Prince usually ignored any advice from Private Secretaries that he did not like, and Lascelles resigned in despair in 1929. Lascelles had tried to educate Edward but had failed. Alexander Hardinge[10] became Private Secretary to Edward VIII during his short reign and continued to act for George VI. Hardinge too had done his best to educate Edward VIII but had not succeeded: in November 1936 he had written to the King warning him of the constitutional difficulties of a marriage with Mrs Simpson and urged that she should leave the country immediately. Edward took offence and reacted to the letter by asking the lawyer Sir Walter Monckton to act on his behalf in finding a solution to the constitutional difficulty. Hardinge as educator had been rejected, and the King effectively appointed Monckton as his chosen alternative, although as Bogdanor has recently pointed out, on other matters Hardinge continued to act as Private Secretary.[11]

After the Abdication, Hardinge became Private Secretary to George VI, remaining until 1943, when he retired at the early age of 49, because, it was rumoured, his ideas on the training of the King did not always coincide with those of the Queen. At that time, Alan Lascelles took over as Private Secretary. His educational duties had begun much earlier: as Assistant Private Secretary he had accompanied George V on a visit to Canada and the United States, had masterminded the detailed arrangements and instructed the King on protocol. He was rewarded with a knighthood during the visit. During the war George VI was heavily dependent on Lascelles, although he also occasionally found his advice contradicted by the Queen. Cannadine summed up the position rather sharply, saying that George VI was 'surrounded by courtiers and equerries whose world-views were, if anything, even more blinkered and reactionary than his own. Indeed, his two Private Secretaries, Alec Hardinge and Alan Lascelles were snobbish, narrow-minded, obscurantist and completely lacking in flexibility or imagination.'[12] Lascelles retired in 1953, shortly after the death of George VI and was replaced by Michael Adeane (a grandson of Lord Stamfordham).[13] Adeane remained as Private Secretary to the Queen from 1953–72. His son, Edward, was Private Secretary to Prince Charles from 1979 to 1985. Hereditary monarchs served by hereditary courtiers?

This short review of some of the Private Secretary 'educators' has illustrated an aspect of the Court which has often been criticised: Private Secretaries, and other senior court officials, have tended to come from a very exclusive social background, with an education which is typically public school, Oxford or Cambridge, and a period of commissioned military service in an elite regiment. Such courtiers represent only a limited section of the Queen's subjects. They identify with only a part of the population rather than the whole nation. John Grigg[14] suggested a solution: recruiting advisors from a much wider social spectrum, including some from other Commonwealth countries. This has so far only been acted upon in a rather half-hearted way.[15]

## THE PRESENT PROBLEM

It is generally agreed, even among those who have criticised the royal family, that there was a period of strong support for the monarchy stretching from the accession of George VI in 1936, reaching a high point in the early years of the reign of Elizabeth II. But it went into decline in the 1980s, reaching a low point in 1992 (the Queen's *'annus horribilis'*) and by 1997 support for the monarchy as an institution sank, for a while, to below 50 per cent. There is some dispute about the reasons for the decline: while the Queen herself was respected, the behaviour of the younger royals, including Prince Charles, received much attention in the popular press, giving the impression of young people with too much money behaving irresponsibly. This bad publicity was linked to the broader issue of the cost of the royal family and the question of value for taxpayers' money. The Queen's private wealth had received regular attention in newspapers, yet when Windsor Castle caught fire in 1992, it was announced that the multi-million-pound bill would be passed on to the taxpayer. This provoked various analyses of the cost of the monarchy and also the taxes that many thought the Queen ought to be paying. Some accused the Windsors of wanting the best of both worlds: claiming to be 'a normal family' when it suited them, but clinging to the privileges of royalty and an extravagant lifestyle.[16] The question of taxation had been under consideration for some time and the Queen had already decided to offer to pay some income tax, but when this was announced it was interpreted as a reluctant decision under pressure, and also as 'too little, too late'. The death of Princess Diana in 1997 added to the unpopularity of the royal family: despite the success of the funeral as a 'royal occasion', the Windsors were criticised for a number of decisions which were alleged to show that they were unsympathetic to Diana as well as being out of touch with public opinion. Could better royal training have helped the avoidance of such bad publicity? Or was it simply a question of public relations? Or were more fundamental changes necessary?

We saw in Chapter 1 that to counter the charge of being remote and out of touch, the royal family (or at least the Way Ahead Group) decided to copy the methods of professional politicians by employing 'spin doctors' and indulging in such modern techniques as focus groups and public opinion polls. But this was to attack the symptoms rather than the cause: underlying the superficial manifestations of unpopularity were deeper social, political, constitutional and educational issues. The fundamental problem was that although the monarchy had survived into the modern age it had failed to adjust sufficiently to the fact that the royal family in a modern democratic society had to be very different from what had worked in Victorian England and in the first half of the twentieth century. The current problem is very complex: it concerns the role of a constitutional monarchy in a country which is not only democratic but in which certain democratic values have become part of the belief system. That change clearly had educational implications which have not yet been addressed. Jonathan Dimbleby's biography of the Prince of Wales, published in 1994, attempted to show Charles's suitability to become king. Cannadine in his review of the book, on the other hand, thought that he had been unsuccessful.[17] As another royal biographer has commented: 'He will need to prove himself more in touch with the progressive thinking and relaxed life-style of a large proportion of his own age-group, who approach the seats of power quite as remorselessly as he approaches the throne. It is the greatest irony of the many innovations in his upbringing, and the many royal "firsts" he has himself achieved, that they have combined to produce the most conventional young Prince of Wales of modern times.'[18]

The British political system is not only a parliamentary democracy but, especially since the end of the Second World War, a system resting on the principle of equality of opportunity. There is, of course, a gap between ideal and reality with this principle; nevertheless there has been a gradual move towards the recognition that equality of opportunity is a desirable aspiration, especially in health, justice, human rights and education. We are still a long way from achieving the ideal, but the principle is only rarely challenged. The ideal of equality of opportunity calls into question the continued existence of such institutions as a House of Lords with a partly hereditary membership. Because that kind of privilege flies in the face of full democracy, it is likely that the House of Lords will be reformed in some way to remove the vestiges of hereditary power. Where would that leave the monarchy? There is a need for a head of state but no enthusiasm for a presidential solution. It has been suggested that there would be far less opposition to the continued existence of the Windsor dynasty if the title of King or Queen continued to be inherited, but that it was made clear in a written constitution that there were no powers attached. In time Prince Charles would become Charles III without any royal powers, unless he decided to opt out. Without the pretence of power it would be easier for other justificatory 'theories' of monarchy to disappear. For example, it has become clear in the last 20 years or so that it is unreasonable and unrealistic for members of the royal family to act as role models for the rest of us. Far better for them to be expected to act in accordance with existing norms and to avoid offensive and ostentatious behaviour. In this respect Charles may be right in wanting to relinquish that part of the role which demands that he be 'Defender of the Faith'. That religious function could be left to the Archbishop of Canterbury, just as political functions should be clearly in the hands of the Prime Minister. Would that leave enough for the royal family to do?

Prochaska has demonstrated that since George III, our monarchy has not only been moving towards a constitutional, powerless position, but has also established itself as the leading role-players in the world of charity.[19] Prochaska also shows that whereas in the period immediately following the Second World War the Labour Party might have opposed such a role on grounds of the need for total centralised planning, today this is no longer the case. Prince Charles has devoted a good deal of his time to the Prince's Trust working especially with the young unemployed. Princess Anne has similarly been very active in Save the Children Fund; and one of the reasons for Diana's popularity was her high-profile work with underprivileged children. It is now generally acknowledged, not least by the Labour Party, that the welfare state is unlikely to be able to meet all possible demands on it; this makes the royal concern for welfare appropriate and possibly useful. Members of the royal family generally seem to have accepted this position of leadership without power. These changes would obviate the necessity for much of the customary advice on constitutional matters. Advisers will still be needed but they would be less politically important to the system than, for example, Lord Stamfordham was to George V. This would also avoid the problem of a king or queen receiving bad advice.[20] These occasions have been rare but still sufficiently numerous to be regarded as a constitutional weakness.

There are some indications that Prince Charles is considering actions along the above lines, probably more radical actions than those endorsed by the other members of the Way Ahead Group. On 12 July 1998 the *Sunday Times* leaked some of the plans of 'Prince Charles, together with close advisers and friends'. It was stated that the plans included a more accessible monarchy which would be less associated with the aristocratic landowning class. One example of ways of achieving that objective was that Balmoral would be handed over to the Scottish National Trust when Charles became king. In the same *Sunday Times* report, Lord St John of Fawsley was quoted as confirming the Prince's wish to establish a more 'inclusive' monarchy, not mixed up with the aristocracy. But Charles would also need to distance himself from some of the upper-class practices which probably cause much greater offence than he realises, fox-hunting and blooding, for example. Has he been advised on this? It may be that private education falls into the same category: identifying with a small elite group rather than the whole nation. The idea of a more inclusive monarchy would answer some of the points made years before by John Grigg.[21] Others have also commented on the 'exclusive' image of the present Queen: for example, Anthony Sampson, writing in 1982, said that 'the Queen's own life has remained almost uniquely unchanged. She still pursues her timeless progress between her palaces and country estates, surrounded by the rituals of nineteenth-century rural life, concerned with racehorses, forestry or corgis. She is still accompanied by friends from landed or military backgrounds, with a strong hereditary emphasis. The Mistress of the Robes is the Duchess of Grafton; the Ladies of the Bed Chamber are the Marchioness of Abergavenny and the Countess of Airlie.'[22] It may also be advisable for the Prince to consider to what extent elaborate royal ceremonies would conflict with a more inclusive monarchy. Is it possible to shed some of the mystique and magic but retain a role as symbolising national consensus?

In an article in the *Sunday Times* about the anniversary of the death of Diana, Pimlott made a number of interesting observations, including a suggestion for the future role of the monarchy.[23] He discussed the idea of a role for the royal family as 'filling the democratic deficit'. He pursued the Galbraith diagnosis in *The Culture of Contentment*, which said that the affluence of the majority had encouraged parties of the left to seek the support of the middle classes even if it meant moving away from the redistributive policy of taxing the rich to provide for the poor. If this diagnosis is correct for Britain, there would be a non-party-political role to play in focusing on the hole in our system left by 'the demise of traditional socialism': an interesting idea of a monarchy more radical than the Labour Party. Some might argue that the Prince's Trust has already moved in that direction in a non-political way. If Diana could bring a little magic into the world of AIDS and leprosy, perhaps Charles could begin to illuminate the problem of youth unemployment.

## EDUCATIONAL IMPLICATIONS

Part of the problem of recent years has been uncertainty about what was required in the role of being a royal, and that may have been a failure of education to some extent, although the constitutional issues are more important. Given the changes suggested earlier in this chapter, what kind of education should future royals receive? The answer is easy in principle, but probably highly controversial in practice. If future royals are to be regarded as normal members of society with no special privileges, then it would seem to follow that their education should be as normal as possible, with some special attention being paid to the five areas outlined at the beginning of this chapter. But what is normal? A fashionable preparatory school, followed by Eton and Oxford? Or the local primary school, a comprehensive secondary school and a provincial university? The principle of 'normal' is easy, the implementation difficult. In recent years, while there have been many moves towards modernising the monarchy, it could be argued that there has been much less progress on the education of princes, even a retreat to the traditional. Whereas Princes Charles, Andrew and Edward followed their father to Gordonstoun, an unconventional – in some respects even progressive – independent school, the next generation of princes have had Eton chosen for them. This will be interpreted by some as a confirmation of the view that the monarchy is too closely connected with the aristocracy and upper classes to be accepted as a truly democratic institution. There are other aspects of educational change which may be important.

In Chapter 1 we showed that since George V, some of the writings of Bagehot[24] have been part of the royal curriculum. This is not an adequate basic text for royals in the context of true democracy. Bagehot was extremely cynical about the operation of Victorian government, and part of his thesis was how to keep an ignorant electorate under control. He therefore used such expressions as 'the magic of the monarchy' and his advice was that rulers should be careful not to let too much light onto it. The words 'magic' and 'mysticism' have continued to be used by many writers on monarchy since Bagehot, but it may be that in the late twentieth century we need a more honest approach rather than the deception that Bagehot seemed to recommend. Bagehot was at most a reluctant democrat, sharing with many upper-class Victorians a contempt for the masses and a fear that the lower orders might one day gain too much power: the monarchy was for such cynics part of the state apparatus to keep the working classes in their deferential place. The monarchy was a safer alternative to the state power of the police force and the Army. That cynical Victorian solution will not do for the twenty-first century: we need sensible constitutional reforms accompanied by a much improved education programme. Queen Victoria once stated that she would not wish to be the sovereign in a democracy: her Windsor descendants, with the possible exception of Edward VIII, were more flexible. John Cannon has suggested that the British monarchy survived when most others were swept away because it came to terms with democracy.[25] But two problems remain: first, the royal family must not simply adjust to democracy; it must become fully part of a democratic society, including its education system. Second, the royal family needs to find a set of useful roles to play which are consistent with democracy.

The specific educational implications of this stress on democracy are reasonably clear. The educational programme of future kings and queens, or those near in line of succession, should be as normal as possible. We have already discussed the problem of interpreting 'normal' in this context, but from age 5 to 16 the problem has been solved to some extent by the existence of the national curriculum.[26] In addition to the requirements of the national curriculum, it would be desirable to ensure adequate progress in some of the key areas discussed earlier in this chapter, such as constitutional history. A moral tutor should also be appointed to supervise some of those aspects of upbringing which were also referred to earlier: for example, the need to ensure that a future king is not corrupted by flattery and deference, what we referred to earlier as the occupational hazard of being royal. This social and moral education should continue into adult life – perhaps until the age of 25 when the role should transfer to carefully selected non-deferential advisors. The national curriculum does not continue beyond the age of 16, but this is just the time when some careful planning may be necessary. One interesting possibility would be to progress from the national curriculum and GCSE examinations at 16 to the International Baccalaureate which could be taken at one of the United World Colleges,[27] such as Atlantic College in Wales. The advantage of this kind of education from 16 to 19 is that it is not only academic but emphasises international understanding and includes community service: in Atlantic College, for example, one community service option is to crew the local lifeboat service. That kind of experience would be closer to what Charles himself benefited from at Gordonstoun, but without the Spartan regime which he disliked so much. Finally, at university a special programme could be planned which would supplement a normal degree course. Such a programme should include understanding the British constitution (but not the Bagehot version), the rise of democracy in England, Europe and the Commonwealth, with further attention to economics and public affairs. A degree such as philosophy, politics and economics (PPE) at Oxford would meet many of these needs, but it should not be assumed that future princes or princesses should necessarily attend either Oxford or Cambridge. There would be much advantage gained from sampling several provincial and Scottish or Welsh universities, or higher education in other parts of Europe or the Commonwealth.

Although the education of Princes William and Henry has been settled up to the end of their school days at Eton, it may not be too late to plan something more imaginative and more appropriate for their post-school education and training.

Many have suggested that the key to the survival of the monarchy is for them to relinquish the vestiges of political power, such as the Queen's Speech on the first day of Parliament. We suggest that there are two other necessary parts to the formula: first, finding a satisfactory new role for a slimmed down royal family; second, a much better educational programme.

The monarchy is in need of reappraisal. It should not be assumed that given time all will eventually come right again; the monarchy needs to adapt consciously and rationally to changing social and political circumstances. Peter Hennessy[28] pointed out that the last time the monarch's role in the constitution was written down was in 1949. Bogdanor's book,[29] despite an over-optimistic view of the monarchy, demonstrates that there are many issues needing attention. There is some evidence that young people may be less tolerant of the *status quo* than their parents.

An important part of the reappraisal should be what Bogdanor describes as converting the magical into the practical. We should no longer be satisfied with what George Bernard Shaw mocked as kings being made by 'universal hallucination'. Prochaska[30] has discussed the development on one important practical tradition, welfare monarchy, which Prince Charles seems to be very willing to adopt. But that in itself will not be enough; welfare monarchy is unlikely to succeed unless it is accompanied by real concern for democracy, including democratic education and education for democracy. To equip future monarchs for that kind of practical democratic role will necessarily involve modernising royal educational practices. In the past few years, there have been countless discussions about the future of the royal family, but few constructive suggestions about changing one of its key elements: royal education. The plans for Princes William and Harry have probably already been made, but the two Princes are likely to witness considerable constitutional changes during their life-times. The real turning point will be when decisions have to be made concerning the upbringing and formal education of *their* children. By then it is likely that something more appropriate for a democratic society will be called for.

NOTES

1. See V. Bogdanor, *The Monarchy and the Constitution* (Oxford University Press, 1995). Chapter 3 gives several examples.
2. D. Cannadine, *History in Our Time* (Yale University Press, 1998), p. 69.
3. Arthur Ponsonby, *Henry Ponsonby: Queen Victoria's Private Secretary: His Life from his Letters* (Macmillan, 1942).
4. Harold Laski, 'The King's Secretary', review of Ponsonby, *The Fortnightly Review*, 158 (December 1942), pp. 389–93.
5. Sir Francis Knollys (later 1st Viscount) (1837–1924). Private Secretary to Edward VII and joint Private Secretary to George V, a Liberal who sometimes disagreed on constitutional matters with his joint Private Secretary, Arthur Bigge, who was a strong Tory.
6. Quoted by K. Rose in his *Kings, Queens and Courtiers* (Weidenfeld & Nicolson, 1985), p. 266.
7. Sir Clive Wigram (later 1st Baron) (1873–1960). The son of an official in the Madras Civil Service. Educated at Winchester College and Royal Military Academy. Commissioned into the Royal Artillery but transferred to the Bengal Lancers. Aide-de-camp to Viceroys Elgin and Curzon. Assistant Private Secretary, 1910–31, when he succeeded Lord Stamfordham as Private Secretary and served until 1936.
8. Rose, *Kings, Queens and Courtiers*, p. 281.
9. Sir Alan Lascelles (1887–1981). Assistant Private Secretary to George V and to the Prince of Wales; Private Secretary to George VI and Elizabeth II. Grandson of the 4th Earl of Harewood and cousin of the 6th Earl. Educated at Marlborough and Trinity College, Oxford.
10. Sir Alexander Hardinge (later 2nd Baron Hardinge of Penshurst) (1894–1960). Private Secretary to King Edward VIII and King George VI. The son of the 1st Baron Hardinge, who had been Viceroy of India. Educated at Harrow and Cambridge, and served in the Grenadier Guards. Appointed Assistant Private Secretary to George V in 1920 and served until 1936, when he became Private Secretary to Edward VIII.
11. Bogdanor, *The Monarchy and the Constitution*, p. 209. On the same page Bogdanor stated that 'It was due in no small part to Hardinge that the monarchy survived the Abdication relatively unscathed.'
12. Cannadine, *History in Our Time*, p. 65.
13. Sir Michael Adeane (1st Baron) (1910–84). Private Secretary to the Queen, 1953–72. Educated at Eton and Cambridge. Aide-de-camp to Lord Tweedsmuir, Governor-General of Canada. Assistant Private Secretary to George VI, 1937.
14. John Grigg, when still Lord Altrincham, wrote an essay in 1957 for the *National and English Review* which criticised some aspects of the royal style. He returned to this subject in *The Monarchy and its Future*, ed. Jeremy Murray-Brown (George Allen & Unwin, 1969).
15. Since 1972 there have been five Private Secretaries: Sir Martin Charteris (1972–77); Sir Philip Moore (1977–86); Sir William Heseltine (1986–90); and Sir Robert Fellowes (1990–99); and Sir Robin Janvrin since February 1999. Only Heseltine came from a Commonwealth country – Australia. See Bogdanor, *The Monarchy and the Constitution*, who devotes a whole chapter to the Private Secretaries.
16. Philip Hall has written a very informative book about the royal finances: *Royal Fortune: Tax, Money and the Monarchy* (Bloomsbury, 1992).
17. Cannadine, *History in Our Time*, p. 72.
18. A. Holden, *Charles, Prince of Wales* (Weidenfeld & Nicolson, 1979), p. 20.
19. Frank Prochaska, *Royal Bounty: The Making of a Welfare Monarchy* (Yale University Press, 1995).
20. See Note 1 above. There was another controversial decision connected with Stamfordham's grandson, Michael Adeane, who played a questionable part in the

choice of Lord Home rather than R. A. Butler as Prime Minister in 1963. Bogdanor mentions others.

21. Lord Altrincham, 'The Monarchy Today', *National and English Review*, 149 (August 1957), pp. 61–6.
22. Anthony Sampson, *The Changing Anatomy of Britain* (Hodder & Stoughton, 1982), p. 4.
23. B. Pimlott, 'After Diana', *Sunday Times*, 30 August 1998.
24. Walter Bagehot (1826–77). For many years editor of the *Economist*. His book *The English Constitution* (1867) was the text used to instruct successive monarchs. But it is considered to be over-simplified and misleading.
25. John Cannon, *The Modern British Monarchy: A Study in Adaptation* (University of Reading, 1987).
26. The national curriculum is not a legal requirement in independent schools, but it would be highly desirable for a prince to be educated in a school which followed the national curriculum.
27. Prince Charles was President of the United World Colleges until 1993, when he handed over to Nelson Mandela.
28. P. Hennessy, *Muddling Through: Power, Politics and the Quality of Government in Post-War Britain* (Gollancz, 1996).
29. Bogdanor, *The Monarchy and the Constitution*.
30. Prochaska, *Royal Bounty*.

# Bibliography

*Note:* All publishers are in London unless otherwise stated.

Adamson, J. W., *A Short History of Education* (Cambridge University Press, Cambridge, 1919).

Aikin, L., *Memoirs of the Court of King James the First,* Vol. I (Longman, Hurst, Rees, Orme & Brown, 1822).

Airy. O. (ed.), *Burnet's History of My Own Time,* Vol. I (Clarendon Press, Oxford, 1897).

Airy, O., *Charles II* (Goupil & Co., 1901).

Akrigg, G. P. V. (ed.), *Letters of King James VI and I* (University of California Press, Berkeley, CA, 1984).

Albert, The Prince Consort, *The Principal Speeches and Addresses of HRH The Prince Consort* (John Murray, 1862).

Alexander, M. V. C., *The First of the Tudors: A Study of Henry VII and his Reign* (Croom Helm, 1981).

Alexandra, Queen of Yugoslavia, *Prince Philip: A Family Portrait* (Weidenfeld & Nicolson, 1966).

Altrincham, Lord, 'The Monarchy Today', *National and English Review,* 149 (August 1957).

*Annual Register for 1762* (R. & J. Dodsley, 1762).

Anon., *A Letter upon Education: Translated from the French of a Royal Author,* 2nd edn (J. Nourse, 1777).

Anon., *Who Should Educate the Prince of Wales?* (Effingham Wilson, 1843).

Arnold-Brown, R., *Unfolding Character: The Impact of Gordonstoun* (Routledge & Kegan Paul, 1962).

Aronson, T., *Prince Eddy and the Homosexual Underworld* (Murray, 1994).

Ashley, M., *James II* (Dent, 1977).

Ashley, M., *Charles I and Oliver Cromwell: A Study in Contrasts and*

257

*Comparisons* (Methuen, 1987).

Ashton, J., *Social Life in the Reign of Queen Anne*, Vol. II (Chatto & Windus, 1882).

Aspinall, A., *Mrs Jordan and Her Family* (Arthur Barker, 1951).

Aspinall, A. (ed.), *The Correspondence of George, Prince of Wales, 1770–1812*, 8 vols (Cassell, 1963–71).

Ayling, S., *George the Third* (Collins, 1972).

Baillie, A. and Bolitho, H. (eds), *Letters of Lady Augusta Stanley: A Young Lady at Court* (Gerald Howe, 1927).

Barnett Smith, G., *The Life of Queen Victoria* (Routledge, 1901).

Bascombe, K., 'Sir Anthony Denny', in D. Dean (ed.), *The Worthies of Waltham*, Part 2 (Waltham Abbey Historical Society, Essex, 1978).

Bathurst, B. (ed.), *Letters of the Two Queens* (Robert Holden, 1924).

Battiscombe, G., *Queen Alexandra* (Constable, 1969).

Beckett, N., 'Henry VII and Sheen Charterhouse', in B. Thompson (ed.), *The Reign of Henry VII* (Paul Watkins, Stamford, Lincs., 1995).

Beer, B. L. (ed.), *The Life and Raigne of King Edward the Sixth by John Hayward* (Kent State University Press, OH, 1993).

Benson, A. C. and Viscount Esher (eds), *The Letters of Queen Victoria, 1837–1861*, 3 vols (John Murray, 1907).

Bergeron, D. M., *Royal Families, Royal Lovers: King James of England and Scotland* (University of Missouri Press, Columbia, MO, 1991).

Berkeley, G. F.-H., *Wellington College: The Founders of the Tradition* (R. H. Johns, Newport, 1948).

Bettam, J., *A Brief Treatise on Education with a Particular Respect to the Children of Great Personages for the Use of His Royal Highness The Prince* (P. Lauren, Paris, 1693).

Bevan, B., *King James VI of Scotland and I of England* (Rubicon Press, 1996).

Bingham, C., *The Making of a King* (Collins, 1969).

Birkenhead, Lord, *Walter Monckton: The Life of Viscount Monckton of Brenchley* (Weidenfeld & Nicolson, 1969).

Birnbaum, N., 'Monarchies and Sociologists: A Reply to Shils and Young', *Sociological Review*, New Series, 3, 1 (1955).

Bogdanor, V., *The Monarchy and the Constitution* (Oxford University Press, Oxford, 1995).

Bolitho, H., *King Edward VIII: His Life and Reign* (Eyre & Spottiswoode, 1937).

Bolitho, H., *George VI* (Eyre & Spottiswoode, 1937).

Boothroyd, B., *Philip: An Informal Biography* (Longman, 1971).

Bowen, M., *The Third Mary Stuart* (The Bodley Head, 1929).

Bowle, J., *Henry VIII: A Biography* (Allen & Unwin, 1964).

Bowle, J., *Charles I: A Biography* (Weidenfeld & Nicolson, 1975).

Bowring, J., *Collected Works of Jeremy Bentham* (William Tait, Edinburgh, 1843).

Bradford, F., *Nelson the Essential Hero* (Macmillan, 1977).

Bradford, S., *King George VI* (Weidenfeld & Nicolson, 1989).

Bradford, S., *Elizabeth: A Biography of Her Majesty the Queen* (Heinemann, 1996).

Bray, W. (ed.), *The Diary of John Evelyn* (Bickers & Son, 1906).

Brereton, H. L., *Gordonstoun* (W. & R. Chambers, 1968).

Brett, A. C. A., *Charles II and His Court* (Methuen, 1910).

Brett, M. V. (ed.), *Journals and Letters of Reginald, Viscount Esher*, 2 vols (Ivor Nicholson & Watson, 1934).

Brooke, J., *King George the Third* (Constable, 1972).

Brown, B. C. (ed.), *The Letters and Diplomatic Instructions of Queen Anne* (Cassell, 1935).

Bruce, M. L., *The Making of Henry VIII* (Collins, 1977).

Buckle, G. E. (ed.), *The Letters of Queen Victoria*, 2nd series, Vol. II (John Murray, 1926).

Burne, A. H., *The Noble Duke of York* (Staples Press, 1949).

Burridge, T., *Clement Attlee: A Political Biography* (Cape, 1985).

Butler, Lord, *The Art of the Possible: The Memoirs of Lord Butler* (Hamish Hamilton, 1971).

*Calendar of State Papers*, Charles I 1639, Domestic (HMSO, 1873).

Cannadine, D., 'The Context, Performance and Meaning of Ritual: The British Monarchy and the "Invention of Tradition", *c.* 1820–1977', in E. Hobsbawm and T. Ranger (eds), *The Invention of Tradition* (Cambridge University Press, Cambridge, 1983).

Cannadine, D., *History in Our Time* (Yale University Press, 1998).

Cannon, J., 'The Survival of the British Monarchy', *Transactions of the Royal Historical Society*, 5th series, 36 (1986).

Cannon, J. (ed.), *The Modern British Monarchy: A Study in Adaptation* (University of Reading, 1987).

Carey, Robert, Earl of Monmouth, *Memoirs* (Constable, Edinburgh, 1808).

Carlson, D. R., 'Royal Tutors in the Reign of Henry VII', *Sixteenth Century Journal*, 22 (1991).

Carlton, C., *Charles I: The Personal Monarch* (Routledge & Kegan Paul, 1983).

Carpenter, E. F., *The Protestant Bishop: Being the Life of Henry Compton, Bishop of London* (Longman, Green, 1956).

Carswell, J. and Dralle, L. A. (eds), *The Political Journal of George Bubb Dodington* (Oxford University Press, Oxford, 1965).

Cecil, D., *Lord M.* (Constable, 1954).

Chakrabongse, Prince Chulua of Siam, *The Education of Enlightened Despots* (Eyre & Spottiswoode, 1948).

Chapman, H. W., *Mary II Queen of England* (Cape, 1953).

Chapman, H. W., *The Last Tudor King* (Cape, 1958).

Charlton, K., *Education in Renaissance England* (Routledge & Kegan Paul, 1965).

Chevenix Trench, C., *George II* (Allen Lane, 1973).

Childs, D., *Britain since 1945: A Political History*, 3rd edn (Routledge, 1992).

Chrimes, S. B., *Henry VII* (Eyre, Methuen, 1972).

Churchill, R. S., *Lord Derby 'King of Lancashire'* (Heinemann, 1959).

Churchill, S., *An Account of the Conduct of the Dowager Duchess of Marlborough* (George Hawkins, 1742).

Chute, M., *Ben Jonson of Westminster* (Hale, 1954).

Clarendon, Lord, *Memoirs of King Charles I* (I. Herbert, 1795 edn).

Clarke, J. S., *The Life of James the Second, King of England* (Page & Foss, Budd & Calker, 1816).

Clarke, M. L., 'The Education of a Prince in the Sixteenth Century: Edward VI and James VI and I', *History of Education*, 7 (1978).

Cokayne, G. E. C. (ed. V. Gibbs), *The Complete Peerage*, Vol. II (St Catherine Press, 1912).

Cole, G. D. H., *Politics and Literature* (Hogarth Press, 1929).

Collinson, P., '"Windows in a Woman's Soul": Questions about the Religion of Queen Elizabeth I', in *Elizabethan Essays* (Hambleden Press, 1994).

Colville, A., *Duchess Sarah* (Longman, Green, 1904).

Connell, N., *Anne: The Last Stuart Monarch* (Thornton Butterworth, 1937).

Cosenza, M. E., *Biographical and Bibliographical Dictionary of the Italian Humanism in Italy, 1300–1800*, Vol. IV (G. K. Hall, Boston, MA, 1962).

Cowper, Mary Countess, *Diary of Mary, Countess Cowper, Lady of the Bedchamber to the Princess of Wales, 1714–20* (Murray, 1864).

Crabitès, P., *Victoria's Guardian Angel: A Study of Baron Stockmar* (Routledge, 1937).

Craigie, J. (ed.), *The Basilikon Doron of King James VI* (The Scottish Text Society, Blackwood, Edinburgh, 1944).

Crawford, M., *The Little Princesses* (Cassell, 1950).

Crawford, M., *Queen Elizabeth II* (George Newnes, 1952).

Cressy, D., *Education in Tudor and Stuart England* (Edward Arnold, 1975).

Creston, D., *The Regent and his Daughter* (Eyre & Spottiswoode, 1947).

Creston, D., *The Youthful Queen Victoria* (Macmillan, 1952).

Crossman, R., *The Diaries of a Cabinet Minister*, Vol. I, 1964–66 (Hamilton/Cape, 1975).

Curties, H., *A Forgotten Prince of Wales* (Everett, 1930).

Curtis, S. J. and Boultwood, M. E. A., *A Short History of Educational Ideas* (University Tutorial Press, 1965).

Dalrymple, J., *Memoirs of Great Britain and Ireland* (A. Strachan & T. Cadell, 1790).

Dalton, H., *Call Back Yesterday: Memoirs, 1887–1931* (Muller, 1953).

Daniel, G., *Some Small Harvest: The Memoirs of Glyn Daniel* (Thames & Hudson, 1986).

Davys, G., *A Plain and Short History of England* (Rivington, 1850).

Defoe , D., *Of Royall Educacion*, ed. K. D. Bülbring (David Nutt, 1895).

De-La-Noy, M., *The King Who Never Was: The Story of Frederick, Prince of Wales* (Peter Owen, 1996).

Dillon, Viscount, 'Some Familiar Letters of Charles II and James, Duke of York, Addressed to their Daughter and Niece, the Countess of Litchfield', *Archaeologia*, 58 (1902).

Dimbleby, J., *The Prince of Wales: A Biography* (Little, Brown, 1994).

Disraeli, I., *Commentaries on the Life and Reign of Charles the First*, ed. B. Disraeli (Henry Colburn, 1851).

Donaldson, F. C., *Edward VIII* (Weidenfeld & Nicolson, 1974).

Donne, W. B., *The Correspondence of King George the Third to Lord North, 1768–1783*, 2 vols (Murray, 1867).

Dowling, M., *Humanism in the Age of Henry VIII* (Croom Helm, 1986).

Duff, D., *Mother of the Queen* (Frederick Muller, 1965).

Duff, D., *Albert and Victoria* (Frederick Muller, 1972).

Duff, D., *George and Elizabeth: A Royal Marriage* (Collins, 1983).

Earle, P., *The Life and Times of James II* (Weidenfeld & Nicolson, 1972).

Edwards, A., *Frederick Louis, Prince of Wales, 1707–51* (Staples Press, 1947).

Edwards, A., *Matriarch: Queen Mary and the House of Windsor* (Hodder & Stoughton, 1984).

Edwards, A., *Royal Sisters: Elizabeth and Margaret, 1926–1956* (Collins, 1990).

Ellot, G. P. (ed.), 'The Diary of Dr. Edward Lake, 1677–8', *Camden Society Miscellany*, 1 (1847), p. 5.

Ellis, H., *Original Letters, Illustrative of English History*, ser. 1, Vol. III, (Harding, Triphook & Lepard, 1825).

Ellis, J. (ed.), *Thatched with Gold: The Memoirs of Mabell, Countess of Airlie* (Hutchinson, 1962).

Elsna, H., *Catherine of Braganza* (Hale, 1967).

Elyot, Sir John (ed. A. T. Eliot), *The Governor* (Ridgway & Sons, 1531, 1834 edn).

Erickson, C., *Bloody Mary* (Dent, 1978).

Erickson, C., *Great Harry* (Dent, 1980).

Erickson, C., *The First Elizabeth* (Macmillan, 1983).

Erskine, E. (ed.), *Twenty Years at Court: From the Correspondence of the Hon. Eleanor Stanley* (Nisbet, 1916).

Esher, Viscount (ed.), *The Girlhood of Queen Victoria*, 2 vols (John Murray, 1912).

Falkus, C., *The Life and Times of Charles II* (Weidenfeld & Nicolson, 1972).

Fisher, G. and H., *Charles: The Man and the Prince* (Robert Hale, 1977).

Fitzgerald, D., *The Life of George the Fourth*, 2 vols (Tinsley Brothers, 1881).

Foot, M., *The Pen and the Sword* (McGibbon & Kee, 1957).

Forbes, G., *My Darling Buffy: The Early Life of the Queen Mother* (Richard Cohen, 1997).

Forester, H. (trans.), *Memoirs of Sophia, Electress of Hanover, 1630–1680* (Bentley & Son, 1888).

Fowler, L. and Fowler, H. (eds), *Cambridge Commemorated* (Cambridge University Press, Cambridge, 1984).

Foxcroft, H. C. (ed.), *Life and Letters of Sir George Savile, Bart, First Marquis of Halifax* (Longman, Green, 1898).

Foxcroft, H. C., *A Supplement to Burnet's History of My Own Time* (Clarendon Press, Oxford, 1902).

Fox-Strangways, A. H., *Cecil Sharp* (Oxford University Press, Oxford, 1933).

Frankland, N., *Prince Henry, Duke of Gloucester* (Weidenfeld & Nicolson, 1980).

Fraser, A., *King James VI of Scotland and I of England* (Weidenfeld & Nicolson, 1974).

Fraser, A., *King Charles II* (Weidenfeld & Nicolson, 1979).

Fulford, R., *George the Fourth* (Duckworth, 1935).

Fulford, R. (ed.), *The Prince Consort* (Macmillan, 1949).

Fulford, R. (ed.), *Darling Child: The Private Correspondence of Queen Victoria and the Crown Princess of Prussia, 1871–1878* (Evans, 1976).

Gathorne-Hardy, J., *The Rise and Fall of the British Nanny* (Hodder & Stoughton, 1972).

Gibbs, F. W., 'The Education of a Prince', *Cornhill Magazine*, Spring (1951).

Gibbs, P., *George the Faithful: The Life and Times of George V* (Hutchinson, 1936).

Giles, J. A. R. (ed.), *The Whole Works of Roger Ascham*, Vol. III (John Russell Smith, 1864).

Godwin, G., 'Edward Lake', in S. Lee (ed.), *Dictionary of National Biography* (Smith, Elder, 1892).

Gore, J., *King George V: A Personal Memoir* (Murray, 1941).

Gore, J., 'George V', in L. G. Wickham Legg (ed.), *Dictionary of National Biography, 1931–1940* (Oxford University Press, Oxford, 1949).

Gotch, J. A., *Inigo Jones* (Methuen, 1928).

Green, D., *Queen Anne* (Collins, 1970).

Greer, D., 'Henry VIII', in *The New Grove Dictionary of Music*, Vol. VIII (Macmillan, 1980).

Gregg, E., 'The Education of Princes: Queen Anne and Her Contemporaries', in J. D. Browning (ed.), *Education in the Eighteenth Century* (Garland Publishing, 1979).

Gregg, E., *Queen Anne* (Routledge & Kegan Paul, 1980).

Grey, C., *The Early Years of the Prince Consort* (William Kimber, 1967).

Grigg, J., 'A Summer Storm', in J. Murray-Brown (ed.), *The Monarchy and its Future* (George Allen & Unwin, 1969).

Haile, M., *Queen Mary of Modena: Her Life and Letters* (Dent, 1905).

Hall, P., *Royal Fortune: Tax, Money and the Monarchy* (Bloomsbury, 1992).

Halpern, J., *The Life of Jane Austen* (Harvester Press, Brighton, 1984).

Hamilton, E., *William's Mary: A Biography of Mary II* (Hamish Hamilton, 1972).

Hansard, T. C., *Parliamentary Debates* (1825).

Harris, F., *A Passion for Government: The Life of Sarah, Duchess of Marlborough* (Clarendon Press, Oxford, 1991).

Harris, J., *Sir William Chambers* (Zwemmer, 1970).

Harris, K., *The Queen* (Weidenfeld & Nicolson, 1994).

Harrison, G. B. (ed.), *The Letters of Queen Elizabeth* (Cassell, 1935).

Harrison, M., *Clarence: The Life of HRH the Duke of Clarence and Avondale* (W. H. Allen, 1972).

Haswell, J., *James II: Soldier and Sailor* (Hamish Hamilton, 1972).

Hatton, R., *George the First: Elector and King* (Thames & Hudson, 1978).

Heald, T., *The Duke: A Portrait of Prince Philip* (Hodder & Stoughton, 1991).

Healey, E., *The Queen's House: A Social History of Buckingham Palace* (Michael Joseph, 1997).

Hennessy, P., *Muddling Through: Power, Politics and the Quality of Government in Post-War Britain* (Gollancz, 1996).

Henson, H. H. (ed.), *A Memoir of the Right Honourable Sir William*

*Anson* (Clarendon Press, Oxford, 1920).

Hibbert, C., *Charles I* (Weidenfeld & Nicolson, 1968).

Hibbert, C., *Edward: The Uncrowned King* (Macdonald, 1972).

Higham, F. M. G., *Charles I: A Study* (Hamish Hamilton, 1932).

Holden, A., *Charles, Prince of Wales* (Weidenfeld & Nicolson, 1979).

Holden, A., *Charles, A Biography* (Weidenfeld & Nicolson, 1988).

Hollis, L., *Eton: A History* (Hollis & Carter, 1960).

Home, J. A. (ed.), *The Letters and Journals of Lady Mary Coke*, 4 vols, (Kingswood Reprints, Bath, 1970).

Howard, A., *RAB: The Life of R. A. Butler* (Cape, 1987).

Howard, P., *The British Monarchy in the Twentieth Century* (Hamish Hamilton, 1977).

Howarth, P., *George VI* (Hutchinson, 1987).

Hughes, A. (ed.), *Seventeenth Century England: A Changing Culture*, Vol. I (Ward Lock, 1980).

Hughes, E. A., *The Royal Naval College, Dartmouth* (Winchester Publications, 1950).

Huish, R., *Memoirs of George the Fourth* (T. Kelly, 1830).

Huish, R., *The History of the Life and Reign of William the Fourth* (William Emans, 1837).

Hutton, R., *Charles the Second: King of England, Scotland and Ireland* (Clarendon Press, Oxford, 1989).

Ingamells, J., *Mrs Robinson and Her Portraits*, Monograph 1, Wallace Collection (Wallace Collection, 1978).

Irving, D., *Memoirs of the Life and Writings of George Buchanan* (Blackwood, Edinburgh, 1817).

James, R. Rhodes (ed.), *Chips: The Diaries of Sir Henry Channon* (Penguin, 1970).

James, R. Rhodes, *Albert, Prince Consort: A Biography* (Hamish Hamilton, 1983).

Jesse, J. H., *Memoirs of the Life and Reign of King George the Third*, 3 vols (Tinsley Brothers, 1867).

Johnson, J. N., *The Life of Thomas Linacre*, ed. R. Graves (Edward Lumley, 1835).

Jones, M. K. and Underwood, M. G., *The King's Mother: Lady Margaret Beaumont, Countess of Richmond and Derby* (Cambridge University Press, Cambridge, 1992).

Jones, T., *Whitehall Diary*, ed. K. Middlemas, Vol. II, 1926–30 (Oxford University Press, Oxford, 1969).

Jordan, W. K. (ed.), *The Chronicle and Political Papers of King Edward VI* (Allen & Unwin, 1966).

Jordan, W. K., *Edward VI: The Young King* (Allen & Unwin, 1968).

# Bibliography

Judd, D., *King George VI: 1895–1952* (Michael Joseph, 1982).

Junor, P., *Charles* (Sidgwick & Jackson, 1987).

Kaye, E., *A History of Queen's College, London* (Chatto & Windus, 1972).

Kenyon, J. P., *Stuart England* (Allen Lane, 1978).

Kilvert, Revd F., *Memoirs of the Life and Writings of the Right Revd Richard Hurd* (Richard Bentley, 1860).

Kishlansky, M., *A Monarchy Transformed: Britain, 1603–1714* (Allen Lane, Penguin, Harmondsworth, 1996).

Kitson Clark, G., *The Making of Victorian England* (Methuen, 1965).

Kroll, M., *Sophia, Electress of Hanover: A Personal Portrait* (Gollancz, 1973).

Lacey, R., *Majesty: Elizabeth II and the House of Windsor* (Hutchinson, 1990).

Laird, D., *Queen Elizabeth the Queen Mother* (Hodder & Stoughton, 1966).

Laski, H., 'The King's Secretary', *The Fortnightly Review*, 158, December (1942).

Latham, R. and Matthews, W. (eds), *The Diary of Samuel Pepys* (Bell, 1971, 1976).

Lee, E., 'Mrs Sarah Trimmer', in S. Lee (ed.), *Dictionary of National Biography* (Smith, Elder, 1899), p. 232.

Lee, S., *King Edward VII: A Biography*, 2 vols (Macmillan, 1925).

Lees-Milne, J., *Harold Nicolson: A Biography* (Chatto & Windus, 1981).

Lees-Milne, J., *The Enigmatic Edwardian: The Life of Reginald, 2nd Viscount Esher* (Sidgwick & Jackson, 1986).

Leslie, A., *Mrs Fitzherbert* (Hutchinson, 1960).

Lloyd, C., *The Queen's Pictures* (Royal Collection Enterprises, 1994).

Loades, D., *Mary Tudor: A Life* (Blackwell, Oxford, 1989).

Longford, E., *Victoria R. I.* (Pan, 1966).

Longford, E., *Royal Throne: The Future of the Monarchy* (Hodder & Stoughton, 1993).

MacCaffrey, W., *Elizabeth I* (Edward Arnold, 1993).

McElwee, W., *The Wisest Fool in Christendom: The Reign of King James I and VI* (Faber & Faber, 1958).

McFarlane, I. D., *Buchanan* (Duckworth, 1981).

Mackie, J. D., *The Earlier Tudors, 1485–1558* (Oxford University Press, Oxford, 1952).

Magnus, L., *Herbert Warren of Magdalen* (John Murray, 1932).

Magnus, P., *King Edward the Seventh: The Most Edwardian of Them All* (John Murray, 1964).

Maitland Club, *Letters to King James the Sixth*, 35 (Edinburgh, 1835).

Malet, C. E., *A History of the University of Oxford*, Vol. II (Methuen, 1924).

Malloy, F., *The Sailor King: William the Fourth, His Court and His Subjects*, 2 vols (Hutchinson, 1903).

Margaret, Duchess of Newcastle, *The Life of William Cavendish, Duke of Newcastle*, ed. C. H. Firth (John C. Nimmo, 1886).

Markham, C. R., *King Edward VI* (Smith, Elder, 1907).

Marlow, J., *The Life and Times of George the First* (Weidenfeld & Nicolson, 1973).

Marples, M., *Princes in the Making* (Faber & Faber, 1965).

Marples, M., *Poor Fred and the Butcher* (Michael Joseph, 1970).

Marshall, D., *The Life and Times of Victoria* (Weidenfeld & Nicolson, 1972).

Marshall, R. K., *Mary I* (Her Majesty's Stationery Office, 1993).

Martin, K., *The Crown and the Establishment* (Hutchinson, 1962).

Martin, T., *The Life of His Royal Highness The Prince Consort*, 5 vols (Smith, Elder, 1875–80).

Mathew, D., *James I* (Eyre & Spottiswoode, 1967).

Melville, J., *The Memoirs of Sir James Melville* (D. Wilson, 1752 edn).

Melville, L., *The First George in Hanover and England*, 2 vols (Pitman, 1908).

Michie, A. A., *The Crown and the People* (Secker & Warburg, 1952).

Middlemas, K., *The Life and Times of George VI* (Weidenfeld & Nicolson, 1974).

Millar, O., *The Age of Charles I* (Tate Gallery, 1972).

Miller, J., *Charles I* (Weidenfeld & Nicolson, 1991).

Mitchell, L. G., *Lord Melbourne 1779–1848* (Oxford University Press, Oxford, 1997).

Montague-Smith, P. W., *The Royal Line of Succession* (Pitkin, 1986).

Morrah, D., *The Work of the Queen* (William Kimber, 1958).

Morrah, D., *To Be A King* (Hutchinson, 1968).

Morton, A. Q., *Science in the Eighteenth Century: The King George III Collection* (Science Museum, 1993).

Mumby, F. A., *The Girlhood of Queen Elizabeth* (Constable, 1909)

Nairn, T., *The Enchanted Glass: Britain and its Monarchy* (Vintage, 1988, 1994).

Nichols, J. G. (ed.), *The Literary Remains of King Edward the Sixth* (Burt Franklin, New York, 1857).

Nicolson, H., *King George the Fifth: His Life and Reign* (Constable, 1952).

Ollard, R., *The Image of the King: Charles I and Charles II* (Hodder & Stoughton, 1979).

Oman, C., *Henrietta Maria* (Hodder & Stoughton, 1936).

Orme, N., *From Childhood to Chivalry: The Education of English Kings and Aristocracy 1066–1530* (Methuen, 1984).

Pakula, H., *An Unknown Woman: The Empress Frederick* (Phoenix, 1997).

Parker, J., *Prince Philip: A Critical Biography* (Sidgwick & Jackson, 1990).

Passmore, B., 'The Prince and the Inspector', *Times Educational Supplement*, 20 June 1997.

Petrie, C. (ed.), *The Letters, Speeches and Proclamations of King Charles I* (Cassell, 1935).

Petrie, S., *The Four Georges* (Eyre & Spottiswoode, 1931).

Pimlott, B., *Hugh Dalton* (Cape, 1985).

Pimlott, B., *The Queen: A Biography of Elizabeth II* (HarperCollins, 1996).

Pimlott, B., 'After Diana', *Sunday Times*, 30 August 1998.

Plowden, A., *The Young Victoria* (Weidenfeld & Nicolson, 1981).

Plumb, J. H., *The First Four Georges* (Batsford, 1957).

Plumb, J. H., *The Penguin Book of the Renaissance* (Penguin, 1964).

Pocock, N., 'Brian Duppa', in L. Stephen (ed.), *Dictionary of National Biography*, Vol. XVI (Smith, Elder, 1888).

Pocock, T., *Sailor King: The Life of King William the Fourth* (Sinclair-Stevenson, 1991).

Pollard, A. F., *The Reign of Henry VII from Contemporary Sources*, Vol. I (Longman, Green, 1913).

Ponsonby, A., *Henry Ponsonby: Queen Victoria's Private Secretary: His Life from his Letters* (Macmillan, 1942).

Pope-Hennessy, J., *Queen Mary* (Allen & Unwin, 1959).

Prescott, H. F. M., *Mary Tudor* (Eyre & Spottiswoode, 1953).

Prince Albert Victor and Prince George of Wales, *The Cruise of Her Majesty's Ship Bacchante, 1879–1882*, 2 vols (Macmillan, 1886).

Prince Philip, HRH Duke of Edinburgh, *Selected Speeches, 1948–1955* (Oxford University Press, Oxford, 1957).

Prochaska, F., *Royal Bounty: The Making of a Welfare Monarchy* (Yale University Press, 1995).

Public Schools Commission, *First Report*, Vol. I (HMSO, 1968).

Purves, L., 'A Period of Silence, Sir', *The Times*, 17 June 1997.

Raphael, D. D., *Hobbes, Morals and Politics* (Allen & Unwin, 1977).

Ray, H. B., 'Eyre Papers', *Miscellanies of the Philobiblon Society*, Vol. 2 (1855–56).

Reeve, I. J., *Charles I and the Road to Personal Rule* (Cambridge University Press, Cambridge, 1989).

Reynolds, E. E., *Thomas More and Erasmus* (Burns & Oates, 1965).

Riddell, Lord, *More Pages From My Diary* (Country Life, 1934).

Ridley, J., *Henry VIII* (Constable, 1984).

Roll, W., *Mary I* (Prentice-Hall, Englewood Cliffs, NJ, 1980).

Rose, K., *King George V* (Weidenfeld & Nicolson, 1983).

Rose, K., *Kings, Queens and Courtiers* (Weidenfeld & Nicolson, 1985).

Roskill, S. W., 'Sir James Ramsay Montagu Butler', in Lord Blake and C. S. Nicholls (eds), *Dictionary of National Biography, 1971–1980* (Oxford University Press, Oxford, 1986).

Ross, G. M., *Leibnitz* (Oxford University Press, Oxford, 1984).

Rowse, A. L., *The England of Elizabeth* (Macmillan, 1950).

Ryan, D., *Roger Ascham* (Oxford University Press, Oxford, 1963).

St Aubyn, G., *Edward VII: Prince and King* (Collins, 1979).

St Aubyn, G., *Queen Victoria: A Portrait* (Atheneum, 1992).

Sampson, A., *The Changing Anatomy of Britain* (Hodder & Stoughton, 1982).

Sandars, M. F., *Princess and Queen of England: Life of Mary II* (Stanley Paul, 1913).

Sargeaunt, J., *Annals of Westminster School* (Methuen, 1898).

Scarisbrick, J. J., *Henry VIII* (Eyre & Spottiswoode, 1997 edn).

Scott, E., *The King in Exile: The Wanderings of Charles II from June 1646 to July 1654* (Constable, 1905).

Scott, W. (ed.), *Memoirs of Count Grammont by Anthony Hamilton*, Vol. I (John C. Nimmo, 1885).

Sedgwick, R. (ed.), *Letters from George the Third to Lord Bute, 1756–1766* (Macmillan, 1939).

Sedgwick, R. (ed.), *Lord Hervey's Memoirs* (William Kimber, 1952).

Selleck, R. J. W., *James Kay-Shuttleworth: Journey of an Outsider* (Woburn Press, 1994).

Sells, A. L. (ed.), *The Memoirs of James II* (Chatto & Windus, 1962).

Shils, E. and Young, M., 'The Meaning of the Coronation', *Sociological Review,* 1, 2 (1953).

Simon, J., *Education and Society in Tudor England* (Cambridge University Press, Cambridge, 1967).

Slaughter, T. R., *Ideology and Politics on the Eve of Restoration: Newcastle's Advice to Charles II* (American Philosophical Society, Philadelphia, 1984).

Smith, A. A., *Our Sailor King* (John F. Shaw, 1910).

Somerset, A., *Ladies-in-Waiting* (Weidenfeld & Nicolson, 1984).

Somerset, A., *Elizabeth I* (Fontana, 1992).

Speck, A. W., *The Birth of Britain: A New Nation, 1700–1710* (Blackwell, Oxford, 1994).

Starkey, D., 'The Legacy of Henry VIII', in D. Starkey (ed.), *Henry*

*VIII: A European Court in England* (Collins & Brown, 1991).

Steeholm, C. and H., *James I of England: The Wisest Fool in Christendom* (Michael Joseph, 1938).

Stephenson, J. (ed.), *A Royal Correspondence: Letters of King Edward VII and King George V to Admiral Sir Henry F. Stephenson* (Macmillan, 1938).

Sterry, W., *Annals of The King's College of our Lady Beside Windsor* (Methuen, 1898).

Stockmar, E. von, *Memoirs of Baron Stockmar*, 2 vols (Longman, Green, 1872).

Storey, R. L., *The Reign of Henry VII* (Blandford Press, 1968).

Strickland, A., *Lives of the Queens of England* (Longman, Green, Reader & Dyer, 1875).

Strong, R., *Henry, Prince of Wales* (Thames & Hudson, 1986).

Strype, J., *Sir John Cheke* (Clarendon Press, Oxford, 1821 [1703]).

Summers, S., 'The Outward Bound Movement', in H. Röhrs and H. Tunstall-Behrens (eds), *Kurt Hahn* (Routledge & Kegan Paul, 1970).

Temperley, G., *Henry VII* (Constable, 1917).

Thompson, D., 'Queen Victoria', *The Historian*, Spring (1997).

Tisdall, E. E. P., *Unpredictable Queen: The Intimate Life of Queen Alexandra* (Stanley Paul, 1953).

Timbs, J., *School-Days of Eminent Men* (Kent & Co, 1858).

Tomalin, C., *Mrs Jordan's Profession* (Viking, 1994).

Torrens, W. M., *Memoirs of the Second Viscount Melbourne*, 2 vols (Macmillan, 1878).

Townsend, W. and L., *The Biography of HRH The Prince of Wales* (Albert E. Marriott, 1929).

Trevelyan, G. M., *England under Queen Anne: Blenheim* (Longman, 1936).

Tucker, M. J., 'The Child as Beginning and End: Fifteenth and Sixteenth Century English Childhood', in L. de Mause (ed.), *The History of Childhood* (Souvenir Press, 1976).

Turner, F. C., *James II* (Eyre & Spottiswoode, 1948).

Tylden-Wright, D., *John Aubrey* (HarperCollins, 1991).

Van der Zee, H. and B., *William and Mary* (Macmillan, 1973).

Vincent, J. E., *His Royal Highness The Duke of Clarence and Avondale* (Murray, 1893).

Wakeford, G., *The Heir Apparent: An Authentic Study of the Life and Training of HRH Charles, Prince of Wales* (Robert Hale, 1967).

Wakeford, G., *Thirty Years a Queen* (Robert Hale, 1968).

Waldegrave, James, Earl, *Memoirs: From 1754 to 1758* (John Murray, 1821).

Wallace, W., *The History of the Life and Reign of William the Fourth* (Longman, 1831).

Walpole, H., *Memoirs of the Reign of King George the Third*, ed. G. F. R. Barker, 4 vols (Lawrence & Bullen, 1894).

Walters, J., *The Royal Griffin: Frederick, Prince of Wales* (Jarrolds, 1972).

Warwick, C., *King George VI and Queen Elizabeth* (Sidgwick & Jackson, 1985).

Waterstone, N. M., *Mary II Queen of England* (Duke University Press, Durham, NC, 1928).

Watkins, J., *Memoirs of Sophia Charlotte, Queen of Great Britain* (Henry Colburn, 1819).

Watkins, J., *The Life and Times of William the Fourth* (Fisher, Son & Jackson, 1831).

Watson, D. R., *The Life and Times of Charles I* (Weidenfeld & Nicolson, 1972).

Watson, Foster, *The Old Grammar Schools* (Cambridge University Press, Cambridge, 1916).

Watson, Foster, 'Juan Louis Vives', in *Encyclopaedia and Dictionary of Education*, Vol. IV (Pitman, 1922).

Watson, J. S., *The Reign of George the Third, 1760–1815* (Oxford University Press, Oxford, 1960).

Weinberger, J. (ed.), *Francis Bacon: The History of the Reign of Henry the Seventh* (Cornell University Press, Ithaca, NY, 1996).

Weintraub, S., *Albert: Uncrowned King* (John Murray, 1997).

Wheeler-Bennett, J. W., *King George VI: His Life and Reign* (Macmillan, 1958).

Whiting, C. E., *Nathaniel Lord Crewe, Bishop of Durham, 1674–1721, and his Diocese* (SPCK, 1940).

Williams, C. H., *England under the Early Tudors* (Longman, Green, 1925).

Williams, N., *The Royal Residences of Great Britain* (Barrie & Rockliff, 1960).

Williams, N., *The Life and Times of Elizabeth I* (Weidenfeld & Nicolson, 1972).

Williams, R., *The Contentious Crown: Public Discussion of the Monarchy in the Reign of Queen Victoria* (Ashgate, 1997).

Willson, D. H., *King James VI and I* (Cape, 1956).

Wilson, P. W. (ed.), *The Greville Diary*, 2 vols (Heinemann, 1927).

Windsor, Duke of, *A King's Story* (Cassell, 1951).

Windsor, Duke of, *A Family Album* (Cassell, 1960).

Woodham-Smith, C. B., *Queen Victoria: Her Life and Times* (Hamish Hamilton, 1972).

Woods, R., *Robin Woods: An Autobiography* (SCM Press, 1986).

Wright, G. N., *The Life and Reign of William the Fourth*, 2 vols (Fisher, Son & Jackson, 1837).

Wyndham, H. (ed.), *Correspondence of Sarah Spencer, Lady Lyttelton, 1787–1870* (John Murray, 1912).

Wynn Jones, M., *The Cartoon History of Britain* (Stacey, 1977).

Young, G., *Poor Fred: The People's Prince* (Oxford University Press, Oxford, 1937).

Young, G. M., *Early Victorian England, 1830–1865*, 2 vols (Oxford University Press, Oxford, 1934).

Ziegler, P., *King William the Fourth* (Collins, 1971).

Ziegler, P., *Mountbatten: The Official Biography* (Guild Publishing Company, 1985).

Ziegler, P., *King Edward VIII* (Collins, 1990).

*Genealogy*

# HOUSE OF TUDOR

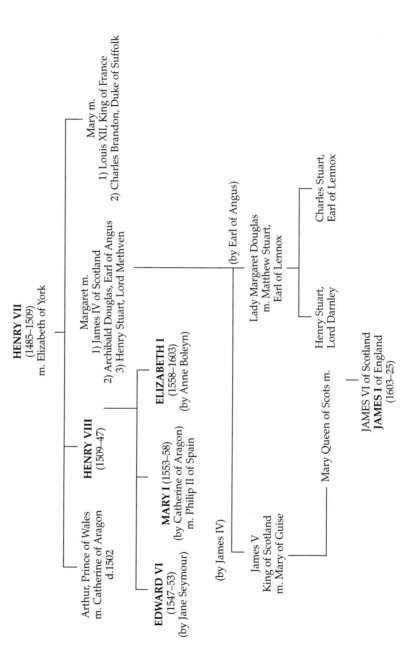

**HENRY VII**
(1485–1509)
m. Elizabeth of York

Arthur, Prince of Wales
m. Catherine of Aragon
d.1502

**HENRY VIII**
(1509–47)

Margaret m.
1) James IV of Scotland
2) Archibald Douglas, Earl of Angus
3) Henry Stuart, Lord Methven

Mary m.
1) Louis XII, King of France
2) Charles Brandon, Duke of Suffolk

**EDWARD VI**
(1547–53)
(by Jane Seymour)

**MARY I** (1553–58)
(by Catherine of Aragon)
m. Philip II of Spain

**ELIZABETH I**
(1558–1603)
(by Anne Boleyn)

(by Earl of Angus)

(by James IV)

James V
King of Scotland
m. Mary of Guise

Lady Margaret Douglas
m. Matthew Stuart,
Earl of Lennox

Mary Queen of Scots m.

Henry Stuart,
Lord Darnley

Charles Stuart,
Earl of Lennox

JAMES VI of Scotland
**JAMES I** of England
(1603–25)

# HOUSE OF STUART

JAMES VI of Scotland and
**JAMES I** of England
m. Anne of Denmark
(1603–25)

Henry Frederick
Prince of Wales
d. 1612

**CHARLES I**
(1625–49)
m. Henrietta Maria of France

Elizabeth m. Frederick V
Elector Palatine of the Rhine
and King of Bohemia

**CHARLES II**
(1660–85)
m. Catharine
of Braganza

Mary m. William II
Prince of Orange

**JAMES II**
(1685–88)
m. 1) Anne Hyde
2) Mary of Modena

Henry,
Duke of
Gloucester

Henrietta Anne

Frederick Henry | Charles Louis | Elizabeth | Rupert of the Rhine | Maurice | Louisa | Edward | Henrietta Maria | Philip | Charlotte | Sophia m. Ernest Augustus, Elector of Hanover

**GEORGE I**
(1714–27)

**WILLIAM III**
(1689–1702)
Prince of Orange

m.

**MARY II**
(1689–94)
(by Anne Hyde)

**ANNE**
(1702–14)
(by Anne Hyde)
m. Prince George of Denmark

Elizabeth | Anne

James,
Prince of Wales
(by Mary of
Modena)

Louisa Maria
(by Mary of
Modena)

# HOUSE OF HANOVER

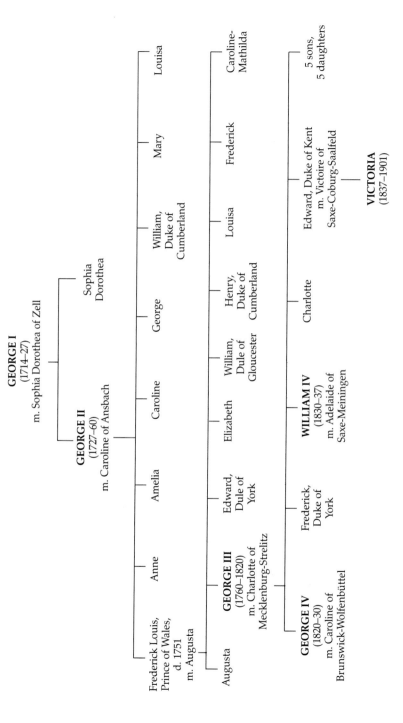

# HOUSE OF SAXE-COBURG AND GOTHA

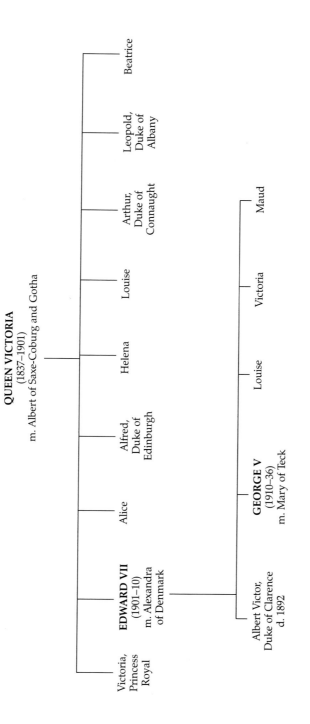

**QUEEN VICTORIA**
(1837–1901)
m. Albert of Saxe-Coburg and Gotha

Victoria, Princess Royal

**EDWARD VII**
(1901–10)
m. Alexandra of Denmark

Alice

Alfred, Duke of Edinburgh

Helena

Louise

Arthur, Duke of Connaught

Leopold, Duke of Albany

Beatrice

Albert Victor, Duke of Clarence d. 1892

**GEORGE V**
(1910–36)
m. Mary of Teck

Louise

Victoria

Maud

# HOUSE OF WINDSOR

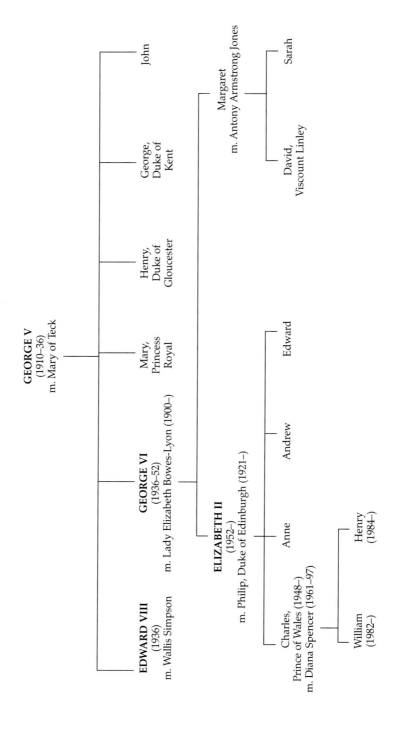

**GEORGE V**
(1910–36)
m. Mary of Teck

**EDWARD VIII**
(1936)
m. Wallis Simpson

**GEORGE VI**
(1936–52)
m. Lady Elizabeth Bowes-Lyon (1900–)

Mary,
Princess
Royal

Henry,
Duke of
Gloucester

George,
Duke of
Kent

John

**ELIZABETH II**
(1952–)
m. Philip, Duke of Edinburgh (1921–)

Margaret
m. Antony Armstrong Jones

Charles,
Prince of Wales (1948–)
m. Diana Spencer (1961–97)

Anne

Andrew

Edward

David,
Viscount Linley

Sarah

William
(1982–)

Henry
(1984–)

# *Index*

279